ILLINOIS, LAND OF LINCOLN

ILLINOIS

Consulting Editors

Paul M. Angle
  Director, Historical Publications
  Illinois Sesquicentennial Commission

Paul E. Woods
  Director, Title III
  Office of the Superintendent
  of Public Instruction

Olive S. Foster
  Director, School Services and
  Editor, *Illinois History*
  Illinois State Historical Library

Sarajane Wells
  Education Director
  Chicago Historical Society

Arvarh E. Strickland, Ph.D.
  Associate Professor of History
  Illinois Teachers College, South

LAND OF LINCOLN

by Allan Carpenter

CHILDRENS PRESS, CHICAGO

This Sesquicentennial Edition of *Illinois, Land of Lincoln* has been made possible through the generous cooperation of the following Chicago corporations, who have taken this means of expressing their faith in the future of free enterprise and their pride in the state of Illinois.

American Typesetting Company	Typography
John Ball & Associates	Photography
Chicago Book Manufacturing	Book and Pamphlet Binding
Ernst Hertzberg & Sons, The Monastery Hill Bindery	Custom Book Covers
Mack-Chicago Corporation	Display and Shipping Cartons
Regensteiner Press	Lithography and Engraving
Bernard E. Ury Associates, Inc.	Public Relations

The author also wishes to express his appreciation for the kind assistance of the following individuals: Otto Kerner, Governor of Illinois; Ralph G. Newman, Chairman, Illinois Sesquicentennial Commission; Woodson W. Fishback, Director of Curriculum, Office of the State Superintendent of Public Instruction; James Leahy, Office of the State Superintendent of Public Instruction; William Nichol, Principal, Dawes School, Evanston; Frederick Gotham, Chicago Historical Society; Mary Frances Rhymer, Curator of Prints, Chicago Historical Society; Raymond R. Becker, Chief, Information and Publication, Department of Business and Economic Development; Wilmer A. Lamar, Executive Secretary, Illinois Association of Teachers of English; W. J. Beecher, Director, Chicago Academy of Sciences; Charles W. Collins, author of *Guide for Beginning Fossil Hunters,* Illinois State Geological Survey; Thomas F. Driscoll, City Editor, *Peoria Journal Star;* Tom Balow, Indexer, and Dr. Eugene Baker, Curriculum Consultant.

See page 208 for a complete list of all illustration credits.

Cover and Body Design by Margrit Fiddle

Library of Congress Catalog Card Number: 68-12827

FIRST EDITION
Second Printing, February, 1968

Third Printing, May, 1968

CONTENTS

The Next 150 Years

*For 150 years Illinois has fulfilled the promise which its
early champions saw in it. Today we are celebrating that century
and a half, but we are doing more than celebrating. We are laying
the groundwork for future growth and future expansion.*

*We have had a great history, but we are even more concerned
with making history than we are in recounting it.*

*The Sesquicentennial is a milestone. It helps us to evaluate
our progress by giving us an incentive to look once
more and see how far we have come. It gives us a new starting point from
which we will go on to an even greater future.*

*If those of us who are heirs of that great past century and a
half will work together to make Illinois first in enterprise, imagination,
opportunity, progress, and achievement we can continue to assert
that this is a great state to work in and a great state to live in!*

Otto Kerner, *Governor*
The State of Illinois

Needed: Another Lincoln

Is there somewhere today in Illinois a boy who, after thirty years of nurture and growth in the Land of Lincoln, will rise up to lead his people in a time of crisis? Is he now enduring with dignity and patience the difficulties of a Negro or Puerto Rican ghetto? Does he come from a poor mining family? Is he helping his family to eke out a living on a marginal farm? Or, by contrast, this time is he "overcoming" the luxury and privilege afforded by being from one of the elite and aristocratic families of the state?

Whoever he is, from wherever he comes, he will face the problems of a world where people have not yet learned to live together in harmony and goodwill and mutual respect, where human dignity is increasingly disregarded, where violence and hatred seem to have become a way of life for constantly greater numbers throughout the world.

He will have to learn how to address himself with all the skill he can find to problems of social integration and human relations; to the awesome growth of urban centers, with their problems of crowding, inequality, transportation, parking and the awful polution of water and air; to the increase and conservation of our natural resources; and to the happy and useful utilization of the growing amount of leisure time available to people.

He will need to consider the many problems involved in the efficient and honest administration of a government on which more and more people will depend. He must also seek to resolve, patiently, firmly, and with the wisdom of Solomon, questions dealing with private business, relations with other nations, and, finally, the ultimate question of war or peace.

He must find new means of promoting religious freedom and toleration while at the same time encouraging his people to hold fast to their beliefs. He must seek solutions for the increasing difficulties encountered in personal relationships and family life, for the fearsome toll exacted by divorce, divided families, experimentation with drugs, and other perils to health and safety if he is to promote a stable, healthy, well-adjusted population.

However perplexing, fearsome and foreboding the problems of today may seem to modern Americans, few would have found comfort in the America of 1860—an America poised on the brink of one of the most bloody wars ever to wreak its havoc on the world—a war followed by a period of the most bitter hatred and violence!

It might have seemed unlikely that, at such time, hope would come from the young town of Chicago in the still pioneering state of Illinois. Yet the events of the third day of the Republican Convention, meeting in the Wigwam building in Chicago on May 18, 1860, may have brought American history to a turning point. That stirring day—one of the many dramatic days in the 150 years of Illinois statehood—was vividly described by the journalist Murat Halstead, who was a participant and eyewitness:

"When the convention was called to order, breathless attention was given the proceedings. There was not a foot square in the wigwam unoccupied. There were tens of thousands still outside, and torrents of men had

11

rushed in at the three broad doors until not another one could squeeze in. . . .

"The applause when Mr. Evarts named Seward was enthusiastic. When Mr. Judd named Lincoln, the response was prodigious, rising and raging far beyond the Seward shriek. Presently, upon Caleb B. Smith seconding the nomination of Lincoln, the response was absolutely terrific. It now became the Seward men to make another effort, and when Blair of Michigan seconded his nomination,

At once there rose so wild a yell,
Within that dark and narrow dell;
As all the fiends from heaven that fell
Had pealed the banner cry of hell.

"The effect was startling. Hundreds of persons stopped their ears in pain. The shouting was absolutely frantic, shrill and wild. . . .

"Now the Lincoln men had to try it again . . . the uproar was beyond description. Imagine all the hogs ever slaughtered . . . giving their death squeals together, a score of big steam whistles going . . . and you can conceive something of the same nature. . . ."

The third ". . . ballot was taken amid excitement that tested the nerves. . . . It was whispered about: 'Lincoln's the coming man—will be nominated this ballot.' . . . The number of votes necessary to a choice were two hundred and thirty-three and I saw under my pencil as the Lincoln column was completed the figures 231½—one vote and a half to give him the nomination. . . . In about ten ticks of a watch, Cartter of Ohio was up. . . . He said: 'I rise (eh), Mr. Chairman (eh), to announce the change of four votes of Ohio from Mr. Chase to Mr. Lincoln.' The deed was done. There was a moment's silence. The nerves of the thousands, which through the hours of suspense had been subjected to terrible tension, relaxed and as deep breaths of

relief were taken, there was a noise in the Wigwam like the rush of a great wind in the van of a storm—and in another breath, the storm was there. There were thousands cheering with the energy of insanity. . . .

"The city was wild with delight . . . a hundred guns were fired from the top of the Tremont House. . . . I left the city on the night train. . . . At every station where there was a village, until after two o'clock, there were tar barrels burning, drums beating, boys carrying rails, and guns, great and small, banging away. The weary passengers were allowed no rest, but plagued by the thundering jar of cannon, the clamor of drums, the glare of bonfires, and the whooping of the boys, who were delighted with the idea of a candidate for the Presidency who thirty years ago split rails on the Sangamon River —classic stream now and forever more— and whose neighbors named him 'honest'."

Eventually, because of the decision made in Chicago, the whole world was to share some of the boys' delight in the selection of the "honest" rail-splitter from Illinois.

There are some who would say that the old virtue of honesty and the traditional qualities of leadership are not enough to meet the crushing problems of modern times. That earlier great Illinoisan, who rose to first rank in world history, seemed to many in his own time little more than an inadequate buffoon, yet the world is still discussing the qualities of his personality which made him equal to the task.

Abraham Lincoln was ". . . cool, careful, earnest, sincere, truthful, fair, self-possessed, not insulting, not dictatorial; was pleasing, good natured; had great strong naturalness of look, pose and act, was clear in his ideas, simple in his words, strong, terse, and demonstrative; he spoke and acted to convince individuals and masses," according to his law partner, W. H. Herndon.

"The President was the kindest man I had ever seen . . . Lincoln was so easy with me, so gentle, that I soon forgot my fright . . . " said William Scott. (Known as the "sleeping sentinel," Scott was one of three men posted on a key bridge leading into Washington. All three fell asleep, but because it was Scott's turn at guard, he was arrested, tried, and sentenced to die. Scott had a good record as a new recruit, and officers and enlisted men alike felt that the punishment was too severe. A petition was drawn up and shown to Lincoln by Major-General George McClellan. Because this was the first case of its kind, Lincoln agreed, only hours before the execution, to pardon Scott.)

Lincoln "had a fantastic sense of humor which kept him from being completely swallowed up by his troubles . . . he interspersed our conversation with all sort of quaint stories, each of which had a witty point, applicable to the subject in hand . . . his laugh was so genuine, hearty and contagious that nobody could fail to join in it," observed Carl Schurz, lawyer, general and politician. And yet he " . . . had a kind of natural dignity, quite sufficient to keep the forwardest of us from clapping him on the shoulder and asking him for a story," wrote the admiring novelist, Nathaniel Hawthorne.

Hawthorne also commented on Lincoln's wisdom and good sense, saying that he possessed " . . . A great deal of native sense . . . honest at heart and thoroughly so, and yet, in some sort, sly—at least endowed with a sort of tact and wisdom that are akin to craft. . . ." However, Carl Schurz implied that his ability rated as that of genius: "He replied to Douglas' arguments and attacks with rapid thrusts so deft and piercing, with humorous retort so quaint and pat, and with witty illustrations so clinching, and he did it all so good-naturedly, that the meeting again and again broke out in bursts of delight by which even many of his opponents were carried away. . . ."

To all these qualities was added a deep reverence as indicated when he wrote to a Mrs. Bixby who had suffered the loss of five sons in the Civil War: " . . . I pray that our heavenly Father may assuage the anguish of your bereavement and leave you only the cherished memory of the loved and lost and the solemn pride that must be yours to have laid so costly a sacrifice upon the altar of freedom."

Herndon noted: " . . . he was a diffident man, somewhat, and a sensitive one. . . ." And yet he " . . . had confidence, full and complete confidence, in himself, . . . relying on no man." He also had confidence " . . . that truth and that justice will surely prevail by the judgment of this great tribunal of the American People," as he himself said in his first inaugural address.

Most important of all, however, Lincoln was the great humanitarian as described by thousands of others as well as by Herndon: " . . . he seemed inspired, fresh from the hands of his Creator. Lincoln's gray eyes would flash fire when speaking of liberty, justice and the progress of mankind. . . ."

Today, perhaps, the nation and the world face even greater problems, deeper anguish and more awful dangers than could have been imagined when Abraham Lincoln went to Washington. In such times, if Illinois' only accomplishment in its second 150 years of life as a state were to create another such man, it might rest content.

The Face of Illinois

If Illinois is thought of as a personality, it certainly has a pleasant face—generally smooth and untroubled, with just enough wrinkles and beauty marks to denote character. Here is a face that glows with gentle confidence and radiates serenity.

Surely this is an interesting face, suggestive of a character that deserves further consideration.

Stretching for 380 miles from north to south, it is a long face, although not a somber one. Most people are surprised to learn that Illinois is both a southern state, with its southernmost tip farther south than Richmond, Virginia, and a northern state, having a northern border farther north than New York City. At its widest point, Illinois extends a substantial 205 miles from east to west. Twenty-three states are larger, and twenty-six are smaller, so that with 56,290 square miles Illinois is about average in size.

From the highest point of 1,241 feet at Charles Mound, near the Wisconsin border, in its whole length of almost 400 miles Illinois descends only 962 feet to its lowest point of 279 feet at the delta at Cairo, where the Ohio and Mississippi rivers converge.

Since mountains are defined as peaks 2,000 feet in height or more, Illinois technically has no mountains. However, residents have grown accustomed to using the term mountains for the extension of the Ozark range which reaches into southern Illinois. There are also picturesque hills and ridges in the northwest area near the Wisconsin border. Many of the rivers and streams of Illinois have high bluffs and terraces which also provide a break in the generally even landscape.

Only in the hilly and rough areas of the state are there any rock outcrops showing.

Most of Illinois is a broad prairie plain, sloping gently from the north and east to the south and west. In the first description ever written about Illinois, Father Jacques Marquette, a Jesuit missionary, exclaimed "we have seen nothing like this . . .," and later he spoke of these "beautiful lands."

Another and later visitor, English author Charles Dickens, had a more down-to-earth view of the Illinois landscape: " . . . there lay, stretched out before my view, a vast expanse of level ground; unbroken, save by one thin line of trees, which scarcely amounted to a scratch upon the great blank . . . a tranquil sea or lake without water, if such a simile be admissible . . . and solitude and silence reigning paramount around. . . ."

Most of the Illinois surface is made up of two general types of soil—prairie and forest. Prairie soils are found principally in the east-central section of the state. These black soils, rich in organic content and lime, have the capacity to hold great amounts of water for long periods, and will sustain crops for a long time without wearing out. Much of the prairie surface soil was brought in over the centuries by the wind and is known as loess.

The forest soils, yellow to yellowish gray in color, with little organic material, are less productive than the prairie soils. They have come to be known as the "clay pan." Rains run rapidly off these soils.

Scientists divide the surface of Illinois into three main physiographic regions, based on the physical characteristics of the land. These regions are: the Central Plains, the

Shawnee Hills, and the Gulf Coastal Plain. The Central Plains include about 90 percent of the state, while the other two regions occupy only a small corner in the south.

"BY THY RIVERS GENTLY FLOWING"

Imagine 24 clouds, each one hanging above a different state. These 24 states are scattered from Montana on the west to Virginia on the east, from Colorado on the south to Minnesota on the north. Suppose that from each of those 24 clouds rain fell on each of the 24 states, including Illinois. At some point on its way to the sea, the water from each of these clouds would pass by or through the state of Illinois.

This is a somewhat fanciful way of illustrating Illinois' very unusual drainage system. This system is, in fact, one of the largest and most complete for any region of this size in the world.

Water giants surround Illinois on three sides—the mighty Mississippi River coursing along the western border for 518 miles, the "beautiful Ohio" gleaming beside the southeast for 113 miles and majestic Lake Michigan sparkling along a shoreline of more than 50 miles on the northeast.

The gentle but continuing slope of Illinois toward the south and southwest keeps the rivers flowing, but there are no great falls or long stretches of white-water rapids. All but a small section of Illinois is drained by the Mississippi River system. However, there is an important divide of the waters a few miles west of Lake Michigan, where an almost invisible crest (or watershed) sends waters flowing southwest toward the Mississippi and the Gulf of Mexico and east into the Great Lakes and eventually to the St. Lawrence River and the Atlantic Ocean.

The community of Summit, southwest of Chicago takes its name from its position astride the "summit" of this watershed.

The third major river boundary of Illinois is the Wabash, emptying into the Ohio River and forming part of the southern half of the boundary with Indiana. In Illinois the principal tributaries of the Wabash are the Embarrass and Little Wabash rivers.

Illinois' main internal river is, naturally, the Illinois, beginning at the meeting of the Kankakee and Des Plaines rivers, southwest of Joliet, and flowing through the state for 273 miles to its junction with the Mississippi just above Alton. On its way, the Illinois accepts the waters of the Du Page, Fox, Vermilion, Spoon, Sangamon and many other smaller rivers. Forty-three percent of the water which falls on Illinois is drained by the Illinois River and its tributaries.

Some of the other rivers of Illinois which drain directly into the Mississippi are the Apple, Rock, Kaskaskia and Big Muddy. The Saline and Cache rivers flow into the Ohio River.

The Pocatonica River dips down from Wisconsin, crosses the border, then as if apologizing for intruding, withdraws again into Wisconsin.

The Mississippi and Ohio rivers come together at the southern tip of Illinois to make one of the world's major river junctions. This delta region between the rivers was compared so often to the land of the Nile in Egypt that this part of Illinois has been known for generations as "Little Egypt." Altogether, the major rivers of Illinois have a total length of 1,277 miles.

Many Illinois rivers have gained fame in story and song. Illinois' official state song salutes its many rivers, beginning: "By thy rivers gently flowing, Illinois..." Illinois

*The Midwest—a twelve-state region in the heartland
of America—contains some of the richest farmland
in the world and is a dialect area of American speech.*

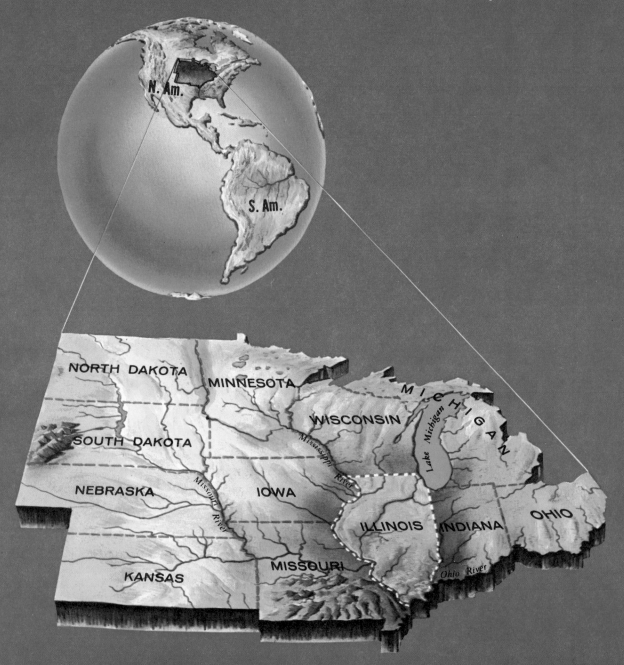

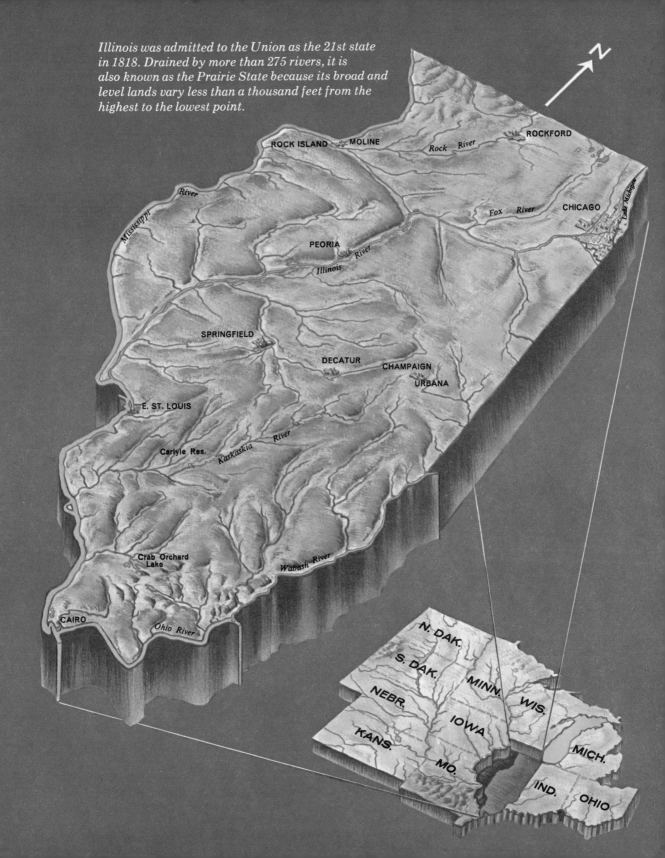

Illinois was admitted to the Union as the 21st state in 1818. Drained by more than 275 rivers, it is also known as the Prairie State because its broad and level lands vary less than a thousand feet from the highest to the lowest point.

ROCK ISLAND MOLINE
ROCKFORD
Rock River
Mississippi River
Fox River
CHICAGO
Lake Michigan
PEORIA
Illinois River
SPRINGFIELD
DECATUR
CHAMPAIGN
URBANA
E. ST. LOUIS
Carlyle Res.
Kaskaskia River
Crab Orchard Lake
Wabash River
CAIRO
Ohio River

N. DAK.
S. DAK.
NEBR.
KANS.
MINN.
IOWA
WIS.
MO.
MICH.
IND.
OHIO

poet Edgar Lee Masters made the Spoon River famous in his *Spoon River Anthology*. Australian composer Percy Grainger wrote a piano selection called *Spoon River*. And, of course, there is the Wabash River, which is famous in song, but it is usually "claimed" by Indiana rather than Illinois.

SPARKLING GEMS

Most Illinois lakes have connections with rivers. Among the 352 natural lakes, perhaps the best known is the Chain of Lakes strung like beaded gems on the necklace of the Fox River in northeastern Illinois. Many relatively small artificial lakes have been made by damming the rivers, especially in the central and southern parts of the state.

Among the total of more than 900 lakes or reservoirs of Illinois, there are no giants within the state. However, there is a giant at the doorstep. Mighty Lake Michigan provides Midwestern Illinois with the coast of an inland sea.

An early Illinois farmstead, typical of the kinds that were built as farms began to dot the prairie lands.

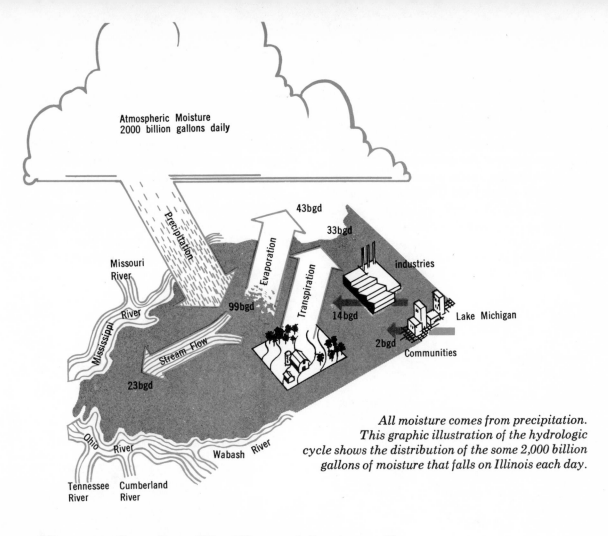

Atmospheric Moisture
2000 billion gallons daily

Precipitation

Evaporation

Transpiration

43bgd

33bgd

industries

Missouri
River

Mississippi River

99bgd

Stream Flow

14bgd

Lake Michigan

2bgd

Communities

23bgd

Ohio River

Wabash River

Tennessee
River

Cumberland
River

*All moisture comes from precipitation.
This graphic illustration of the hydrologic
cycle shows the distribution of the some 2,000 billion
gallons of moisture that falls on Illinois each day.*

Everybody Talks About It

As both a "southern" and a "northern" state, Illinois has considerable variation in weather. It lives up to expectations, with a climate ranging from a humid continental, cool summer in the north to a humid subtropical, warm summer in the extreme south.

The length of the growing season in each area demonstrates the difference between the climate of the north and the south. Only about 160 days are free from frost on the average in the north, while at Cairo the growing season averages 211 days. For the state as a whole, the number of frost-free days varies from 160 to 190 days. However, major crops seldom suffer from a serious freeze.

Oceans and tall mountain ranges, which greatly influence climate and weather, are so distant from Illinois that there are few moderating influences in the state. Lake Michigan is the only weather modifier of any consequence, and its effects are not felt very far inland from the lakeshore. Weather changes come quickly, and the long distances across which wind-bearing pressure areas must move assure great extremes. The eastward movement of pressure areas and masses of polar air meeting with tropical air masses from the Gulf of Mexico make for sudden and sometimes violent changes.

Most moisture is brought up from the Gulf of Mexico, and this precipitation, which is well distributed throughout the state, is one of the major assets of Illinois' climate. Average precipitation in Illinois ranges from 32 inches in the extreme northeast to more than 46 inches in the extreme south. The recorded amounts of precipitation not only vary across the state but also from year to year.

Variation in snowfall is extreme: from 9 inches in the south to more than 33 inches in the north. In the years of heaviest snowfall, some regions have reached 60 inches.

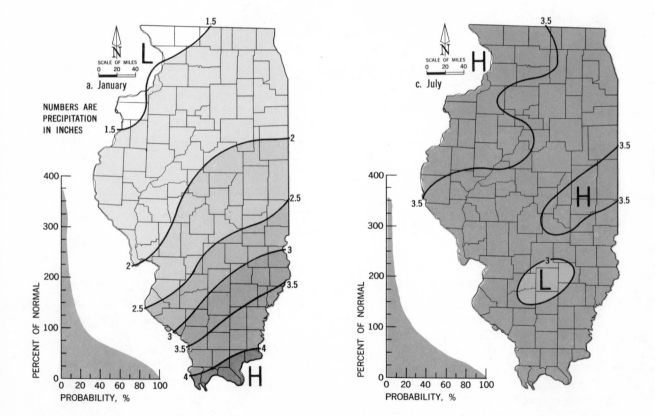

Normal precipitation in January and July.

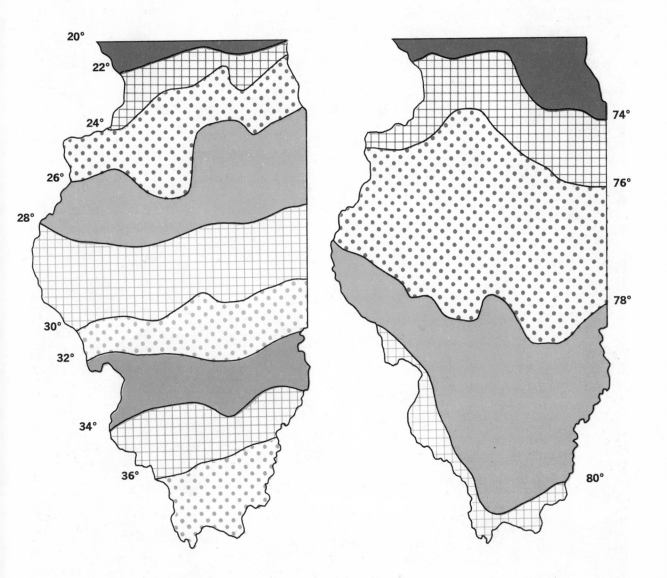

Mean temperature in January and July.

*This diorama at the Chicago Academy of Science shows Chicago
as it appeared 300 million years ago. The ancestor
of the dragonfly, in foreground, measured 28 inches across.*

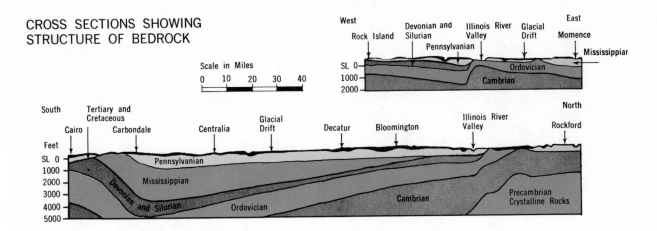

CROSS SECTIONS SHOWING
STRUCTURE OF BEDROCK

Scale in Miles
0   10   20   30   40

West   Devonian and   Illinois River   Glacial   East
    Rock Island   Silurian   Valley   Drift   Momence
                                    Pennsylvanian   Mississippiar
SL 0   Ordovician
1000   Cambrian
2000

South   Tertiary and   North
         Cretaceous
    Cairo   Carbondale   Centralia   Glacial   Decatur   Bloomington   Illinois River   Rockford
                                             Drift   Valley
Feet
SL 0   Pennsylvanian
1000
2000   Mississippian
3000   Devonian   Precambrian
4000   and Silurian   Ordovician   Cambrian   Crystalline Rocks
5000

My How You've Changed!

The earth is changed by many forces. Some of these are sudden and violent, while others, such as erosion by wind, water and glacier, work so slowly that the changes wrought are hardly apparent over hundreds or thousands of years. Another of the slowly working forces is pressure—the transforming power of tremendous weights of earth and rocks.

Most stupendous of all are the forces beneath the surface, which can push up a vast range of mountains, or erupt with explosions of lava, ash and gas to create new mountain ranges or endless miles of volcanic matter.

Although there is no evidence of volcanic activity in Illinois, nor are there any lofty mountain ranges, the changes in the area over many hundreds of millions of years have been almost unbelievable.

Who today can imagine Illinois as a place with a sweltering tropical climate, not a land but a sea? Yet many millions of years ago a bay of the Gulf of Mexico, known as the Silurian Sea, occupied the entire Mississippi Valley; land as far north as present Chicago was covered with water, and little coral creatures, extracting the lime from seawater, built up their reefs in the shallow waters over much of what is now Chicago.

Today this limestone bedrock lies under the whole city, beneath the clays and sand, and even extends into present Lake Michigan, coming close to the surface only in raised areas such as Stony Island. This underlying rock is known as Niagara limestone because it was formed at about the same time as the limestone bedrock over which Niagara Falls now pours. When engineers had to dig under Addison Street in Chicago during construction of the Kennedy Expressway, they were surprised to run straight into the buried coral reef at Logan Square.

When the forces beneath the surface pushed the level of the land up, the shallow seas slowly receded. Eventually the land sank and the water returned again. This happened many times, and each time deep deposits of sand, clay and the shells of marine animals were left. Pressed down by the weight of new deposits, the older deposits turned into the sandstone, shale and limestone found as bedrock throughout the present state. In White County, in southern Illinois, these sedimentary rocks reach the amazing depth of 12,000 feet. Beneath these sedimentary rocks lies the granite of the very remote period known as Precambrian, the earliest era of geological history.

Not until about 60,000,000 years ago did the last of the seas subside. After this the land remained permanently above the surface except for the small southern tip of Illinois, which is the northern extreme of the vast coastal plain which extends from the Gulf of Mexico to above the present-day Cairo area. This delta region around Cairo was built up gradually by particles of earth, sand and stone carried down and deposited by the rivers. This process is a continuing one. The Mississippi River delta is perhaps the most conspicuous example.

Over millions of years the bodies of countless generations of animals and sea creatures were buried beneath new layers of sediment as the seas came and went. Even the wind carried additional deposits of soil. Great pressures and the forces of decay turned the buried organisms into the petroleum now found in much of Illinois. Similarly, coal was formed by deposits of trees and other plant matter over untold centuries.

CONTINENTS OF ICE

About 60,000,000 years ago, for some unknown reason the climate changed; the region of present Illinois was no longer a tropical paradise. Far to the north, where it had become very cold, snow fell almost continually. As the snow mounted to the almost unbelievable depth of two or three miles it formed huge masses of ice known as glaciers. Gradually, as the pressure increased, these ice masses began to spread southward.

On four separate occasions, with inexorable force, these tremendous glaciers—as large as a continent—moved over much of what is now the state of Illinois. In front of them, like the blade of a bulldozer, they pushed great mounds of boulders, rocks, sand, dirt or whatever happened to be in their way. In many places the glaciers brought rich soils, stolen from farther north, and invaluable supplies of many minerals for the soil.

Hills were leveled and valleys were filled in with the materials brought by the glaciers as they carried everything before them. This leveling off process is the reason for the smooth surface of much of Illinois. The surface material (drift) left by the glaciers varies from a few feet to 500 feet in thickness.

When the temperatures increased, each of the glaciers slowly melted. Then the temperature turned cold once more, and the process was repeated.

The third period of glaciation, beginning about 150,000 years ago, covered so much of what is now Illinois that it is known as the Illinoisan glacier. This glacier reached almost to the southern tip of the present state, the most southerly penetration of any North American glacier. However, this glacier began to melt before it could level the stubborn Illinois Ozarks, and the southern tip of the state was left as an unglaciated, or driftless, region. Most of Calhoun County on the west, together with part of the surrounding area, and the northwest corner of present Illinois are the only other areas of the state that escaped the glaciers. These areas are

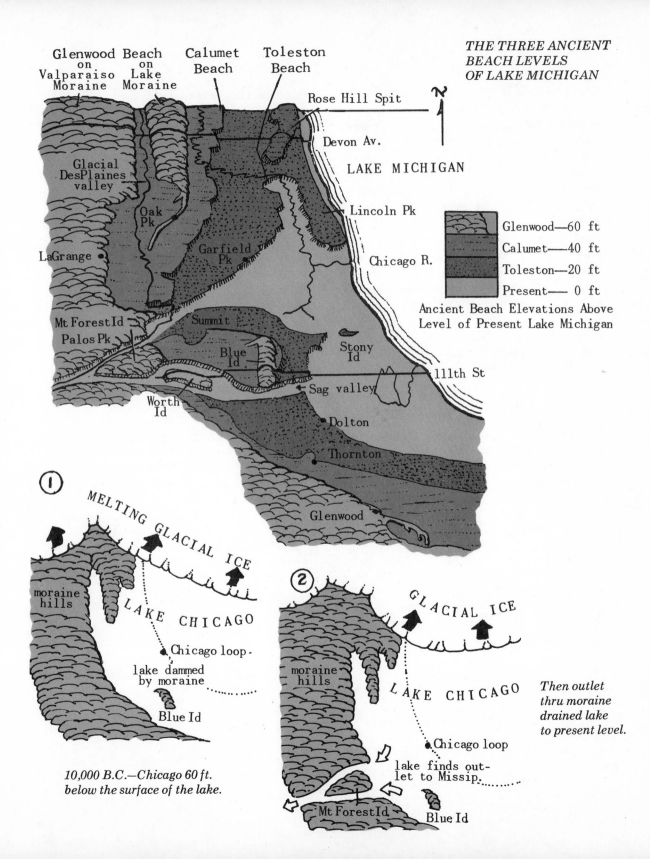

THE THREE ANCIENT
BEACH LEVELS
OF LAKE MICHIGAN

Glenwood on Valparaiso Moraine

Beach on Lake Moraine

Calumet Beach

Toleston Beach

Rose Hill Spit

Devon Av.

N

LAKE MICHIGAN

Glacial DesPlaines valley

Oak Pk

Lincoln Pk

Chicago R.

Garfield Pk

LaGrange

Glenwood—60 ft
Calumet—40 ft
Toleston—20 ft
Present—— 0 ft

Ancient Beach Elevations Above
Level of Present Lake Michigan

Mt Forest Id
Palos Pk

Summit

Blue Id

Stony Id

111th St

Worth Id

Sag valley

Dolton

Thornton

Glenwood

① MELTING GLACIAL ICE

moraine hills

LAKE CHICAGO

Chicago loop

lake dammed by moraine

Blue Id

10,000 B.C.—Chicago 60 ft.
below the surface of the lake.

② GLACIAL ICE

moraine hills

LAKE CHICAGO

Then outlet
thru moraine
drained lake
to present level.

Chicago loop

lake finds out-
let to Missip.

Mt Forest Id

Blue Id

called driftless because, having escaped the glaciers, they do not have the huge amounts of glacial drift—clay, sand, gravel and boulders—found in glaciated regions.

The fourth and last of the great glaciers, known as the Wisconsin, entered only a small portion of northeastern Illinois, but it left some of the largest mounds of terminal rubble known to science. Called terminal moraines, these piles of rock, sand, and earth are left where the edges of glaciers melt. Some of these terminal moraines, which make up the hills in northeastern Illinois, have taken the names of the communities built on them, such as the Bloomington, Shelbyville, Marseilles and Valparaiso moraines. The last is considered to be one of the largest glacial moraines in existence.

WATERY AFTERMATH

Melting of the glaciers left tremendous amounts of water to form huge lakes or to run off in vast raging torrents. Lake Chicago, the name given to the mammoth ancestor of present Lake Michigan, was much larger than the lake is now—a kind of super Lake Michigan.

Near what is now Palos Park, south of Chicago, this great body of water burst through the moraines that hemmed it in and formed the ancestral Des Plaines and Illinois rivers. These mighty prehistoric streams, far larger than they are at present, roared across the countryside. The ancient Illinois River formed a great gorge as much as two miles wide and 200 feet deep. The broadening series of terraces and bluffs far on either side of the present river show where the ancient river flowed in its various stages.

The prehistoric Des Plaines River was the immediate outlet for Lake Chicago, and its gorge was immensely larger than at present. There were other similar mighty ancestral rivers, such as the Fox, now much reduced from its former glory.

What remains of Lake Chicago today is the familiar Lake Michigan, which is classified as a glacial lake. Illinois also can thank the glaciers for leaving the many lakes which provide recreation for the northern part of the state.

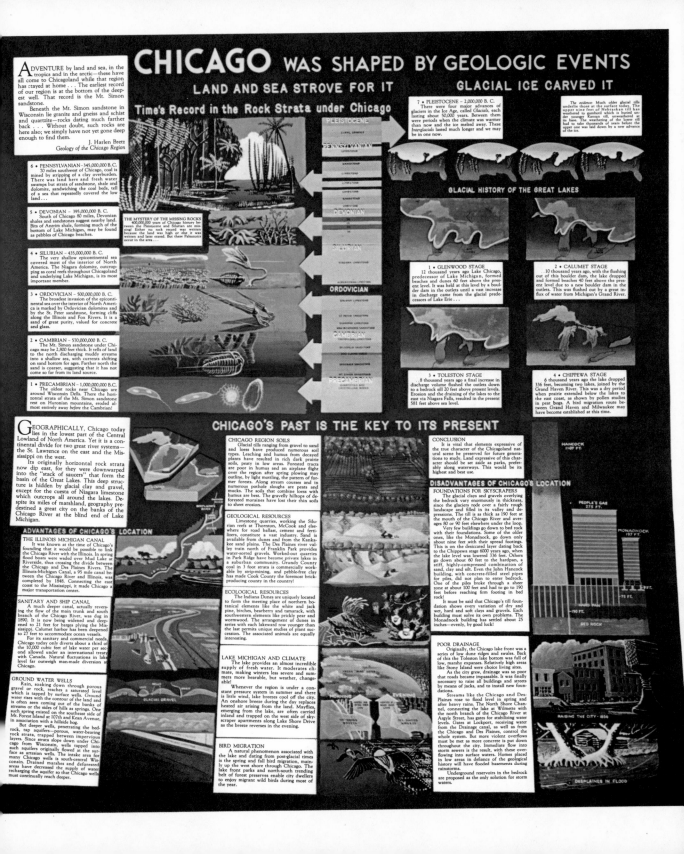

CHICAGO WAS SHAPED BY GEOLOGIC EVENTS

ADVENTURE by land and sea, in the tropics and in the arctic—these have all come to Chicagoland while that region has stayed at home . . . The earliest record of our region is at the bottom of the deepest well. That record is the Mt. Simon sandstone.

Beneath the Mt. Simon sandstone in Wisconsin lie granite and gneiss and schist and quartzite—rocks dating much farther back . . . Without doubt, such rocks are here also; we simply have not yet gone deep enough to find them.

J. Harlen Bretz
Geology of the Chicago Region

LAND AND SEA STROVE FOR IT

Time's Record in the Rock Strata under Chicago

PLEISTOCENE
PENNSYLVANIAN
DEVONIAN
SILURIAN
ORDOVICIAN
CAMBRIAN
PRECAMBRIAN

6 • PENNSYLVANIAN – 345,000,000 B.C.
70 miles southwest of Chicago, coal is mined by stripping of a clay overburden. There was land here and fresh water swamps but strata of sandstone, shale and dolomite, sandwiching the coal beds, tell of a sea that repeatedly covered the low land . . .

5 • DEVONIAN – 395,000,000 B. C.
South of Chicago 80 miles, Devonian shales and sandstones suggest nearby land. Bits of Antrim shale, forming much of the bottom of Lake Michigan, may be found as pebbles of Chicago beaches.

THE MYSTERY OF THE MISSING ROCKS
400,000,000 years of Chicago history between the Pleistocene and Silurian are missing! Either no rock record was written because the land was high or else it was written and later erased. But these Paleozoics occur in the area . . .

4 • SILURIAN – 435,000,000 B. C.
The very shallow epicontinental sea covered most of the interior of North America. The Niagara dolomite, outcropping as coral reefs throughout Chicagoland and underlying Lake Michigan, is its most important member.

3 • ORDOVICIAN – 500,000,000 B. C.
The broadest invasion of the epicontinental sea over the interior of North America is marked by Ordovician dolomites and by the St. Peter sandstone, forming cliffs along the Illinois and Fox Rivers. It is a sand of great purity, valued for concrete and glass.

2 • CAMBRIAN – 570,000,000 B. C.
The Mt. Simon sandstone under Chicago may be 2,800 feet thick. It tells of land to the north discharging muddy streams into a shallow sea, with currents shifting on sand bottom for ages. Farther north the sand is coarser, suggesting that it has not come so far from its land source.

1 • PRECAMBRIAN – 1,000,000,000 B.C.
The oldest rocks near Chicago are around Wisconsin Dells. There the horizontal strata of the Mt. Simon sandstone rest on Huronian mountains, eroded almost entirely away *before* the Cambrian!

GLACIAL ICE CARVED IT

7 • PLEISTOCENE – 2,000,000 B. C.
There were four major advances of glaciers in the Ice Age, called *Glacials*, each lasting about 50,000 years. Between them were periods when the climate was warmer than now and the ice melted away. These *Interglacials* lasted much longer and we may be in one now.

The evidence: Much older glacial tills underlie those at the surface today. The upper nine feet of Nebraskan till has weathered to gumbotil which is buried under younger Kansan till, unweathered at its base. The weathering of the lower till had to take thousands of years before the upper one was laid down by a new advance of the ice.

GLACIAL HISTORY OF THE GREAT LAKES

1 • GLENWOOD STAGE
12 thousand years ago Lake Chicago, predecessor of Lake Michigan, formed beaches and dunes 60 feet above the present level. It was held at this level by a boulder dam in the outlets until a vast increase in discharge came from the glacial predecessors of Lake Erie . . .

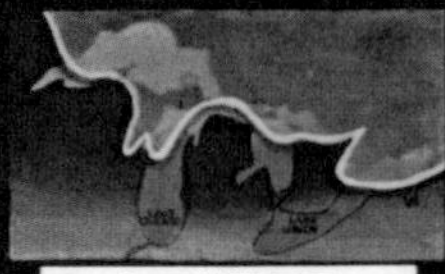

2 • CALUMET STAGE
. . 10 thousand years ago, with the flushing out of this boulder dam, the lake dropped and formed beaches 40 feet above the present level due to a new boulder dam in the outlets. This was flushed out by a great influx of water from Michigan's Grand River.

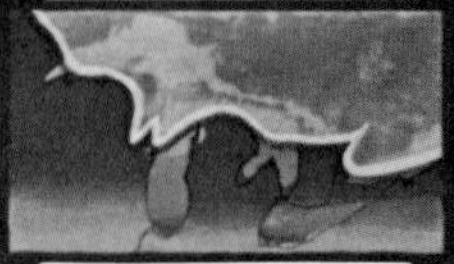

3 • TOLESTON STAGE
. . 8 thousand years ago a final increase in discharge volume flushed the outlets down to a bedrock sill 20 feet above present levels. Erosion and the draining of the lakes to the east via Niagara Falls, resulted in the present 581 feet above sea level.

4 • CHIPPEWA STAGE
6 thousand years ago the lake dropped 336 feet, becoming two lakes, joined by the Grand Haven River. This was a dry period when prairie extended below the lakes to the east coast, as shown by pollen studies in peat bogs. A bird migration route between Grand Haven and Milwaukee may have become established at this time.

CHICAGO'S PAST IS THE KEY TO ITS PRESENT

GEOGRAPHICALLY, Chicago today lies in the lowest part of the Central Lowland of North America. Yet it is a continental divide for two great river systems—the St. Lawrence on the east and the Missisippi on the west.

Its originally horizontal rock strata now dip east, for they were downwarped into the "stack of saucers" that form the basin of the Great Lakes. This deep structure is hidden by glacial clay and gravel, except for the cuesta of Niagara limestone which outcrops all around the lakes. Despite its miles of marshland, geography predestined a great city on the banks of the Chicago River at the blind end of Lake Michigan.

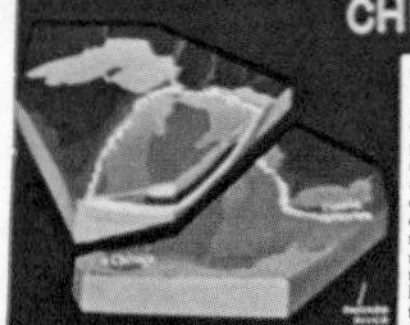

ADVANTAGES OF CHICAGO'S LOCATION

THE ILLINOIS MICHIGAN CANAL
It was known at the time of Chicago's founding that it would be possible to link the Chicago River with the Illinois. In spring flood boats were waded over Mud Lake at Riverside, thus crossing the divide between the Chicago and Des Plaines Rivers. The Illinois-Michigan Canal, a 95 mile canal between the Chicago River and Illinois, was completed by 1848. Connecting the east coast to the Mississippi, it made Chicago a major transportation center.

SANITARY AND SHIP CANAL
A much deeper canal, actually reversing the flow of the main trunk and south branch of the Chicago River, was dug in 1890. It is now being widened and deepened to 21 feet for barges plying the Mississippi. Calumet harbor has been deepened to 27 feet to accommodate ocean vessels.

For its sanitary and commercial needs, Chicago today only diverts about a third of the 10,000 cubic feet of lake water per second allowed under an international treaty with Canada. Natural fluctuations in lake level far outweigh man-made diversion at Chicago.

GLACIAL GRAVEL

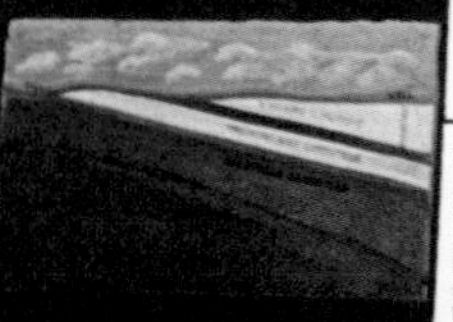

GROUND WATER WELLS
Rain, soaking down through porous gravel or rock, reaches a saturated level which is tapped by surface wells. Ground water rises with the contour of the land and is often seen coming out of the banks of streams or the sides of hills as springs. One such spring existed on the southeast side of Mt. Forest Island at 107th and Kean Avenue, in association with a hillside bog.

But deeper wells, penetrating the bedrock, tap aquifers—porous, water-bearing rock strata, trapped between impervious layers. Since strata slope down under Chicago from Wisconsin, wells tapped into such aquifers originally flowed at the surface as artesian wells. The intake area for many Chicago wells is south-central Wisconsin. Drained marshes and deforested areas have decreased the supply of water recharging the aquifer so that Chicago wells must continually reach deeper.

EVENING

CHICAGO REGION SOILS
Glacial tills ranging from gravel to sand and loess have produced numerous soil types. Leaching and humus from decayed plants have resulted in rich dark prairie soils, peaty in low areas. Forested tracts are poor in humus and an airplane flight over the region after spring plowing may outline, by light mottling, the pattern of former forests. Along stream courses and in numerous pothole sloughs are peats and mucks. The soils that combine loess with humus are best. The gravelly hilltops of deforested moraines have lost their thin soils to sheet erosion.

GEOLOGICAL RESOURCES
Limestone quarries, working the Silurian reefs at Thornton, McCook and elsewhere for road ballast, cement and fertilizers, constitute a vast industry. Sand is available from dunes and from the Kankakee sand plains. The Des Plaines river valley train north of Franklin Park provides water-sorted gravels. Worked-out quarries in Park Ridge have become private lakes in a suburban community. Grundy County coal in 3 foot strata is commercially workable by strip-mining, and pebble-free clay has made Cook County the foremost brick-producing county in the country!

ECOLOGICAL RESOURCES
The Indiana Dunes are uniquely located to form the meeting place of northern botanical elements like the white and jack pine, birches, bearberry and tamarack, with southwestern elements like prickly pear and wormwood. The arrangement of dunes in series with each lakeward row younger than the last permits unique studies of plant succession. The associated animals are equally interesting.

LAKE MICHIGAN AND CLIMATE
The lake provides an almost incredible supply of fresh water. It moderates climate, making winters less severe and summers more bearable, but weather, changeable!

Whenever the region is under a constant pressure system in summer and there is little wind, lake breezes cool off the city. An onshore breeze during the day replaces heated air arising from the land. Mayflies, emerging from the lake, are often carried inland and trapped on the west side of skyscraper apartments along Lake Shore Drive as the breeze reverses in the evening.

BIRD MIGRATION
A natural phenomenon associated with the lake and dating from post-glacial times is the spring and fall bird migration, mainly up the west shore through Chicago. The lake front parks and north-south trending belt of forest preserves enable city dwellers to enjoy migrant wild birds during most of the year.

CONCLUSION
It is vital that elements expressive of the true character of the Chicagoland natural scene be preserved for future generations to study. Land expressive of this character should be set aside as parks, preferably along waterways. This would be its highest and best use.

DISADVANTAGES OF CHICAGO'S LOCATION

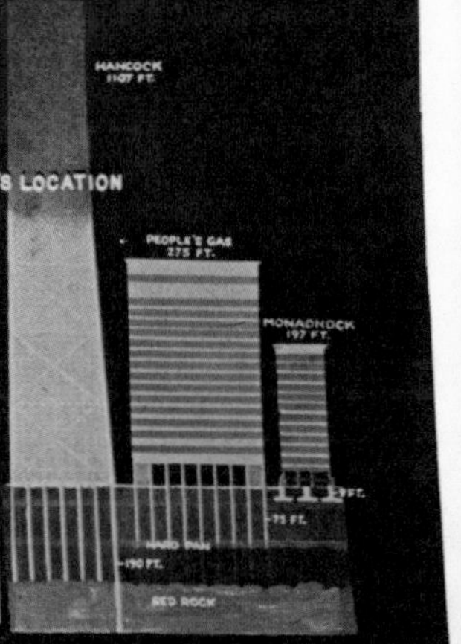
HANCOCK
1107 FT.
PEOPLE'S GAS
275 FT.
MONADNOCK
197 FT.
75 FT.
HARD PAN
190 FT.
RED ROCK

FOUNDATIONS FOR SKYSCRAPERS
The glacial clays and gravels overlying the bedrock vary enormously in thickness, since the glaciers rode over a fairly rough landscape and filled in its valley and depressions. The till is as thick as 190 feet at the mouth of the Chicago River and averages 80 or 90 feet elsewhere under the loop.

Very few buildings go down to bed rock with their foundations. Some of the older ones, like the Monadnock, go down only about nine feet with their spread footings. This is on the desiccated layer dating back to the Chippewa stage 6000 years ago, when the lake level was lowered 336 feet. Others go down about 60 feet to the hardpan, a stiff, highly-compressed combination of sand, clay and silt. Even the John Hancock building, with concrete-filled steel pipes for piles, did not plan to enter bedrock. One of the piles broke through a sheer zone at about 100 feet and had to go to 190 feet before reaching firm footing in bed rock!

It must be said that Chicago's till foundation shows every variation of dry and wet, hard and soft clays and gravels. Each building must solve its own problems. The Monadnock building has settled about 25 inches—evenly, by good luck!

RAISING THE CITY - 1856

POOR DRAINAGE
Originally, the Chicago lake front was a series of low dune ridges and swales. Back of this the Toleston lake bottom was full of low, marshy expanses. Relatively high areas like Stony Island were choice living sites.

As the city grew, drainage was so poor that roads became impassable. It was finally necessary to raise all buildings and streets by means of jacks, and to install new foundations.

Streams like the Chicago and Des-Plaines rose to flood level in spring and after heavy rains. The North Shore Channel, connecting the lake at Wilmette with the north branch of the Chicago River at Argyle Street, has gates for stabilizing water levels. Gates at Lockport, receiving water from the Drainage canal, as well as from the Chicago and Des Plaines, control the whole system. But more violent overflows must be met as more concrete is put down throughout the city. Immediate flow into storm sewers is the result, with these overflowing into surface waters. Homes placed in low areas in defiance of the geological history will have flooded basements during rainstorms.

Underground reservoirs in the bedrock are proposed as the only solution for storm waters.

DESPLAINES IN FLOOD

Evidence of Ancient Life

Not long ago young Chicago specimen hunters from a number of schools hired a bus to take them to Thornton quarry. There they enthusiastically collected so many fossils and rocks that the bus broke down under the weight. Such enthusiasm illustrates how much interest and fascination we continue to have in finding traces of the prehistoric world.

Fossils—the petrified remains of once living plants and animals—provide a record of the life that existed here millions of years ago. Almost all fossils are found in sedimentary rock—sandstone, limestone, shale. Generally only the hard parts, such as shells or bones are preserved. Rarely are such forms of life as jellyfish and worms, which have only soft, fleshy parts easily subject to decay, found in fossil form.

Among the vertebrate fossils (those with backbones) found in Illinois are dinosaurs, the elephant-like mammoths and mastodons, giant beaver, bison, and deer. Although complete or even partial skeletons of these animals are not common here, teeth, tusks, and bones are on exhibit in many local museums throughout the state.

Most of the Illinois fossils are primitive types such as the foraminifera, the one-celled animals which help geologists to identify oil-bearing rocks. Other common types of fossils found include the sponges and corals. In many places shells of clams, snails and brachiopoda (fossil mollusca) are preserved with little change, and appear much as they were the day they were buried at the bottom of the prehistoric sea. Marine worms, which burrowed into the sand or mud of the sea floor, are seldom found as fossils, but their trails and holes are common.

The plant fossil materials that make up the coal beds of Illinois are the remains of primitive trees and plants that grew in the swamps during the coal age. When the plants died, they fell into the water and were preserved as peat that later became coal.

Many fine fossils found in the coal and overlying shales represent the roots, trunks and leaves of the plants. A few of the insects that lived in the trees also are preserved. Perhaps the most famous collecting site for plant fossils is the Mazon Creek area near Braidwood in northeastern Illinois, where beautifully preserved impressions of ferns, tree leaves and a few insects have been gathered for museums all over the world. These are considered among the finest ever to be uncovered.

Insects are among the rarest of fossils, yet more than 130 different kinds have been taken from the coal-age rocks of Illinois, nearly all from Mazon Creek. Some of the prehistoric insects, such as cockroaches, dragonflies and damselflies, are still very much with us. Others, such as the giant dragonfly, which was a monster almost two feet in length, have long been extinct—and perhaps this is just as well.

Mounds, Men, and Monsters

"While Skirting some rocks, which by Their height and Length inspired awe, We saw upon one of them two painted monsters which at first made Us afraid, and upon Which the boldest savages dare not Long rest their eyes. They are as large As a calf; they have Horns on their heads Like those of a deer, a horrible look, red eyes, a beard Like a tiger's, a face somewhat like a man's, a body Covered with scales, and so Long A tail that it winds all around the Body, passing above the head and going back between the legs, ending in a Fish's tail.

"Green red and black are the three Colors composing the picture. Moreover, these 2 monsters are so well painted that we cannot believe that any savage is their author; for good painters in france would find it difficult to paint so well,—and, besides, they are so high up on the rock that it is difficult to reach that place Conveniently to paint them . . ."

This first comment on the works of prehistoric people in Illinois was recorded by Father Jacques Marquette in his fascinating diary. Even more interesting, the bluff monsters have become one of the real prehistoric mysteries. No Europeans had been known in the region previously, yet, as Father Marquette said, the paintings seemed to be beyond the skill of primitive people.

Later travelers rediscovered the figures, still glowering down from the cliff just north of present-day Alton, and disagreed on just what they saw. In 1699, only 23 years after Marquette made his discovery, Father St. Cosmé viewed the rock and found the figures much worn away. He said they seemed to be about 30 feet long and 12 feet high, with the wings of a bat.

In the early 1800's, a writer said he counted 10,000 bullet holes on or near the paintings, and one of the monsters had disappeared. Apparently the superstitious Indians shot at the paintings every time they passed by. The bullets were rapidly wearing the remaining figures away. Later the cliff was blasted apart for rock used to make railroad ballast.

Fortunately, a German publisher had sent an artist to Illinois in 1839 and had published the artist's sketch of the remaining figure in a book entitled *Das Illustrirte Mississippithal* (*The Valley of the Mississippi, Illustrated*). Here the figure was called *Piasa Bird* or *Thunderbird*, the name which is given in Europe to similar figures.

Modern travelers along the river highway near Alton may be as surprised as Father Marquette to see the great Piasa Bird glowering down from the cliff just as it once did. The people of Alton have had a colorful 30-foot likeness of the Piasa Bird reproduced, placing it close to the original site as a reminder of Illinois' prehistoric past.

MANY CULTURES

The Indians who were found in the Illinois region when early European explorers came are known as the protohistoric peoples (meaning that they lived just before recorded history). These Indians were apparently not related to the prehistoric peoples and knew little or nothing about them, so that just who the earliest peoples were and what became of them is a mystery.

A painting of the original Piasa Bird by a German artist, done in 1839 for the now rare book Das Illustrirte Mississippithal.

No relics have been found reaching back to the earliest days of prehistoric occupation in Illinois, but objects have been found which can be identified quite accurately as being eight or ten thousand years old, and the region undoubtedly was occupied thousands of years earlier. The legends of the Indians who were in the region when the first Europeans came tell of the awful ages of ice, and these ended about 10,000 years ago. Artifacts found include beautifully fluted flint spearheads. These primitive Indians lived in small family groups and hunted the mastodon.

The next cultural stage, called the Archaic, appeared about 8000 B.C. and lasted about 7,000 years. The great cultural advance of this period was the manufacture and use of such tools as the axe, adz and gouge. Archaic campsites also yield many grinding stones, used to process foods gathered from local trees and plants. Indications of temporary shelters have been found, but very rarely. These people did some of the earliest working of metals in history, but the metal was pounded and shaped rather than smelted.

As time went by, more advanced cultures came to the region. The group known as Early Woodland people dates from about 2500 B.C. to 500 B.C. They made the important advance of bringing pottery making to the Illinois area, using a characteristic clay tempered with grit. They also introduced small permanent houses and probably built the first burial mounds. Even more important, they began to practice agriculture and to raise crops. The Middle Woodland Indians reached a cultural peak in social activity, arts and crafts. This was due to the increase of leisure provided for them by the growing of crops.

The remarkable Hopewell people, the principal builders of mounds, were part of this culture period. In their burial mounds, which were frequently raised over log tombs, have been found a number of surprisingly beautiful pottery pieces of great artistic merit. Among those discovered are figurines in the forms of people, birds and animals. Materials found in their campsites—mica from the east, copper from the north, seashells and alligator teeth from the Gulf Coast—show that the Hopewell people must have been great traders. This being the case, they doubtless learned many things from the different people with whom they traded, and added to their knowledge and skills from these contacts. This culture lasted about 1,300 years, until A.D. 1200.

After A.D. 800 or 900 there was an abrupt decline in culture. However, some original work was done in this Late Woodland period. Using enormous amounts of material and untold man-hours, these people perfected the technique of building effigy mounds in the shape of reptiles, turtles, birds and other forms. The effigy mounds are thought to have had a part in their religious observances.

The next period of prehistoric culture was known as the Mississippian because a large number of villages built by these people were found abandoned along the Mississippi River. They were also scattered about Illinois. Their village sites show that they built long, oval houses covered with bark mats, probably housing many families.

Some of these villages probably had populations in the hundreds, indicating that they had highly developed agriculture which could support large numbers of people. Hoes of flint, bone and shell are found, along with milling stones for grinding flour. Hunting and fishing added to the food supply.

Extensive garbage pits, known as kitchen middens, give detailed information about the diet of the Mississippians. Shells of mussels, clams and snails are found along with the bones of fish, birds, mammals and even reptiles. Mammal bones are those of squirrels, deer, elk and bison; birds include turkeys, cranes, ducks and geese. Charred corncobs are also found, along with nut shells and other food remains.

The Mississippian peoples made pottery in many forms, together with other clay items such as smoking pipes, beads and effigies. Crushed shell was often used to strengthen the clay.

THE MOUND BUILDERS

There are more than 10,000 mounds raised by prehistoric people in Illinois—more than in any other state. Because the mounds are the most evident inheritance of the prehistoric people, they have been lumped together under the term "Mound Builders."

Ninety percent of the mounds probably were used as burial places. Some were built up constantly; when a body was buried, earth would be piled on. As more bodies were buried the mound gradually grew.

Some of the mounds were the effigy mounds already mentioned, while others were flat topped in the form of pyramids. Temples or other important buildings were placed on the flat top.

In the center of a number of smaller mounds near Cahokia stands Monk's Mound, reputed to be the largest artificial earthwork in the world. An archaeologist, Professor Cyrus Thomas marveled, "When we stand at the base of the great Cahokia Mound and study its vast proportions, we can scarcely bring ourselves to believe it was built without

An old illustration of some of the prehistoric
earth mounds at Cahokia. The largest of the mounds
in the area, and possibly in the world,
is Monks Mound, which covers nearly 17 acres at its base
and rises to a height of 100 feet. It is estimated
to contain 21,600,000 cubic feet of earth.

some other means of collecting and conveying material than that possessed by the Indians. But what other means could a lost race have had?

"The Indians had wooden spades, baskets, skins of animals, wooden and clay vessels and textile fabrics; they also had stone implements. It should be remembered that Cahokia is unique in respect to size being more than treble in contents that of any other true mound in the United States." It must have taken thousands of people many years to build Monk's Mound by carrying this immense amount of material in baskets and vases.

The Cahokia mounds were first studied scientifically in 1921 by Professor W. K. Moorehead of the University of Illinois.

One of Illinois' most interesting records of prehistoric people was made in the excavation of the Dickson mounds—now a state memorial near Lewiston, southwest of Peoria. What makes this excavation particularly important is the fascinating way in which the old tombs have been exposed. The more than 200 skeletons so far discovered are shown partially uncovered on the precise spot where they were laid to rest at an unknown time in the past.

A shelter has been built over the excavations and visitors may view the skeletons just as they were uncovered. With a slight shudder one visitor expressed what might have been the sentiments of all when he said, "Who knows what priest, leader of men, or even great ruler lies here, with his bones exposed to the rude gaze of thousands? Perhaps here is one who in his own time and for his own people was a Pharaoh or a Caesar—a Diogenes or a Sequoyah."

Even more poignant is the burial uncovered at Oakwood Mound near Joliet. Here most of the burials were of women and children. The confusion of the graves indicates that many people died suddenly and were hastily buried. The bodies of five pairs of skeletons were found here—mothers and their children, each pair clasped together in the bony embrace of death.

OTHER REMAINS

Illinois is dotted with various kinds of remains of early peoples, many of them having had little or no scientific study. Unusual are the seven stone "forts" found in the Ozark area. These "forts" were built on cliffs or bluffs, with a thick stone wall covering the exposed approach. They may have been used for protection, or perhaps even as traps for the capture of buffalo.

In what is now Union County, the prehistoric peoples mined flint from a quarry, flint of a particular kind found only there. It is interesting that flint brought from this quarry has been found in mounds in several other states, some quite distant, showing that Indians of various regions traded with one another for necessities.

Illinois is not as rich in pictographs and petroglyphs as some other areas. Pictographs are the pictures such as the Piasa Bird, painted on the walls of caves or rocks, and petroglyphs are the drawings gouged, scratched or carved into the surface. No one has been able to learn the meaning of any of these works, even though those in Illinois are generally of more recent date, and may even have been done during the historic period. However, the storied Piasa Bird probably must rank among the best known of such prehistoric work.

A Land of "Superior Men"

"When one speaks the word 'Illinois' it is as if one said in their language, 'the men,'—As if the other Savages were looked upon by them merely as animals. It must be admitted that they have an air of humanity which we have not observed in the other nations that we have seen upon our route."

This description by Father Marquette was the first ever written about the Illini Indians who gave Illinois its name. When the region first became known to European explorers the most important inhabitants were the members of six related tribes who had joined together in a loose confederation or government. These were the Michigamea, Moingwena, Peoria, Tamaroa, Cahokia and Kaskaskia tribes. They spoke of themselves as the Iliniwek (shortened to Illini), which means, in effect, "superior men." As Father Marquette indicates, perhaps they had some reason for this boast.

The early French explorers gave a French spelling to the name Illini, which became the familiar Illinois. The confederated Illini occupied much of central Illinois, spreading over onto the Iowa side of the Mississippi.

"... their language ... on the whole resembles allegonquin, so that we easily understood each other," Father Marquette pointed out. Actually, the Illini were members of the Algonquin family, a great group of tribes speaking the Algonquin language.

Father Marquette gave a fascinating description of the Illini: "They are of a gentle and tractable disposition; have several wives, of whom they are Extremely jealous; they watch them very closely and Cut off Their noses or ears when they misbehave. I saw several women who bore the marks of their misconduct.

"Their bodies are shapely; they are active and very skillful with bow and arrows. They also use guns, which they buy from our savage allies who Trade with our french. They use them especially to inspire, through their noise and smoke, terror in their Enemies; the latter do not use guns, and have never seen any, since they live too Far toward the West.

"They (the Illini) are warlike, and make themselves dreaded by the Distant tribes ... The Captains are distinguished from the warriors by wearing red Scarfs. These are made with considerable Skill from the Hair of bears and wild cattle. They paint their faces with red ocher ... They live by hunting, game being plentiful in that country, and on indian corn, of which they always have a good crop. Consequently, they have never suffered from a famine. They also sow beans and melons, which are Excellent ... Their Cabins are very large, and are Roofed and floored with mats made of Rushes. They make all Their utensils of wood and Their Ladles out of the heads of cattle, whose Skulls they know so well how to prepare. . . .

"There remains no more, except to speak of the Calumet (peace pipe). There is nothing more mysterious or more respected among them. Less honor is paid to the Crowns and scepters of Kings than the Savages bestow upon this. It seems to be the God of peace and of war, the Arbiter of life and of death. It has but to be carried upon one's person and displayed, to enable one to walk safely through the midst of Enemies

La Salle visiting an Illini village, as portrayed by the American artist George Catlin, famous for his Indian portraits and scenes of tribal life.

—who, in the hottest of the Fight, lay down Their arms when it is shown. For that reason, the Illinois gave me one, to serve as a safe-guard among all the Nations through whom I had to pass during my voyage. . . .

"It is fashioned from a red stone, polished like marble, and bored in such a manner that one end serves as a receptacle for the tobacco, while the other fits into the stem; this is a stick two feet long, as thick as an ordinary cane, and bored through the middle. It is ornamented with the heads and necks of various birds. . . .

"The Calumet dance, which is very famous among these peoples, is performed solely for important reasons: sometimes to strengthen peace, or to unite themselves for some great war; at other times, for public rejoicing. . . ."

OTHER ILLINI CUSTOMS

Lodges of the Illini were long, covered by reed mats woven by the women. The lodges housed as many as ten families; there were usually four or five fires in each house. Illini burial customs varied. Some placed the bod-ies in trees until only the skeletons were left. Then the remains were buried. Others placed the dead in shallow graves, burying them with items the dead might need on their way

Indians on the move used a travois, an arrangement of poles supporting a net or platform, to carry their belongings.

to a home beyond the earth. Sometimes calumets, tobacco, corn, bows or cooking utensils were buried in this way.

Women and children prisoners of war were generally held as slaves, but men prisoners suffered many tortures, particularly by fire; their hearts were cut out and eaten by their captors with the hope that they would be able to assume the courage of their dead enemies.

As Father Marquette points out, men could take a number of wives. A first wife's sisters, nieces or aunts could all be claimed by a man who was a good enough hunter to support them. Wives could not remarry for a year after the death of a husband; the penalty for disobeying this was death, and the erring woman's scalp was hung over the lodge of her late husband's family.

MANY PLACES—MANY TRIBES

There was a great deal of movement of Indian tribes in what is now Illinois. Maps showing various tribes in certain areas might be accurate for a given time, but a few years later many different tribal locations would have to be shown. This movement was increased by the fact that the fierce and hostile Iroquois of New York and some of their eastern relatives gradually came farther and farther west on raiding parties.

They drove many tribes from their homes, and these had to seek homes in the West. Tribes that occupied Illinois at one time or another include the Winnebago, Kickapoo, Piankashaw, Chippewa, Sauk and Fox, Ottawa, Miami, who were probably relatives of the Illini, and Shawnee. The Potawatomi, who were latecomers into the northeast around the Chicago area, were prominent in the later pioneer history of Illinois.

The Indians had innumerable legends about almost every subject, some of the most interesting being those of the Potawatomi. In one of these legends the story is told of the great flood (probably referring to the rising of prehistoric Lake Chicago) and of the creation of man. After the flood the Great Spirit, Kitchemonedo, made a man; when he became lonely he sent a sister for him. Then the

Great Spirit sent five suitors to the sister. Their names were Usama (tobacco), Waupako (pumpkin), Eshkossimin (melon), Kokees (bean) and Tamin (maize).

The girl rejected the first four. They fell dead as soon as they were rejected; after they were buried, the familiar tobacco, melons, pumpkins and beans sprang from their graves. After turning down four braves, she finally accepted Tamin. They were married, and all the Indians were descended from them.

When the first Europeans came into the region, they estimated that the six Illini tribes numbered as many as 10,000 people. One of the largest villages was that of the Kaskaskia on Lake Peoria. At one time it had almost 500 lodges. Each year the nations of the Illini had a gathering at Kaskaskia, and it is thought that as many as 8,000 delegates came to some of the larger meetings.

The Indian village built where the Rock River meets the Mississippi is said to have been one of the largest Indian villages in North America. Another very large Indian community was near Starved Rock.

These large populations were not to last. The Illini were attacked by the Iroquois, then by their neighbors to the north. Over the years they began to drink excessively and these once "superior men" faded from the scene. When the last of them left Illinois for Oklahoma in the early 1800's, they numbered only 150.

Old prints showing the Potawatomi chiefs Me-No-Quet (above) and Wa-Baun-See (below). Chief Wa-Baun-See has adopted some of the European style of dress.

Three Flags Flying

"I thank thee, Black Gown, and thee, O frenchman, for having taken so much trouble to come to visit us. Never has the earth been so beautiful, or the sun so Bright, as today; Never has our river been so Calm, or so clear of rocks, which your canoes have removed in passing; never has our tobacco tasted so good or our corn appeared so fine, as we now see Them. Here is my son, whom I give thee to Show thee my Heart. I beg thee to have pity on me and on my Nation.

"It is thou who Knowest the great Spirit who has made us all. It is thou who speakest to Him and who hearest his word. Beg Him to give me life and health, and to come and dwell with us, in order to make us Know him." Thus spoke the Illini Indian chief.

Father Jacques Marquette, the Black Gown, and Louis Jolliet, the Frenchman, indeed had "taken trouble" to visit the Illini in 1673. They had come from the distant lands of French Canada, they had been the first to discover the northern portion of the Mississippi River, and they were hopeful that it might lead them to the goal of much of the early exploration of America. This was to find an easy route to the rich trade of the Orient.

Father Marquette spoke wistfully of his hope that the river he called the Pekitanoui (Missouri) would prove to be the long-sought route to the East: "Judging from the Direction of the course of the Missisipi, if it continue the same way, we think it discharges into the mexican gulf," he wrote with great disappointment. "It would be a great advantage to find the river Leading to the southern sea, toward California; and, As I have said

that is what I hope to do by means of the Pekitanoui."

Of course, there were other reasons for the voyage. Father Marquette very sincerely hoped to bring Christianity to the Indians. Jolliet wanted to reinforce the claim of the French to all of North America west of the Appalachian Mountains. He also looked for new lands for settlement, for growing opportunities for French settlers both from Canada and from the mother country.

On their way south, Marquette and Jolliet only skirted the shores of Illinois, along the Mississippi. On their way back, however, after reaching as far south as present Arkansas, Marquette continued his account, "We therefore reascend the Missisipi which gives us much trouble in breasting its Currents. It is true that we leave it at about the 38th degree, to enter another river (the Illinois), which greatly shortens our road, and takes us with but little effort to the Lake of the Illinois (Lake Michigan)."

He praised the land: ". . . . its fertility of soil, its prairies and woods; its cattle, elk, deer, wildcats, bustards, swans, ducks, parroquets and even beaver . . . That (river) in which we sailed is wide, deep, and still for 65 leagues. In the spring and during part of the summer there is only one portage of half a league. We found on it a village of Illinois called Kaskaskia, consisting of 74 cabins.

"They received us very well, and obliged me to promise that I would return to instruct them (in religion). One of the chiefs of this nation, with his young men, escorted us to the Lake of Illinois (Michigan), whence at last, at the end of September, we reached

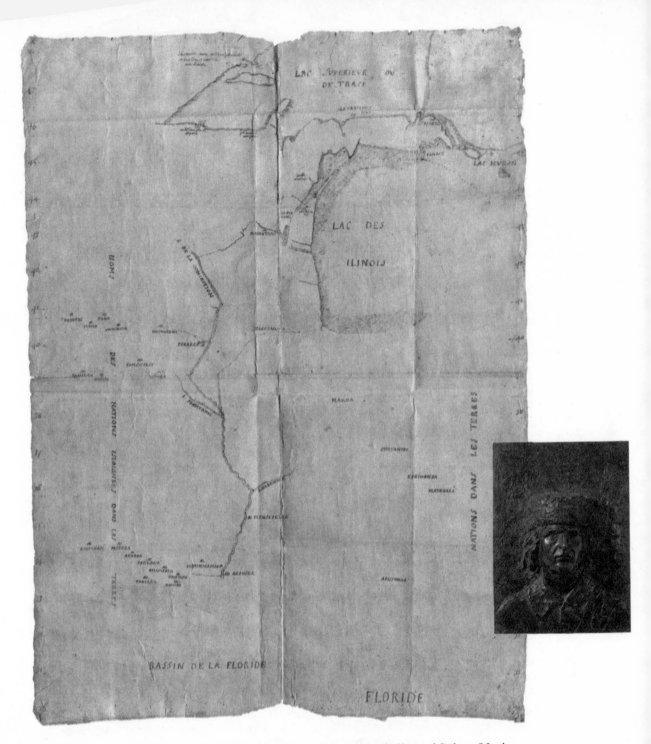

This map, reproduced from the original in the archives of the College of Sainte-Marie in Montreal, is said to be the only document of its kind to have survived the epic journey of Father Marquette and Louis Jolliet. The bust of Jolliet (inset) is a half-relief bronze plaque. See also the portrait of Marquette on page 128.

the bay des puantz (Green Bay), from which we had started at the beginning of June.

"Had this voyage resulted in the salvation of even one soul, I would consider all my troubles well rewarded, and I have reason to presume that such is the case. For, when I was returning, we passed through the Illinois of Peouarea (Peoria), and during three days I preached the faith in all their Cabins; after which, while we were embarking, a dying child was brought to me at The water's edge, and I baptized it shortly before it died, through an admirable act of providence for the salvation of that Innocent soul."

Theirs had been one of the truly memorable explorations of world history. In addition to discovering the upper Mississippi, they had made another discovery which may have been even more important—the great water route that someday would do its important part to make Illinois the world's transportation hub. It is remarkable that Jolliet had a vision of this. He could foresee that the route he and his partner had just traveled would someday tie together a whole continent. At what is now the community of Lyons, the party had been led by the Indians to leave the Des Plaines River and make a short portage to the Chicago River. This brought them to Lake Michigan, providing easy passage with a few portages to the French settlements of the Great Lakes, the St. Lawrence River and eventually to Europe.

Although New Orleans and the exact route of the Mississippi were not yet known, Jolliet must have realized that the route they had followed could place men in fairly easy reach of one another on a water route with only a few breaks from the Gulf of Mexico to the Gulf of St. Lawrence.

As the Frenchmen followed their friendly Indian guides to the outlet of the Chicago River, they made history in another way. They became the first white men to set foot on the site of the future city of Chicago.

Could Jolliet have foreseen a city here? Probably, for he wrote of the region south of Chicago as "Most beautiful and suitable for settlement . . . a settler would not there spend ten years in cutting down and burning trees; on the very day of his arrival, he could put his plow into the ground. Thus he would easily find in the country food and clothing."

BLACK GOWN RETURNS

Keeping his promise to return to the Indians, Marquette left Green Bay again October 25, 1674, to spread the word of Christianity to the people. Because Father Marquette was not well, and the weather was extreme, he and his party did not reach the mouth of the Chicago River until December 4. Here they decided to spend the winter "two leagues" above the mouth of the river, becoming in a sense the "first residents" of Chicago.

With his health partially restored, Marquette went on in the spring, down the Illinois River to the village of the Kaskaskia Indians, across the river from Starved Rock. On Easter he set up the first mission in what is now Illinois—the Mission of the Immaculate Conception of the Blessed Virgin.

After he had given the Indians some instruction in the new religion, Marquette asked all of the leaders to assemble in a great council. More than five hundred chiefs and elders gathered in a scene which must have been picturesque and even a little awesome. On a rope strung between two trees hung four large pictures of the Virgin Mary, carefully brought by Marquette for just such an occasion. Each picture was suspended by taffeta ribbons.

Father Marquette's crude winter quarters on the banks of the Chicago River in 1675, as painted by Charles S. Winslow.

The leaders sat on woven mats, bearskins, or even luxurious buffalo skins. Around them in this woodland setting stood a thousand of the leading young men, representatives of the various tribes. At the far fringes of the crowd, in a respectful fashion befitting their status, stood the women and children.

In the center stood the admired Black Gown. Father Marquette presented the leaders with ten gifts, each one a symbol of one part of the message he wished to give them; he then concluded with a mass. Another great council was held two days later.

Sadly, Father Marquette's health had failed again; he knew he was dying and asked to be returned to his beloved Mackinac at the head of Lake Michigan. However, he died in what is present-day Ludington, Michigan, before he could reach his destination.

The first epic of Illinois' recorded history, and one of the most noteworthy, had been concluded.

LA SALLE AND THE IRON HAND

Next on the scene in Illinois was the renowned discoverer and empire builder René Robert Cavelier, whose French title—Sieur de La Salle—gave him the name by which he is generally known. With his assistant, Henri de Tonti, La Salle came overland across what is now northern Indiana to the Kankakee River, and from there to the Illinois River.

He met the Illinois tribe of the Peoria, who had a large settlement in the region of Lake Peoria. In January, 1680, La Salle and his men established the first French foothold in the Illinois country and named it Fort Crèvecoeur (Fort Heartbreak). It was located on the Illinois River, about two miles south of Lake Peoria. It was La Salle's plan to build a string of forts stretching from the Great Lakes to the Gulf of Mexico. These, he felt, would strengthen the French hold on the region and provide bases for trade.

*A view of Fort Crevecoeur,
the first European settlement
in what is now Illinois.*

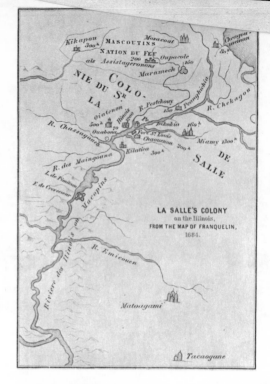

LA SALLE'S COLONY
on the Illinois,
FROM THE MAP OF FRANQUELIN,
1684.

*This map, drawn in 1684,
shows the locations of both
Fort Crevecoeur and
Fort St. Louis
on the Illinois River.*

Leaving a small garrison at Fort Crève-coeur under the command of Tonti, La Salle himself returned for supplies. In his absence, faced by hostile Indians and mutinous men, Tonti had to abandon the fort. When La Salle came back he found the post deserted, but finally located Tonti at Mackinac Island.

In 1682 the two men set out again. They descended the Mississippi River to its mouth at the Gulf of Mexico, the first white men to complete the journey. Arriving on April 9, 1682, they took formal possession of the great valley in the name of France. On their return they completed the construction of Fort St. Louis at Starved Rock.

The following year La Salle was deprived of his authority and returned to France, leaving Tonti in the Illinois country. After obtaining the right to colonize the Mississippi Valley, La Salle set sail for the mouth of the river. Unable to find the Mississippi because the coastline looked the same everywhere, he finally landed in Texas. In 1687, while on a third futile attempt to reach the Mississippi by traveling overland, La Salle was murdered by his men.

However, in 1690 his friend Tonti received much the same rights that had been given La Salle in the Mississippi Valley. Tonti was known as "Iron Hand" by the Indians who were greatly in awe of his artificial hand.

In 1691 Tonti moved Fort St. Louis back to the Peoria region. There it came to be called Fort Pimiteoui, which means "Fat Lake" in Indian, probably because Lake Peoria there makes a large bulge in the Illinois River. The modern city of Peoria claims that this settlement should be considered as the first permanent European community in Illinois. However, settlement around Fort Pimiteoui was not entirely continuous after 1691, and the area was almost deserted during the American Revolution.

For eleven or twelve years Tonti gave his energies to establishing the settlement of the Mississippi Valley. He encouraged settlers to come to the region, persuaded missionaries to set up missions and established regular routes for bringing in trade supplies.

By the year of his death in 1704, Tonti had succeeded in creating a system of forts stretching from the St. Lawrence River in Canada to Biloxi on the Gulf of Mexico. He had accomplished much of the dream of his leader and former associate, La Salle, of building a French empire in the Mississippi Valley. The fur trade which was established in the vast Mississippi area continued to be important for many years.

TRUE BEGINNINGS

In 1699 priests of the Seminary of Foreign Missions under the leadership of Father Jean François Buisson de St. Cosmé built a chapel and house on a place where the Tamaroa Indians kept a summer colony, on the Mississippi River, just south of present East St. Louis. Around the mission a community known as Cahokia grew up, and this is usually considered the first permanent settlement in the present state of Illinois.

Members of the Jesuit order however, contended that they had the exclusive right to conduct all missionary activity in the Mississippi Valley. To assert their rights, the Jesuit fathers, in 1703, moved their Mission of the Immaculate Conception from the present site of St. Louis to a place about sixty miles below

Cahokia, where an Indian village of the Kaskaskia stood not far from the mouth of the Kaskaskia River. They called their settlement Kaskaskia.

Around these two communities—Cahokia and Kaskaskia—in a region known as the American Bottom, grew much of the French settlement of the Illinois area, with Kaskaskia as the largest and most important.

THE FRENCH PERIOD

A strange chapter in history was concerned with the ambitious company built up by a speculator in France named John Law, who was given the French rights for commercial development of the entire Mississippi Valley. Because his company grew so fast and finally burst so explosively, it came to be known popularly as the "Mississippi Bubble."

The Mississippi Bubble did succeed in bringing a number of settlers into the Illinois country, but aside from some additional trade, that was about the only result in the Illinois region, and there was not much difficulty there when the bubble burst. However, the failure of this grand scheme greatly delayed any further development of the entire Mississippi region, especially to the north. France was almost bankrupt, and there was neither time nor money for the mother country to devote to the colonies in Louisiana.

In 1717 the French organized the Mississippi Valley into a colony known as Louisiana, and one of the districts of this colony was called Illinois, the first time the term had ever been used for what is now the state.

The chief district official was a commandant, who not only supervised the military and governed the people but also was in charge of fur trading, farming and other activities. Assisting the commandant were a

La Salle on the Mississippi,
from an old drawing.

Robert Cavelier, Sieur de La Salle,
from a portrait by G. P. A. Healy.

doctor, a notary, an interpreter and a judge. The militia of each village was headed by a captain under the control of the district judge. Church wardens maintained a kind of semi-official position as mayors.

French settlements in Illinois grew slowly. Probably there never were more than 2,000 French settlers in the entire state. Yet this small group managed to grow crops of grain which helped to feed the whole Mississippi Valley as far south as New Orleans.

The French settlers were good-natured and easygoing. They enjoyed nothing so much as dancing or playing their favorite card games. They accepted the Indians and treated them as equals, often marrying the women. Life of a community centered around the Catholic church or mission.

Life was simple; few things could be imported, and not much generally could be brought with them, so that settlers mostly had to make-do with whatever the country offered or they could grow or make with their own hands. Houses were simple but sturdy; furniture was homemade from the local forests. Sometimes a man who became a little better at making furniture than his neighbors

could barter it to others for meat, grain or vegetables. Women spun cloth for the clothes which they made themselves or used skins of animals for rough shirts or pants. The soap was boiled using lye made from charcoal and fats saved from cooking and butchering. It was usually strong enough to take off most of the dirt and considerable skin.

In 1718 Pierre Duque, Sieur de Boisbriant, arrived in the American Bottom to build a new fort. He finished the work in 1720 and named the place Fort de Chartres in honor of the Duke of Chartres. The settlement followed, and before long there was a local saying, "All roads lead to Fort de Chartres."

CHANGING HANDS

French-controlled areas were being slowly surrounded by British interests pressing down from Hudson's Bay holdings in the far north. British colonies on the East Coast were also beginning to move traders and even scattered settlers into the lands claimed by both the French and English between the East Coast and the Mississippi River.

One of the bloodiest of all Indian battles

Prairie du Rocher was one of the French communities that sprang up as a result of John Law's Mississippi Bubble. French was still widely spoken there as late as 1900.

in Illinois occurred in 1730 when a group of 300 Fox braves with their families was attacked near the present town of Plano by French soldiers, aided by their own allied Indian tribes.

The Fox dug in and held out during a three-week siege, but when they tried to slip away during a storm, they were pursued, and the following day great numbers of them were slaughtered.

All up and down the Mississippi the French were forced to fight the Chickasaw and other Indian groups who received support from the British.

In 1751 the French appeared to feel that heroic measures were necessary to keep their control of the country. To improve their strength in the region, they spent three years in building a new Fort de Chartres which they considered to be impregnable. They placed the foundations in 1753 and finished the great work in 1756.

Four acres of land were enclosed inside the massive walls, which were 18 feet thick. The four bastions each included eight embrasures, 48 loopholes for rifles, along with a box for a sentry. A guardhouse inside the walls also contained a chapel with adjoining rooms for priests. There was an administration building, a carriage house with loft for pigeons, and barracks stretching in two long rows to house the troops. A heavy powder magazine was set some distance from the other buildings for safety.

Meanwhile, war with the British had been erupting all across the East. Known as the French and Indian War, the conflict raged until the British captured the centers of French control on the St. Lawrence River in Canada.

By 1763 the war was over, but the French remained in control in Illinois until 1765.

The French fleur de lis flag flying over Fort de Chartres was lowered, while the commandant's eyes filled with tears. This was the last place on the North American continent where the French flag remained flying. The story is told that even the impassive Indians wept as the British flag, bearing the Cross of St. George, triumphantly ascended the flagpole, under the direction of the new British commander, Captain Thomas Stirling.

The great fort, thought to be mightiest in all of North America, had fallen without standing a single siege.

The British manned the fort for some time, but the Mississippi River began to take over, and by 1772, the British destroyed all that remained of the proudest military fortification of the West.

Little remains of the French occupation of Illinois. The most permanent reminders of their presence are the names of such communities as La Salle, Creve Coeur, Des Plaines, Du Quoin, Marseilles, Monticello and Paris.

UNDER THE BRITISH

The years of British occupation were uneasy ones. The British had been restricted in their take-over of Illinois by the hostilities of the Indians under Chief Pontiac. The Indian tribes were suspicious of the English and unhappy over the change from French to English control. The Illinois country was unbelievably remote from the centers of British government in the new world.

In 1769 the famed Chief Pontiac was murdered, presumably by Illini warriors, in Cahokia. To revenge their leader, his tribes of Potawatomi, Ottawa and Chippewa hurried from the north to make war on the Illini

*A room in one of the better French houses in Illinois
as re-created by the Chicago Historical Society.*

and left only scattered remnants of this once great tribe.

This was the struggle that gave birth to the legend from which Starved Rock received its name. A group of Illini fled to the top of the rock where they were safe from the pursuing tribes. However, their food and water at last gave out; they tried to let buckets down for water, but the enemies cut the ropes. Finally, after many died of thirst and famine, the attackers managed to reach the rest and put them to death. Although this story is widely believed, it has never been authenticated.

The population of the region was reduced when many of the most influential and wealthy French inhabitants moved across the river to St. Louis, which had recently been founded. Only the region east of the Mississippi was turned over to Britain by France. Spain had been given the Mississippi Valley regions west of the river to keep them from falling into British hands.

After Fort de Chartres was abandoned, the British commander governed from Kaskaskia with a small force of men. The British, however, were never able to form much more than a makeshift government in the Illinois territory, and they found the French settlers almost impossible to deal with. Settlers from the British colonies to the east were not attracted to Illinois, and conditions in Illinois were generally deplorable.

THE SPARK OF REVOLUTION

The Revolutionary War came to Illinois with the activities of young George Rogers Clark of Virginia, who had a growing reputation as a leader of American opposition to Britain. He went to Governor Patrick Henry of Virginia with a daring and imaginative plan to capture the western country and was given a commission by the governor to carry out this plan. Much of this region had long been claimed as a part of Virginia.

Gathering up a tiny army of 175 men in Kentucky and Ohio, Clark and his forces drifted down the Ohio River on flatboats until they reached Fort Massac, and then they set out for Kaskaskia, the unimpressive seat of British government.

The British commander, Rocheblave, a Frenchman, did little but send complaining letters to England about his situation. When Clark and his men arrived on July 4, 1778, the second anniversary of American independence, they received a friendly reception and took the town without resistance.

The main French settlement in the Midwest had been Vincennes, in present Indiana, just across the Wabash River from what is now Lawrenceville, Illinois. Father Pierre Gibault, a beloved priest at Kaskaskia, volunteered to make the difficult journey to Vincennes, and he was able to persuade the people there to come over to the American side. There was no English garrison there.

When the British commander at Detroit, Henry Hamilton, heard of this, he marched on Vincennes with 600 men and retook it in December, 1778. Hamilton was sure Clark could not attack until spring, so he kept only a small force of men at Vincennes and dismissed the rest for the winter. One of the rich traders of the town, courageous Francis Vigo, made the dangerous journey to Kaskaskia to bring this news to Clark. Without Vigo's hard journey, Clark might never have learned how the garrison at Vincennes had been weakened.

Clark expected that in the spring Hamilton would gather a large army again which might easily drive the American forces out of

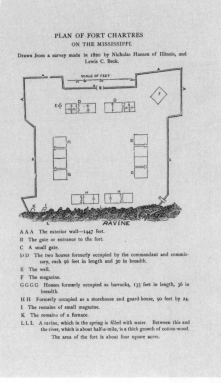

*Plans of Fort Chartres,
from a survey made in 1820.
See also the photographs
of the original powder magazine (F)
and the restoration
of this building on page 190.*

the West forever. Yet it seemed impossible for any force to march across the 240 miles from Kaskaskia to Vincennes during the winter. Clark wrote to Virginia's Governor Henry, "I know the case is desperate, but, Sir, we must either quit the country or attack Mr. Hamilton. No time is to be lost. Was I sure of a re-enforcement I should not attempt it. Who knows what fortune will do for us? Great things have been effected by a few men well conducted. Perhaps we may be fortunate." He was right; he and his men were soon to perform one of the "great things" of American history.

In perfect secrecy, on February 5, 1779, Clark marched from Kaskaskia at the head of only about 170 "Long Knives," as the men were called because of the deadly knives they carried. There had been a great deal of chilly rain, and most of the Illinois lowlands were flooded. This meant long stretches of wading through icy water. Sometimes the men could barely keep their rifles and ammunition dry.

A drummer boy helped to maintain their morale with his antics, such as floating across a flooded marsh on his drum. But there was little else to be cheerful about. Approaching Vincennes, they could not even light fires to dry their clothes and had to remain soaked. Their supply boat failed to keep up with them, and they went without food the last two days.

The daring and brilliant capture of Vincennes on February 25, 1779, belongs to Indiana history, although it was made possible in part by twenty American flags sewed by the women of Kaskaskia. The flags were used to make the enemy think that Clark had 20 complete divisions of men. Even though limited in size, the action was one of the most important of the Revolution in several respects. It kept much of the then "Far West" quiet and laid the foundation for America's later successful claim to the whole vast region. Without the work of Clark and his Long Knives, the entire area known as the Northwest Territory might have remained a part of Canada.

During the rest of the Revolutionary War there were a few attacks by the British with their Indian allies, but these were beaten off. When Cahokia was attacked in 1780, Clark successfully came to its aid. Military action finally ceased, except for a few Indian raids incited by the British.

George Rogers Clark (1752-1818), American Revolutionary general and conqueror of the Northwest Territory.

THE WESTERN FRONTIER

Almost as soon as word of Clark's successes in Illinois reached Virginia, the Virginia Assembly, on December 9, 1778, established far-off Illinois as a county of Virginia. The Treaty of Paris in 1783, which ended the Revolutionary War, gave formal recognition of America's claims to Illinois and all of the Northwest Territory.

However, owning and governing are two different matters. After Clark's troops were withdrawn in 1780, the area had almost no government. In 1784, a strange figure, John Dodge, once respected by George Washington, seized the remains of the fort at Kaskaskia and set himself up as a kind of ruler— a tyrant of the worst sort. Whenever the people tried to send messengers for help, they would be found murdered. This continued for two years and Father Gibault wrote, "Breaking of limbs, murder by means of a dagger, sabre, or sword (for he who wills carries one) are common, and pistols and guns are but toys in these regions. . . . The most solemn feasts and Sundays are days given up to dances and drunkenness . . . and a thousand other disorders which you are able to infer from these."

How familiar this sounds to anyone who has seen an American "Western." Usually thought of only in connection with the Far West, such conditions were familiar to the frontier as it moved across the continent. The frontier was just as much the "wild west" when it was in Illinois as when it reached Wyoming, Colorado or New Mexico.

THE NORTHWEST TERRITORY

However, changes were soon to come. In 1784, Virginia gave up all claims in Illinois and ceded the area to the central government, and plans went forward to provide a real government for the new American West. A truly amazing act was passed, known as the Ordinance of 1787, establishing the pattern for all future territories to proceed toward statehood in a regular and orderly manner. In setting the example for the expansion of the democratic way of life in all of the territories, the Ordinance must rank along with the Declaration of Independence and the Constitution of the United States.

The Ordinance of 1787 provided organization for a new unit of government to be known as the Northwest Territory. In addition to Illinois, it included Indiana, Ohio, Michigan, Wisconsin and part of Minnesota. General Arthur St. Clair, a hero of the Revolution, was named territorial governor, at the newly formed town of Cincinnati, Ohio.

Governor St. Clair came to Illinois, and at Kaskaskia organized the area west of the Wabash, "modestly" giving it his own name —the County of St. Clair. Cahokia, Kaskaskia and Prairie du Rocher were all made county seats, because a choice of one would have proved unpopular with the others.

Although the settlement that ended the Revolutionary War had seemed final, Britain had never given up the hope that someday all or part of the former colonies might be regained. In the west, British leaders encouraged the Indians to attack settlers to retain control of their ancestral lands.

In 1794, after some serious defeats, American forces finally won a great victory over the Indians in the Battle of Fallen Timbers in Ohio. Following this, in the Treaty of Green Ville (now called Greenville) in 1795, the Indians gave up vast areas including thirty-six square miles at the mouth of the Chicago River (the heart of present Chicago), territory around Peoria and also around the mouth of the Illinois River. By 1809 a large part of southern and western Illinois had been ceded by the Indians.

THE FLOOD OF SETTLEMENT

With great areas of new land open for settlement and with the lands of the East long in private hands, the opportunities for people to make a new life for themselves in the West seemed tremendously attractive. Veterans of the Revolutionary War were offered some of the new lands in part payment for their services, and others found the idea of moving west equally attractive.

Journeying overland, where there were no roads, was almost impossible, but the broad waters of the Ohio River provided a ready-made highway. Travelers who could afford such luxurious travel came to Pittsburgh, Pennsylvania, or other locations on the river and its tributaries. There they made or purchased flatboats (a sort of raft with cabin) and drifted down the river to their new homes, steering as best they could with a sweep-like rudder on the back of the flatboat. The adventures with pirates, Indians, rapids, floods and other dangers on such a trip were more than enough for most lifetimes, and many never reached their destinations. Many others traveled up the Mississippi River from the southern states.

Most of those who did arrive in Illinois went up the inland rivers and built their homes along or near the waterways, even though this meant that the land would have to be cleared of the trees which were almost always found on river bottoms. There were good reasons for choosing such locations. On the treeless prairies there would have been no timber to construct homes, no firewood, fence logs and often no water. Besides, the open stretches of prairies seemed to be an alien land, with no protection from foes or weather. It was said, too, that if the prairie could not grow trees, it lacked fertility.

In this period settlers were still almost entirely on their own, but it was not long before local experts in several trades could be called upon, in exchange for goods or services. Such artisans as blacksmiths were in demand. A good smith did far more than shoe horses; he made tools and simple farm implements and much of the rather primitive hardware and equipment found in pioneer homes and repaired almost anything made of metal. There were cabinetmakers, carpenters and potters in growing numbers.

While almost every household still had members who could spin and weave, more and more cloth was being brought in at this period, mostly from abroad at high prices. There might even be a widow or spinster who could be employed for dressmaking, and possibly even a jack-of-all-trades who could serve as a tailor.

Downriver from the East and upriver from New Orleans, the amount of manufactured goods—pots and pans, pins and needles, and even a few grand items such as bedsteads—were brought in to be exchanged for the products of the country. Since there was almost no currency or coins, barter and exchange were nearly universal.

Manufacturing was confined almost entirely to milling and salt making. Mills were built where waterpower would turn the mill wheel, and at harvest time there would be a constant stream of farmers bringing their grain to the mill to be ground into flour or meal. Usually this was paid for by giving the miller a fixed percentage of the grain. Where the supply of timber was adequate, sawmills were set up, also using waterpower, and boards became available for building in place of whole or split logs.

Some pioneer Illinois homes were built of brick, which usually was manufactured right on the site from clay found on the property.

SHAKEN BY NATURE AND WAR

In 1800 the Northwest Territory was divided, and a new Territory of Indiana, which included much of present Illinois, was created. In 1809 Illinois became a territory in its own right and Ninian Edwards was appointed territorial governor. Present Wisconsin was included in this territory.

The year 1811 brought two firsts—the first steamboat on the Ohio and the first major earthquake to be recorded in the area. The quake was centered on the Mississippi River not far below Cairo, but it was felt over a vast area. Less violent quakes continued to panic the region for almost a year.

Another kind of violence erupted in 1812 when Britain and the youthful United States went to war for the second time. However, except for some sharp clashes with the Indians, who were encouraged by the British to make trouble, the war was hardly felt by the people living in the Illinois territory.

One of these Indian clashes has come to be known as the Fort Dearborn Massacre. Far from the settled regions of Illinois, on the shores of remote Lake Michigan, was built an outpost named in honor of Henry Dearborn, then the Secretary of War and a former hero of the Revolution. Although the fort had a rugged stockade, enclosing barracks, blockhouses and stores, it was abandoned on the orders of General Hull, commander of the American forces in the Northwest. About 100 soldiers and settlers set out for Fort Wayne, but were massacred or captured before they had gone two miles. Only one family escaped. (The story of the establishment of Fort Dearborn and the massacre is given in greater detail on page 86 ff.)

There was other scattered fighting with the Indians throughout the territory during the War of 1812. One of these clashes was the battle of Campbell's Island, in the Mississippi River near present-day Rock Island. A young war chief named Black Hawk was defeated there by American forces under Major John Campbell. Chief Black Hawk was to become better known at a later date.

STATEHOOD

During all of Illinois' territorial period Ninian Edwards occupied the governor's chair. In 1812 Illinois had been made a territory of the second class. Five years later, the area did not really seem ready for statehood, but as the present Governor Otto Kerner has pointed out, "When statehood came to Illinois, it came with a rush."

Ninian Edwards (1775-1833), governor of the Illinois Territory and one of the first United States Senators from the new state.

Inspired by a young newspaperman, Daniel Pope Cook, the Illinois territorial legislature sent a memorial to Congress asking for Illinois statehood. The memorial called for the lead mines and salt springs to be reserved for the benefit of the state. It also contained the foresighted request for "all gifts and privileges as had been previously made and given to the states of Ohio, Indiana and Mississippi."

The greatest problem faced on the path to immediate statehood was that the Ordinance of 1787 required a population of 60,000 before a territory could become a state. Best figures available placed Illinois' population at only 40,258. The legislature authorized a census but made certain that it would be

The Fort Dearborn Massacre, August 15, 1812.
Attacked by the Potawatomi Indians after abandoning the fort,
12 of the militia, 26 of the regular troops,
most of the children and two of the women were killed.
All of the others, except the Kinzie family, were captured.

conducted as slowly as possible, with the hope that Congress would approve statehood before the census could be finished.

When the memorial for statehood reached Congress, it became the responsibility of the territorial delegate to Congress, who had all the privileges of a Congressman except the vote, because he did not represent a state. This delegate for Illinois was Nathaniel Pope, one of the most remarkable and effective of all the territorial delegates in the country's history. Because of their position, many delegates had little influence or authority. Few really accomplished much in Congress. Pope, however, had a way of getting his associates to follow his lead. He was helped, moreover, by the fact that Missouri

was also applying for statehood, and many people in Congress preferred to move ahead on the application of Illinois because they opposed admission of a slave state, at least before a free state was ready.

One of the most remarkable and far-reaching of Nathaniel Pope's accomplishments was the adoption of his amendment to the proposed statehood legislation. The northern boundary of Illinois had been placed at the same latitude as that of Indiana, 10 miles north of the southern tip of Lake Michigan. Pope's amendment raised the Illinois boundary 41 miles north of this.

The additional territory added to Illinois by this move covered 8,000 square miles, including most of 14 present counties, the city

and port of Chicago—altogether an area which now includes about three-fifths of the total population of Illinois.

Another remarkably foresighted Pope provision provided that three percent of the five percent of Federal land revenue usually granted to the state would be used for education. One-sixth of this three percent would be specifically set aside for a college or university. When this was passed, it assured Illinois of an advantage not enjoyed by many other states for providing better education.

The original memorial had reached Congress on January 16, 1818; legislation for Illinois statehood passed the House on April 13, was approved by the Senate the next day, and sent to the President on April 18.

The first Illinois state constitution was adopted August 26, 1818, without being submitted to a vote of the people—the only time this has occurred in the history of the progress of the various colonies and territories to statehood. On December 3, 1818, Illinois became the 21st state of the United States. Shadrach Bond was elected as the first governor and Ninian Edwards and Jesse B. Thomas, the first United States Senators.

Nathaniel Pope gave further evidence of his far-seeing qualities when he wrote home: "We will enter upon a state government with better prospects than any state ever did— the best soil in the world, a mild climate, a large state with the most ample funds to educate every child in the state."

Life in a Young State

"The eye sometimes surveys the green prairie without discovering on the illimitable plain a tree or bush, or any other subject, save the wilderness of flowers and grass," a traveler from England wrote not long after Illinois became a state. "On other occasions the view is enlivened by groves dispersed like islands on the plain, or by a solitary tree rising above the wilderness."

Another author, Frederick Gerhard, wrote in *Illinois as It Is* "Hints to Immigrants"— "A pair of good horses, a wagon, a cow, a couple of pigs, several domestic fowl, two ploughs (one for breaking the prairie, and the other for tillage), together with a few tools and implements are all that is necessary for a beginning. A log house can soon be erected."

These comments are good indications that Illinois was still a pioneer state, but changes were to come rapidly. The frontier communities resounded with increasing bustle. The stream of newcomers continued to come floating down the Ohio in every kind of vessel. Steamboats were increasingly common. They stopped at Shawneetown, Cairo or other Illinois river towns with goods and passengers. There was frequent and regular steamboat service on the smaller rivers, and the Illinois River eventually was served by steamboats as far as Ottawa.

The newcomers were of all types and kinds: first, hunters and roving people, who loathed crowded communities; then those who were too poor to do anything but squat on poorer land; later, many who had stock and capital to establish large operations; and finally even a sprinkling of educated men bringing fresh attitudes to the frontier.

One of the most fascinating developments was the mushroom growth of Galena, typical of the mining boomtowns that were to follow later in the Far West. The lead mines of the Fever River district had attracted developers as early as John Law's promotions in 1717. The lead had been exploited and valuable resources misused by scattered miners until the Federal government took control in 1807.

By 1826 the first post office in northern Illinois had been established at Galena, the town which had been named for its principal product, sulphide of lead. A government mining lease was granted as early as 1822; a smelter began operations in 1823 and shipped out 210 tons of ore. By 1845 the output was 27,000 tons a year, and the Galena area produced more than 80 percent of the country's lead supply. Within a few years, however, Galena suffered a rapid decline. The lead gave out.

THE BLACK HAWK WAR

This was a period of growing Indian unrest. In 1829 the government ordered the Sauk and Fox to leave their lands in northwestern Illinois. Some of them obeyed and crossed the Mississippi to Iowa; others stayed on, disregarding the order. The settlers took over vacated Indian property and plowed land which had been ancient burial grounds of the Indians; disputes naturally arose. Seeing the land which they loved threatened,

United States troops, camped in the shadow of the Mississippi bluffs, prepare to launch an attack against Black Hawk.

the Indians made trouble. The settlers asked the governor for help, complaining that the Indians "threaten our lives if we attempt to plant corn, and say that we have stolen their land from them, and they are determined to exterminate us."

After a volunteer army was called and marched toward the Indian holdings, Black Hawk, the Sauk war chief, gave up and joined his fellow tribesmen across the Mississippi. However, the following year, 1832, Black Hawk and his followers returned to Illinois, saying the treaty was not legal. They had not planned to make war, apparently intending to go to Wisconsin and plant crops.

When troops fired on and killed two braves carrying a flag of truce, the Black Hawk War began. There were several small battles in this little war in northern Illinois and southern Wisconsin. Finally with his back to the Mississippi, Black Hawk offered to surrender, at the same time trying to get his people across the Mississippi and back into Iowa. Ignoring the plea for a truce, the troops attacked in what has come to be known as the Battle of Bad Axe, in Wisconsin. An American gunboat killed most of the Indian women and children who were on the rafts in the river, and in a senselessly savage slaughter wiped out a large part of the Indian force.

The casualties of the Black Hawk War were about 72 on the government side and as many as 600 Indians. Black Hawk was imprisoned for a while. After his release, he went back to his people and died on the Sauk reservation in Iowa in 1838 at 71.

By the end of 1832, most of the other Indian tribes had ceded their lands and left the state. Just 160 years after Father Marquette had first met the Indians of Illinois, the white man had driven them out.

GROWTH AND CHANGE

Because the earliest settlement of Illinois had taken place in southern Illinois, many towns in that region had been settled for generations. Some were flourishing and able to boast of culture and society, while the sleepy little village on Lake Michigan only had 200 inhabitants when it was organized in 1833 as a town with the name of Chicago.

However, a few years before, an event in New York State laid the basis for the dramatic growth of Chicago, a growth which probably surpassed that of any city in history. The Erie Canal had opened in 1825. This made a water route over which travelers and goods could be brought much less expensively from the established Atlantic Coast cities to the frontier of Illinois. The location of Chicago was the most convenient on the Great Lakes.

The year after Chicago was organized, 225 sailing ships docked there. Agricultural products began to arrive in Chicago from the rest of the state to be shipped to the East by boat. Travelers coming by the water route, with destinations all over the Middle West, left their boats at Chicago; they wanted hotels to stay in and transportation into other parts of the country. Chicago was going to provide all this and more. Chicago was on its way.

In the Battle of Bad Axe, the American gunboat, Warrior, *slaughtered Indian women and children who were attempting to escape across the Mississippi.*

*An artist's conception of how the great Mormon temple
at Nauvoo would have looked had the Mormons
not been driven out before it was completed.*

"BEAUTIFUL PLACE"

Even more rapid and spectacular, for a time, was the growth of another Illinois community. In 1839, Joseph Smith, founder of the Church of Jesus Christ of the Latter Day Saints, better known as Mormons, had brought his followers to the banks of the Mississippi in Illinois after they had been driven from Missouri. Smith wrote, "The place was literally a wilderness . . . but believing that it might become a healthy place by the blessing of Heaven to the Saints, and no more eligible place presenting itself, I considered it wisdom to make an attempt to build a city."

He named the community Nauvoo, and soon, incredibly, it was a city, peopled by rapidly growing numbers of enthusiastic hard-working Mormons. Missionaries went over the world to attract converts to the new faith and the new city. Mormon literature was given to thousands. Within five years Nauvoo had grown so amazingly that it was the largest city in Illinois.

Joseph Smith became a powerful leader in Illinois politics. He received a charter for Nauvoo which made him almost independent of the control of the state. He even organized and controlled his own militia. Because his followers voted in a block, following Smith's lead, he might even have influenced the results of elections. He announced in 1844 that he would be a candidate for President of the United States, and most of his followers heartily supported him.

Non-Mormons, known as Gentiles, became suspicious and distrustful. Stories and rumors about the Mormons began to spread. There was a split in a part of the Mormon leadership. When some of the dissenting Mormon leaders opposed Smith and published a newspaper denouncing his policies, Smith had the press destroyed.

For this, Smith and his brother, Hyrum, the Prophet, were taken to jail at Carthage. The region was thrown into turmoil, and Governor Thomas Ford rushed to Nauvoo to tell the Saints that their leaders would have a fair trial. However, Carthage was strongly anti-Mormon. A militia group which had gathered there intent upon trouble was broken up by the governor, but members of the militia disguised themselves, attacked the jail and on June 27, 1844, killed the two Mormon leaders.

For a time civil war seemed to threaten Illinois. The Mormon charter was revoked; all during the summer mobs of both sides met and fought, until the new Mormon leader, Brigham Young, announced that the Mormons would move once again to a new home, this time in the Far West.

All of Nauvoo became a wagon factory as the Saints prepared their transportation. They knew that they would lose most of the large investments they had made in Nauvoo. In February, 1845, the first group crossed the Mississippi with Young, and about a thousand a week left from that time on. "The ferry boats were crowded," says one account, "and the river bank was lined with anxious fugitives, sadly waiting their turn to pass over and take up their solitary march to the wilderness."

When it appeared that some Mormons might stay on in spite of everything, their neighbors once again attacked the town until all had left. Soon Nauvoo was a ghost city.

THE LONG NINE

Kaskaskia had been the first capital of the new state, but in 1819 the capital was moved to Vandalia, which was the seat of state government for 20 years. To Vandalia in 1834 came a new member of the state legislature— tall, lanky Abraham Lincoln. He joined with a group of eight other legislators, who were known as the "Long Nine" because they all were over six feet tall.

One of the principal goals of the Long Nine was to have the capital moved to Springfield. Other legislators were anxious to get bills approved for canals and other improvements. The Long Nine shrewdly carried out a campaign to trade their votes on improvements for votes to move the capital. The result was a triumph for the Long Nine, and on February 25, 1837, the legislature chose Springfield as the new capital.

Illinois not only had a new capital but also a new political figure—Abraham Lincoln—who would soon be heard from.

Whether It "Can Long Endure"

Few slave owners were as generous as Edward Coles, son of a wealthy Virginia planter. When he came to Illinois, Coles immediately freed his slaves. The story is told that he set them free in the middle of the Ohio River, the boundary of freedom. Coles gave each of his freed slaves 160 acres of land.

Slavery in Illinois had a long, sad history, and for all practical purposes lasted until the 1850's. The early French settlers had owned slaves, and later, during what is known as the Mississippi Bubble, large numbers of Negroes were brought in to work the lead mines.

Although the Ordinance of 1787 had forbidden slavery in any part of the Northwest Territory, as early as 1796 and 1802 petitions were sent to Congress to do away with this prohibition and permit slavery in Illinois. At this time, of course, southern Illinois was the only part of the area that was occu-

pied, and most of the residents had come from other slaveholding states.

The Constitution of 1818, under which Illinois was admitted to the Union, provided that "neither slavery nor involuntary servitude shall hereafter be introduced into this state." This did not affect those who were already in slavery. The notorious Shawneetown saltworks, where Negro slaves labored under cruel conditions, were specifically protected in their use of slaves in the "salines." There were also many indentured servants, who had supposedly "agreed" to serve their masters for extended periods of years; these

An angry proslavery mob in Alton burns Elijah Lovejoy's warehouse and destroys his presses. On November 7, 1837, the 35-year-old abolitionist was killed while protecting a new press.

were "held on long terms that made them slaves in all but name," according to the well-known historian Theodore C. Pease.

Large numbers of the leading figures in Illinois favored a new constitution permitting slavery. The legislature approved a measure calling for a convention to draft a new constitution, but the people of Illinois, perhaps surprisingly but certainly to their credit, were ahead of the politicians and rejected the convention proposal in the election of August 2, 1824.

The censuses continued to show slaves in Illinois through 1840, and the practice of holding indentured servants as slaves in all but name continued into the 1850's.

As northern Illinois began to be settled with increasing numbers of people from the antislave northeastern states, the opponents of slavery grew in Illinois, but so also did those who favored slavery. Illinois kept its

"infamous black laws, which stripped Negroes whether slave, indentured or 'free' of almost all their civil rights."

Driven from Missouri where a mob had destroyed his newspaper, Elijah Lovejoy came to Illinois. Here, through his Alton *Observer*, he became the leading figure in the fight against slavery. Alarmed at the growing amount of abolition literature in 1837, the legislature forbade the distribution of abolitionist newspapers and labeled as illegal the circulation of abolition petitions to Congress. In November, 1837, an enraged mob at Alton descended on Lovejoy's printing office. While trying to protect his press, Elijah Lovejoy was shot and killed.

FREEDOM MOVEMENT

No amount of intimidation or suppression could quiet the Abolitionist movement. The number of antislavery societies increased. In 1840 a Liberty party was established in the state, and by 1846 it had a majority of support in 13 counties of the North.

A typical society was that at Quincy. At one meeting of this society a large crowd gathered, summoned by circulars which urged proslavery men to meet and "help clean out the Abolitionists." The meeting was in a church known as the "Lord's Barn," where Dr. David Nelson was minister. As soon as the mob began to pelt the building with stones, those in the meeting seized the hatchets, clubs and muskets they had brought and dashed out of the church. The startled mob scattered, and the meeting was finished without further difficulty.

In 1847 a convention was called to write a new constitution for Illinois. In the resulting constitution, approved by the people in 1848, slavery was forbidden, but the legislature was required to write a law banning free Negroes from coming into the state. This was done in 1853 with a bill making it punishable by a heavy fine to bring a free Negro into Illinois. Negroes entering Illinois were subject to arrest and fine, and in case of inability to pay the fine and court costs, they could be required to pay such costs in labor. In numerous cases free Negroes, of whom there were several groups in Illinois, were sold into slavery or kidnapped and taken to slave states to be sold. In addition, fugitive slaves could be claimed and repossessed by their masters upon payment of costs. However, in spite of the restrictions and disabilities placed upon them, many free Negroes made contributions to their communities.

A growing number of Illinoisans were willing to disregard the law, risk disgrace and do whatever they could to help Negroes. Some of the most effective work was the spiriting of Negroes from the South to safety in Canada over a series of routes and resting places known as the underground railroad.

As Governor John Lourie Beveridge later pointed out in a speech, the underground railroad was "chartered not by law, but in moral convictions; engineered not by science, but through charity; constructed not with money, but out of love; freighted not with commerce, but with downtrodden humanity; operated not for the benefit of stockholders, but for the escape of the fugitive fleeing from the hand of his oppressor."

The stories of the personalities and the stations of the underground railroad in Illinois have become almost legendary, and it is often difficult to find the truth. Owen Lovejoy, brother of the martyred Elijah, was one of the leaders of the movement in Illinois, as was Peter Stewart, sometimes called president of the underground railroad. However, all evidence suggests that the Illinois underground railroad was "a makeshift, improvised method for helping fugitive slaves rather than a smoothly operating system." It is probable that the determination of the slaves to be free was more important in getting them to freedom than any help they received on the way.

"WE CANNOT ESCAPE HISTORY"

In the 1850's Illinois had a strange resemblance to the nation as a whole—a northern section which was generally opposed to slavery and a southern section which was generally in favor of it. Even more strange is the fact that Illinois, alone, produced the two men who became the greatest national symbols of those two viewpoints.

Stephen A. Douglas, Senator from Illinois, had long been a power in national politics. In

1854 he sponsored the Kansas-Nebraska Bill, permitting settlers in American territories to choose for themselves whether the region would be free or slave. This bill replaced the provision in the Missouri Compromise, 1820-21, which prohibited slavery in portions of the Louisiana Purchase above 36° 30′ (the southern boundary of Missouri).

At this time, Abraham Lincoln was not well known in national politics, although he was "acquainted with almost everybody" in Illinois. He had abandoned politics for the practice of law, but the Kansas-Nebraska Act stirred him to return to political life.

As a Whig, he was defeated in a bid for the Senate in 1855. However, he took an active part in the meetings which led to the formation of the Illinois Republican party at Bloomington in 1856. Dissatisfied Whigs, Democrats and Abolitionists joined to form the new party which heard Lincoln make his famous "lost speech," lost because he spoke extemporaneously, and the remarks were not taken down in whole.

In this speech Lincoln asked how those who denied freedom to some could hope to keep their own freedom. He asserted that Abolitionists would remain in the Union, and that any steps by the South to secede from the Union would be countered with force.

Illinois elected its first Republican governor, William H. Bissell, in 1856, and Lincoln became a power in the Republican party. In 1858, he decided to run for Senator against the incumbent, the great Stephen A. Douglas, who already was prominent as a possible candidate for the Presidential election in 1860.

To bring the issues of the Senatorial campaign to the people, the two men agreed to meet in a series of debates across the state. Lincoln invited Douglas to debate following their speeches on consecutive nights at the Tremont House in Chicago. The choice of the seven locations by Douglas represented the Illinois congressional districts at that time. They are said to have completed the arrangement for these debates in the modest Bryant Cottage in Bement.

On August 21, 1858, a crowd of 10,000, twice the size of the city, gathered in Ottawa to hear the first Lincoln-Douglas debate. The New York *Evening Post* described the scene: "By wagon, by rail, by canal the people poured in, till Ottawa was one mass of active life. Men, women, and children, old and young, dwellers on the broad prairies, had turned their backs on the plough, and had come to listen to these champions of the two parties. Military companies were out; martial music sounded, and salutes of artillery thundered in the air. Eager marshals in partisan sashes rode furiously about the streets. Peddlers were crying their wares at the corners, and excited groups of politicians were canvassing and quarreling everywhere."

For three hours the debate went on, with the crowd heckling their opponent and cheering their favorite.

A plaque marks the location of the second Lincoln-Douglas debate at Freeport on August 27, 1858. The plaque quotes Lincoln's famed warning that "This government cannot endure permanently half slave and half free," and the assertion of Douglas, "I am not for the dissolution of the Union under any circumstance."

The third debate was held in the village of Jonesboro on September 15. The story is told that Lincoln and his friend Horace White rocked on the porch of the old Union House Hotel in Jonesboro on the night before the debate while observing Donati's comet as it appeared to sweep across the sky.

Springfield, July 31. 1858.

Hon. S. A. Douglas.

Dear Sir.

Yours of yesterday, naming places, times, and terms, for joint discussions between us, was received this morning— Although, by the terms, as you propose, you take *four* openings and closes to my ~~three~~, I accede, and thus close the arrangement— I direct this to you at Hillsboro; and shall try to have both your letter and this, appear in the Journal and Register of Monday morning—

Your Obt Servt.
A. Lincoln

Lincoln's letter accepting the terms for the historic series of debates with Stephen Douglas.

When Lincoln's carriage clattered down the main street of Charleston, bringing him to the fourth debate, it passed under a banner showing Lincoln as he had appeared coming down the muddy street of Charleston 28 years before when he first arrived in Illinois with his parents. There was even a spirited parade in honor of that early event.

In the debate there on September 8, a throng of 12,000 jammed around the speaker's platform. A seven-car train had even brought an enthusiastic group from Indiana for the event. When Douglas charged Lincoln with having voted to keep supplies from American troops during the war with Mexico, Lincoln jumped up and grabbed a Douglas supporter who knew the facts, forcing him to deny Douglas' accusation.

Carl Sandburg quotes a listener to that debate as having said, "I don't keer fur them great orators. I want to hear just a plain common feller like the rest on us, that I kin foller an' know where he's drivin'. Abe Linkern fills the bill."

On the blustery day of October 7, the fifth debate was held at Old Main on the campus of Knox College at Galesburg. The sixth was held October 13, in Washington Park in Quincy, and the last took place at Alton on October 15.

The meetings between these two great men have been described as among the best known and most important of such debates in history.

It is probable that if the people had been able to vote directly for Lincoln, he would have been elected to the Senate. However, at that time the legislature elected United States Senators, and Lincoln failed. After the defeat he wrote to a friend, "Quit that. You will soon feel better. Another 'blow-up' is coming; and we shall have fun again."

POWWOW IN A WIGWAM

Such a chance for "fun" was to come sooner than he might have expected. The debates with Douglas had been fully reported across the country and had made Lincoln nationally important. If Douglas were the national leader of one side, it seemed obvious that Lincoln might be considered the national leader of the other. He traveled the country widely, gaining a reputation, and climaxed his speaking tour with the famous lecture at the Cooper Union in New York.

The 1860 State Republican Convention at Decatur selected Lincoln as its favorite son and sent its delegates to the national convention at Chicago. For its first great test as a convention city, Chicago had built an enormous temporary wooden convention hall known as the Wigwam, at the present southeast corner of Lake Street and Wacker Drive.

Many distinguished men were candidates for the nomination. However, Lincoln had strong support. He wisely refused to come to Chicago and remained home at Springfield. Many delegates felt that Lincoln's relative obscurity was in his favor, since he had not yet made many enemies. He possessed great appeal for the masses, and many political experts were sure that no one but Lincoln could carry Illinois, Indiana, New Jersey

The Wigwam, a temporary wooden building erected in Chicago for the Republican National Convention of 1860.

Lincoln and Douglas, pitted against each other for election to the Senate in 1858, engaged in a series of seven debates. Although Douglas won the election, it was Lincoln who made the more lasting mark.

and Pennsylvania—which were absolutely essential to a Republican victory.

In the first ballot Indiana gave all of its votes to Lincoln and led the way for his nomination on the third ballot. Senator Douglas was nominated by the Democrats to run for the Presidency to oppose Lincoln. However, Douglas' Democratic party was split by the slavery issue, with a Southern Democratic candidate and a fourth candidate, both running in opposition to both Douglas and Lincoln.

The situation of having both major candidates for the Presidency from one state was and still is unique in American history. Here were two of Illinois' most famous sons competing against one another, as they had on other occasions—this time for the highest office in the land.

Lincoln, of course, was the winner of what was probably the most heartbreaking election of American history, and he took the oath of office as President on March 4, 1861. When Lincoln could not find a place to lay his hat to make his inaugural address, it is said that Stephen Douglas gestured for the familiar stovepipe headgear of the new President, and the former opponent held it throughout the speech as an unspoken gesture of loyalty.

CIVIL STRIFE

In southern Illinois there was extravagant talk of forming a separate state of Egypt which would be free to join the Confederacy. Douglas hurried from Washington and worked long and hard to persuade leaders of southern Illinois to remain loyal. He had worked so hard in his last years that even the strength of the "Little Giant," as he was called, was drained. He died in June, 1861.

Another who was notably responsible for persuading southern Illinoisans to remain with the Union was John A. Logan, later a Civil War general.

Invasion of southern Illinois was another realistic fear. The war and impending invasion found Illinois almost completely unprepared for war, as was most of the rest of the country. The militia was unorganized, with few guns and supplies, and training was spotty. Richard Yates, wartime governor of Illinois, called the legislature into special session and did much to prepare the state and organize the people for the struggle.

A daring Illinois man, Captain James H. Stokes of Chicago, helped to overcome the early arms shortage. There were supplies at the St. Louis arsenal, but this was surrounded by a howling mob trying to keep the arms from going to Union troops.

Captain Stokes managed to get into the arsenal and remove 10,000 muskets and ammunition to a steamboat which he had arranged to have ready at the dock. When the captain of the boat asked for sailing orders, Stokes said, "Straight to Alton in the regular channel."

"What if we are attacked?" asked the captain. "Then we will fight," replied Stokes.

"But what if we are overpowered?"

"Then run the boat to the deepest water and sink her," Stokes answered. Fortunately, the boat reached Alton safely. Here even the women and children helped to unload the desperately needed cargo of arms for Illinois soldiers.

Another Illinois hero of the early war was Colonel Elmer Ephraim Ellsworth. He had been a law student in Lincoln's office at Springfield before the war. Colonel Ellsworth led his troops across the Potomac from Washington to capture Alexandria,

RECRUITS

FOR THE

STAND BY YOUR COUNTRY

36TH ILLINOIS REG'T!

Now is your time to enlist in an old Regiment, that has been in the field nearly three years, and has *re-enlisted* for three years or during the war.

All able bodied men, between the ages of 18 and 45, who have heretofore been enlisted, and have served for not less than nine months, who shall re-enlist, will be considered as

VETERAN VOLUNTEERS,

and will be entitled to receive one months pay in advance, and a bounty and premium of $402. New recruits will receive one months pay in advance, and a bounty and premium of $302. Recruits will be allowed to select the Company which they may wish to serve in.

Each recruit, Veteran or otherwise, will receive

SEVENTY-FIVE DOLLARS

In cash before leaving General Rendezvous, $75 at the first regular payment thereafter, $50 in six months, and the remainder of the bounty in regular instalments till all is paid. The pay, bounty and premium for three years. will average $34 per month for Veterans, and $31 30 per month for all others, not Veterans, and the monthly rate of compensation will increase as the term of service is diminished. If the Government shall not require these troops for the full period of three years, and they shall be mustered honorably out of the service before the expiration of their term of enlistment, they shall receive, upon being mustered out, the *whole amount of bounty remaining unpaid*, the same as if the full term had been served.

All wishing to join the "Old 36th," can do so by calling at the Re-cruiting Station at Elgin, or the Branch Station at Bristol, Kendall County, or Crystal Lake, McHenry County.

GEORGE D. SHERMAN,

Major 36th Illinois, Commanding Recruiting Party.

Virginia, on May 24, 1861. They were successful in driving out the Southern troops. Then Ellsworth spotted a rebel flag flying from a hotel. He ran to the roof and ripped the flag from its mast. As he was returning to the street, he was shot and killed by the owner of the hotel.

President Lincoln gave Colonel Ellsworth a funeral in the White House. At the funeral the President burst into tears and said, "My boy! My boy! Was it necessary this sacrifice should be made?"

The murder of the young colonel from Illinois became widely known, and the words "Remember Ellsworth" served as a rallying cry throughout the North. He was the first Union officer to die in the Civil War.

With the threat of invasion still hanging over southern Illinois, Governor Yates called on a former army officer and veteran of the Mexican War to defend the Cairo region. Ulysses Simpson Grant left his home in Galena for headquarters in Cairo, where as a brigadier general he commanded the District of Southeastern Missouri, including southern Illinois. Grant prevented Illinois from becoming a battleground of the Civil War. At Cairo Grant mounted his campaign against Forts Henry and Donelson, beginning a successful march into the South.

This was the beginning of Grant's steady rise in influence from lieutenant general, to commander of all Union armies in 1864 and finally to the Presidency.

Troops from Illinois played a major part in Grant's campaign to open up the Mississippi River, and Illinois soldiers were on hand in many of the major campaigns of the war—especially in the battles at Murfreesboro, Vicksburg and Shiloh, and with General Sherman at Atlanta, and on Sherman's "March to the Sea."

One of the most noted and daring military actions of Illinois regiments in the war was known as "Grierson's Raid." General Benjamin H. Grierson led a Union cavalry troop through the Confederate lines from Tennessee all the way to a meeting with other Federal troops in far off Baton Rouge, Louisiana.

Two Illinois men made unique contributions to winning the war by writing songs which helped morale among Union troops. George F. Root wrote the famous *Tramp, Tramp, Tramp, the Boys Are Marching*, *The Battle Cry of Freedom* and *Just Before the Battle, Mother*. During the war possibly the most famous of all the wartime songs was *Marching Through Georgia*, written by Henry Clay Work.

The effect such songs had is shown by a quotation said to come from a Confederate soldier, "I shall never forget the first time I heard *Rally Round the Flag*. T'was a nasty night during the 'Seven-days Fight.' I was on picket, when just before taps, some fellow on the other side struck up that song and others joined in the chorus. Tom B. sung out, 'Cap., what are those fellows made of? Here we've licked them six days running, and now on the eve of the seventh they're singing *Rally Round the Flag*.' I tell you that song sounded to me like the knell of doom and my heart went down into my boots, and it has been an up-hill fight with me ever since that night."

Illinois civilians also deserve much credit for their constant work for the Union cause throughout the war. Notwithstanding strong southern leanings at the war's beginning, the people of Illinois were generally loyal, in spite of a troublesome minority of "Copperheads," who were opposed to the war. Sometimes they caused disturbances such as that at Paris in February, 1864. A group of several hundred Copperheads planned to meet there and attack the city. However, Federal troops managed to quell the Copperheads with only a few skirmishes.

For the most part, the activities of Copperheads did not pose as much of a threat in Illinois as they did in some other states.

The exact figures on Illinois enlistments in the Civil War cannot be determined. There were so many short-term enlistments and so many reenlistments which might or might not have been listed as new personnel that precise figures have been impossible to obtain. One often-quoted source places the figure of servicemen from Illinois at 259,092. Only New York, Pennsylvania and Ohio furnished more troops, but these states had much larger populations than Illinois.

Illinois lost 34,834 men, including 1,700 who died in Confederate prisons. This was 16.5 percent of the total number of Illinois men in uniform.

In one aspect of service Illinois had an almost incredible record. The Civil War draft regulations provided that any man who was financially able to do so could pay for a substitute for him in the service, at the rate of $300. This was common practice in the East. To Illinois' credit, only fifty-five men in the state chose to avoid military service this way—a very low figure compared to the almost 260,000 who did serve.

A number of Illinois generals other than Grant gained reputations in the war. Major General John A. Logan was one of the best-liked and most respected military leaders. General John M. Palmer, General John Pope, General Stephen A. Hurlbut, General Elon H. Farnsworth, General Micael Lawler

and General Richard Oglesby were others who distinguished themselves.

Illinois' Senator Lyman Trumbull earned a particular distinction by drafting the Thirteenth Amendment to the United States Constitution. This simple statement declares, "Neither slavery nor involuntary servitude, except as a punishment for crime whereof the party shall have been duly convicted, shall exist within the United States, or any place subject to their jurisdiction." Illinois added further to its own laurels by being the first state to ratify this significant amendment, which put an end forever to the legality of slavery.

Regrettably, Illinois and the nation were soon to lose their greatest citizen to martyrdom. Only six days had passed after the surrender of General Robert E. Lee to General Grant at Appomatox in Virginia, which was the practical end of the war, when Abraham Lincoln was shot by John Wilkes Booth and died on April 15, 1865.

Even many of those who had bitterly opposed him paid tribute to the fallen President. The Chicago *Times*, which had been so strongly against the war that it had been stopped from publishing for a time for disloyalty, admitted that all must surely "realize something of the magnitude of the concerns involved in his lease of existence."

One of the strangest, one of the most pathetic episodes in American history was the long, roundabout slow passage of the somber funeral train bearing Lincoln's body "home" to Springfield, past weeping, mourning crowds, stopping many places where entire communities held memorial services in tribute to the great man.

*As thousands watched in sorrowful silence, the body
of Abraham Lincoln was brought home to Springfield.*

A Maturing State

One of the most famous of all veterans' organizations, the Grand Army of the Republic, or GAR, was founded at Springfield on April 6, 1866, by an Illinois regimental surgeon, Dr. Benjamin F. Stephenson. The first two national commanders of the GAR were also from Illinois.

Ground was broken for the present Illinois capitol at Springfield in 1868. It was first occupied in 1876, but another 12 years passed before the capitol was fully completed.

Illinois' great wartime hero, General Ulysses Simpson Grant, became President in 1869. Another Illinois wartime hero, General John A. Logan, served for 13 years in the United States Senate, beginning in 1871.

This same year there occurred one of the worst disasters ever to hit the state. The origin of the Chicago Fire is hazy, but legend has the O'Leary cow kicking over a lantern and starting the conflagration. Whether or not the story is true, it is certain that a fire did start behind the DeKoven Street cottage of Patrick O'Leary on the night of October 8, 1871. It was, however, only one of many fires that weary fire fighters had to combat that night.

Carried by the strong winds which had persisted for several days, the fires swept across the city. Some threw a few belongings into wagons; others took what they could under their arms. The streets were so crowded little movement was possible. Embers and sparks flew through the air and ignited many in the crowd. Thousands waded into the icy waters of the lake to escape the flames, and even there the hair of many caught fire from sparks.

The heat of the flames was so incredibly intense that it could be felt a hundred miles away in Holland, Michigan. The fierce heat melted coins, bottles, and glass tumblers. Some of the melted lumps and other interesting reminders of the great fire can still be seen in the Chicago Historical Society Museum in Lincoln Park.

In 27 hours, 17,450 buildings had been destroyed, including homes of a third of Chicago's population, 1,600 stores, 28 hotels, bridges, railroad buildings, public buildings and 60 factories. A few buildings still standing as survivors of the fire are Old St. Mary's Church and the Water Tower.

The fire had scarcely begun to cool when people started to salvage and rebuild. Burned out Chicago newspapers published issues the second day. Help poured in from all over the world. Queen Victoria, Alfred Lord Tennyson, Robert Browning, John Ruskin and other famous British people contributed more than 12,000 books from their personal libraries to replace a Chicago public library that did not exist.

Within two years almost no trace of the fire could be seen, but where the former Chicago had been made mostly of flimsy wooden buildings, much of the new city was of firm and permanent construction. The amazing reconstruction of Chicago must rank among the major accomplishments in the field of city building.

GROWING PAINS

The rapid advance of Illinois as a manufacturing state (see page 150 ff.), caused a

*The Chicago Fire, which started the night of October 8, 1871, is one of
the most famous disasters in American history. Several hundred people lost their
lives and some $200,000,000 worth of property was destroyed.*

great deal of unrest between labor and management. Labor unions were formed, but for many years they were dealt with harshly by management. In spite of adverse laws, the use of detectives, and of strike breakers, workers made some advances.

Illinois led all the other states with a law in 1867 providing that "eight hours of labor . . . shall constitute and be a legal day's work, where there is no special contract or agreement to the contrary." However, this pioneer eight-hour day had little practical effect. In 1871, the state made it possible for employers to lease convict labor to compete with free workers.

In the early 1880's labor recorded a number of gains. However, some labor groups made plans to arm and possibly use force. A hundred thousand workers went on strike in Chicago in April, 1886. Police broke up a

In this map of Chicago, the area in red shows the portion of the city that was destroyed by the Great Fire of 1871. Fully a third of Chicago's population was left homeless.

quarrel between strikers and nonstrikers and six workmen were killed.

On May 4 a rally was called to "denounce the latest atrocious act of the police." About 3,000 came to the meeting on Desplaines Street between Randolph and Lake streets, near the Haymarket. The mayor of Chicago, the first Carter Harrison, was on hand to watch the meeting. When the mayor decided that the meeting would be orderly and when rain reduced the crowd to about 500, he left and remarked to Police Inspector John Bonfield, "Nothing is likely to happen that will require interference."

As soon as the mayor had left, Bonfield ordered 200 policemen to scatter the gathering. Just as the policemen arrived, someone (His identity has never been discovered), threw a bomb. The explosion killed 8 policemen, wounded 65, and killed an undetermined number of civilians.

The reaction was swift and directed against all labor, which suffered for years because of this single irresponsible act. Eight of the labor leaders in the Haymarket Riot were tried, seven were sentenced to death and one was given a 15-year sentence. On the night they were to die, Governor Richard J. Oglesby commuted the sentences of two to life in prison. One committed suicide and four were hanged on November 11, 1887.

Six years later Governor John P. Altgeld pardoned the remaining three prisoners,

A bird's-eye view of the Columbian Exposition of 1893. In the center is the Manufacturer's Building. At the far right can be seen the Museum of Science and Industry, the only Exposition building still remaining.

pointing out the gross unfairness in the conviction of eight men for a crime committed by an unknown person. Although his courageous act was hailed by many, Governor Altgeld was said to have committed "political suicide" by this act because it infuriated large numbers of voters. Today, however, it seems to be a matter of simple justice.

BETTER THAN FAIR

A happier note was sounded at Chicago in 1893. The city had been selected to be host for the celebration of the 400th anniversary of the discovery of America by Columbus, in what was to be called the World's Columbian Exposition. An unoccupied prairie site, then far south, now Jackson Park, was selected, but the enormous job of draining the swamps, making lagoons, sewers and roadways and constructing the huge buildings delayed the opening for a year, so that the first Chicago World's Fair did not open until 1893.

The World's Columbian Exposition was one of the most beautiful of any such fair in history. Certainly it was further ahead of its time than most fairs. Considering the in-

finitely greater value of the dollar in those days, it probably also was far and away the most expensive.

People crowded to Chicago all summer from everywhere in the country and from all over the world. They admired the gleaming white buildings, the beautiful calm lagoons and the professional landscaping. Everything that was new in engineering, agriculture and transportation was shown in exhibits from throughout the world.

This was the fair that invented the term midway and this first Midway, covered with thrilling new rides, introduced "naughty" Little Egypt and other excitement, which some Chicagoans thought was not quite proper for their city.

Seeing their great fair, most Illinoisans, many of whom had never before left their farms, felt that they had come into a wonderful new world for the first time; in a very real sense the fair was an amazing revelation to people scarcely a generation away from pioneering.

Theodore Dreiser wrote an excellent summation of the fair: "All at once and out of nothing, in this dingy city of six or seven hundred thousand which but a few years before had been a wilderness of wet grass and mud flats, and by this lake which but a hundred years before was a lone silent waste, had now been reared this vast and harmonious collection of perfectly constructed and showy buildings, containing in their delightful interiors, the artistic, mechanical and scientific achievements of the world."

Although the temporary buildings soon were torn down after the fair, few visitors ever forgot the glimpse of a new kind of beauty which had come into their lives for a while. More than 700,000 crowded onto the grounds for the last night.

CHANGING TIMES

The fair provided a graphic demonstration of the rapidly changing ways of life which had come already or which soon would. The role of electricity was dramatized. Electric motors were already replacing the clumsy steam engines in factories. The miracle of electric light was unfolding in the city, although it would still be two or three generations before every farm would have this then unbelievable helper. Only twenty years after telephones had been introduced, their use was revolutionizing the cities and would soon be in general use even in the rural areas.

The vast increase in manufacturing had made life easier and had provided cheaper and better means of obtaining the necessities of life and of increasing the number of luxuries for hosts of people. Already so many workers had been attracted from the farms to the factories that Illinois, even at this early date, had less than half of its population left in rural areas.

Unskilled workers, however, were still laboring long hours for only a few dollars a week. Labor leaders and others were concerned about the often oppressed working man and brought some gains to numbers of workers, especially among skilled trades. Although by today's standards the cost of living seemed incredibly low, the rise of eggs to 10 cents a dozen from a former 8 cent price, or the rise of a whole chicken from 25 to 35 cents could signal real hardship for people whose income might be no more than $10 a week.

There were no guarantees of employment. Workers thrown off the job by the hiring of cheaper labor, changing conditions or other reasons had no workmen's compensation or other means of support while they looked for a new job. There were few pension plans.

At the time of the fair, the severe depression of 1893 was causing great hardship. In many ways this was the worst depression of a hundred years. Farmers and mine workers came to the cities, where thousands who were already there were also out of work and reduced to asking for charity.

Recovery from this setback took about five years. During this period, in 1894, President Grover Cleveland sent Federal forces to Illinois to put down a strike of Pullman Company workers and the American Railway Union. One of the accomplishments of the period was the winning of an eight-hour day for mine workers in 1897, after a successful strike. The practice of requiring workers to buy from the company stores also was abolished in some instances.

In 1898, a coal mine at Virden scuttled this agreement and brought in 300 new workers along with 85 guards. A strike and riot resulted, and compelled Governor John R. Tanner to assert: "These avaricious mine owners who have so far forgotten their duty to society as to bring this blot upon the fair name of our state have gone far enough . . .

Towering over everything at the Columbian Exposition of 1893
was the awe-inspiring Ferris wheel invented by George Ferris.
This huge wheel, 264 feet high, with cars as big as streetcars,
gave visitors a spectacular view of the fair and the city.
Opposite: *At night electric lights*
turned the fair into a brilliant world of color.

AT NIGHT IN THE GRAND COURT

and I say now to all such and others that this is a thing of the past, that it shall not be tolerated in Illinois while I am governor."

Illinois captured the attention of the world in another field with the "River that flows backwards." Sewage from Chicago had been dumped into the Chicago River. This drained into Lake Michigan uncomfortably close to the source of the city's drinking water. The larger Chicago grew, the more unhealthy its drinking water became.

To remedy this situation, an imaginative engineering plan was conceived. The flow of the Chicago River was reversed—away from its mouth. Instead of flowing to the sea through the Great Lakes and the St. Lawrence River, it was made to turn backward

and flow through the Des Plaines, Illinois and Mississippi rivers into the Gulf of Mexico, taking the sewage with it.

This required dredging the South Branch of the Chicago River to a much greater depth so that it would reverse its flow, digging a new canal through the Illinois divide connecting the Chicago and Des Plaines rivers, and installing locks so that water and boats could travel from one level to another. The plan also required putting locks at the mouth of the Chicago River to control the flow of Lake Michigan into the system.

Provision was made for ships to use the waterway. When the Chicago Sanitary and Ship Canal was finished in 1900, experts called it a great engineering feat.

150 and Going Strong

A new century found Illinois well on the road to supremacy in many fields—in agriculture, manufacturing, minerals and literature, among others—all described in more detail later.

Greater concern with the health, safety and welfare of the people was expressed by the passage of many laws and creation or improvement of various state agencies. Civil service was established for some Illinois government employees in 1910; workmen's compensation acts were approved in 1911 and amended in 1913 and 1917. The Illinois Department of Labor was set up in 1917.

WORLD WAR AND UNEASY PEACE

When World War I finally became a "hot war" for the United States in 1917, American Allies desperately needed men, food and war materials. All of these Illinois was in a position to provide. The amount of service given by Illinois in all three of these fields was probably well above the country's average.

Only three months after the declaration of war, 351,153 men and women from Illinois already had entered military service.

Frank O. Lowden, wartime governor of Illinois, helped to establish the State Council of Defense, which cooperated with all wartime groups in furthering the war effort. Great Lakes Naval Training Station, Camp Grant and Fort Sheridan were three leading military centers in Illinois during the war.

After the war, Illinois, along with the rest of the nation, entered a period sometimes known as the Roaring Twenties. This was a time during which many of the old taboos and restrictions were loosened or altogether forgotten. There was much talk of the "lost generation of youth."

From 1920 to 1933 the Eighteenth Amendment to the Constitution was in effect throughout the United States. During this period, called Prohibition, it was illegal to manufacture, sell or transport liquor. People began to make, sell and buy liquor in secret. Gangsters gained control of many of the illegal activities.

Illinois was plagued by the operations of gangsters who made their headquarters in Chicago and the suburbs. Such names as Al Capone were prominent in the news, and the bodies of men known to be members of various gangs kept turning up with disturbing regularity in a growing series of unsolved gangland slayings. This method of eliminating competitors reached its lowest depths when several gangsters were gunned down in a mass murder known as the St. Valentine's Day Massacre in Chicago.

Chicago's reputation suffered throughout the world, and many people of other countries still know Chicago only as the place where the gangster was king.

More important but not so spectacular were the constant efforts made for improvement in almost every field, highlighted by such events as the International Eucharistic Congress of 1926, with its final session at St. Mary of the Lake Seminary in Mundelein.

The twenties appeared on the surface to be a period of unlimited prosperity. Illinois held third place among all the states in per capita wealth, in manufacturing and in population. But because of its dependence on

*A dramatic view of the great fair known as the Century of Progress,
held in 1934 to celebrate the 100th anniversary
of Chicago's incorporation as a town.*

manufacturing, Illinois was hard hit by the great depression of the 1930's.

The unemployed marched to the state capital restlessly asking for assistance. Mines were slowed; the courts could not keep up with the many foreclosures of farms and homes; banks closed in wholesale numbers; a final touch of disaster was added by some of the worst drought years ever experienced in the Midwest.

One bright spot in the depression was the second world's fair to be held in Chicago and the second to be held during a great depression. This one, celebrating the 100th anniversary of Chicago's incorporation as a town, was known as the Century of Progress.

Nothing like it had ever been seen before. Its buildings were angular and modern. The brilliant colors and striking night lighting made up almost the only decoration. Exhibits formed an amazing array of the promise of a world that might come with the passing of the depression. A form of display known as the diorama was used extensively for the first time in the Century of Progress exhibits and won great praise.

An even greater innovation was the moving or mechanical type of display, many of these operated by the visitor himself. The science hall assembled probably the greatest summary of science and its prospects ever gathered under one roof up to that time, and

The Avenue of Flags at the Century of Progress.

much of this was moved to the new Museum of Science and Industry when the fair was over. The fair was held over for a second season in 1934, and when the lofty towers of the sky ride were toppled by blasts of dynamite and the fair went into history, Illinoisans felt as if they were losing an old friend. They were somewhat consoled by the fact that this was one of the few world's fairs in history ever to show a profit.

Recovery from the depression and drought was slow and imperfect. Expanded oil opera- tions in southern Illinois offered a bright spot, but the worst flood in the history of the Ohio River brought hardship to that area in 1937. One by one the cities of the river- side—Cincinnati, Louisville, Paducah—were overwhelmed as the flood crest swept in- exorably downriver. Newsreel photographers gathered at Cairo as the crest approached. Women and children fled the city; three feet of emergency levee was quickly thrown on top of the existing levees. The flood rose to within four inches of the top and remained there for what seemed an eternity, then slowly began to subside. Among all the cities in the path of the flood only Cairo had escaped.

WORLD WAR II

For the second time in the lifetime of many people, the world was engulfed in war, which came to the United States with the bombing of Pearl Harbor, December 7, 1941. Governor Dwight H. Green called a special wartime session of the state legislature and the state prepared to do its part in the defeat of the German and Japanese powers.

During the war, Illinois contributed a discovery which was to change the world completely, yet because of the extreme necessity for secrecy only a handful of people were aware of it until years had passed.

The setting for this event was a laboratory which had been built underneath the grandstand of the University of Chicago's stadium, known as Stagg Field. Scientists had believed for some time that there was tremendous power in the atom. Of course, the work was extremely complex, but the scientists were convinced after study by some of the best minds that if enough uranium could be put together into a single pile and if they could control the exact amount at all times, they might be able to prove in this test that the power of the atom could be released to produce a chain reaction.

Enrico Fermi, the great Italian scientist, was living in America, and he was placed in charge of the project in Chicago. He and his associates started out to build what looked like a large brick oven, which they called the pile. Inside were layers of uranium and graphite, piled together.

There were many unusual things necessary for the project which could not be explained then because of the secrecy of their work. One thing they needed was a large balloon-cloth bag. The order was given to the Goodyear Rubber Company to make the bag, and the company engineers were greatly puzzled about what anyone would want with a square balloon. When it was finished, the army's new square balloon was the target of many jokes.

Meanwhile, the work at Stagg Field continued, and on December 2, 1942, the scientists felt that their uranium pile had reached the "critical" size; that is, it was ready for testing.

At 8:30 A.M. some of America's most distinguished scientists gathered in what had been the squash court of the stadium. Only 42 people were on hand to watch history being made. As the day wore on, the scientists felt they were getting closer. Finally, according to a government report, "Precisely at 3:25 P.M., Chicago time, scientist George Weil withdrew the cadmium-plated control rod. In this single action man had unleashed the controlled energy of the atom.

"As those who witnessed the experiment became aware of what had happened, smiles spread over their faces and a quiet ripple of applause could be heard. It was a tribute to Enrico Fermi, Nobel Prize winner, to whom, more than to any other person, the success of the experiment was due."

That night Mrs. Fermi happened to be giving a party for a number of the scientists who had seen the experiment come to a climax, but she knew nothing about the work that had been done. Later Mrs. Fermi said she could not understand why everybody was complimenting her husband.

Neither she nor anyone else could know that the work of her husband and his fellow scientists had just paved the way for the

United States, in actual fact, to build the first atomic bomb.

When Dr. Arthur Compton telephoned his report on the experiment to Dr. James B. Conant, he said in code, "The Italian navigator (Fermi) has landed in the New World."

"How were the natives?" asked Conant.

"Very friendly," was the reply.

Another important wartime contribution was made by the University of Illinois, whose engineers, chemists and zoologists discovered a method for decontaminating water. This proved to be of critical importance to American armed services struggling with many unsafe water sources throughout the world.

With unparalleled concentration, business and industry, the working forces of Illinois, turned their attention to winning the war. The flood of wartime products reached a grand total value of $54,400,000,000.

The Naval Training Station at Great Lakes supplied one third of the entire enlisted personnel of the fleet during the war. Fort Sheridan near Chicago, Scott Field near Belleville and Chanute Field at Rantoul all played important parts in training servicemen. An unusual type of training was given at Camp McDowell, near Naperville, where several hundred men were taught sabotage and espionage. In more popular terms, they were trained as spies. An Italian-American group from Camp McDowell went behind the Nazi lines with a mission of blowing up an important Nazi tunnel. Although they were in uniform when they were captured, all were executed as spies, contrary to international law.

Altogether, more than 900,000 men and women from Illinois saw service during World War II. Of these, 19,000 were women. The long sad lists of casualties grew until at the end of the war they included the names of 27,000 from Illinois. Of these, 26 received their country's highest citation—the Congressional Medal of Honor.

IN THE AGE OF ATOMS AND SPACE

Since the time of Marquette and Jolliet, boats have been stopping at the site of Chicago. As the waterways were enlarged from the sea, both from the Gulf of St. Lawrence to the east and the Gulf of Mexico southward, more commerce could come to Illinois by water. However, only the smaller ocean-going ships could arrive at Chicago because the canals and locks leading along the St. Lawrence River and past Niagara Falls were not large enough, nor was the channel deep enough for large vessels. For years there had been talk of enlarging the St. Lawrence water route, but the work was not finished until 1959, when the St. Lawrence Seaway was completed at great cost as a joint project of the United States and Canada. An International Trade Fair, featuring a visit from Queen Elizabeth II of England, celebrated the opening in Chicago.

Although remote from Illinois, the Seaway had an immediate effect on the state. New sea trade began to arrive at Chicago almost at once. For the first time Chicago and other Illinois ports were opened to the ocean shipping of the entire world. Now more than half of the world's ships are able to travel the St. Lawrence Seaway and put in at Illinois ports.

Since the opening, the tonnage through the St. Lawrence Seaway to Chicago has grown. It is now the largest inland seaport.

The scientists who experimented with atomic energy on the squash court of the University of Chicago must have hoped that the atom could be used for peaceful purposes as well as for atomic bombs. Dr. Fermi was dead, but others of the group, surely, were pleased when nuclear power from the atom was used in 1960 to generate electricity at the Dresden, Illinois, power plant, for sometime the largest all-nuclear power plant in North America.

In 1967 preliminary work was started on a project which would keep Illinois in the forefront of the Atomic Age. The tiny village of Weston, a Chicago suburb, was selected by the Atomic Energy Commission to be the site for the world's largest atom smasher, technically known as a nuclear accelerator. This $300,000,000 project was eagerly sought by all of the major states. The enormous prospects of development and economic expansion it opened up are typical of the progress so often experienced by Illinois.

As the year 1968 approached, Illinoisans across the state began to wonder what kind of celebration would be worthy of the 150th anniversary of Illinois statehood.

In 1965 the legislature created an Illinois Sesquicentennial Commission, headed by historian and Lincoln authority Ralph G. Newman. As Mr. Newman pointed out, "The dramatic history of our State as it approaches its 150th birthday is worthy material for a Homer, a Francis Parkman, a Thomas Carlyle or, in our own time, such talented sons of Illinois as Allan Nevins, Pete Akers, or Paul Angle.

"The Illinois Sesquicentennial Commission will concern itself with every aspect of our state's physical, cultural, and industrial assets. We will recount the drama of the early days of Illinois, the beauties, advantages and opportunities of present-day Illinois, and the magnificent promise of a future Illinois."

And so in 1968, Illinois enthusiastically examined its fascinating past and hopefully contemplated its future.

"I Will!": A Short History of Chicago

The site of Chicago has been occupied since prehistoric times, probably by many tribes and peoples. The first settlement known to history was the Indian village which sprang up around Father Pierre Pinet's Mission of the Guardian Angel in 1696. The river which flowed by was neither great nor strong but it was called Checagou, which means strong or mighty in the Indian language. Possibly this was a reference to the wild onions which grew along the banks, and were certainly strong enough even for the Indians. In any event, it was this strange expression which gave Chicago its distinctive name.

Although the French controlled the region for almost a hundred years, they left no permanent settlement at the site of Chicago, nor did the British establish one. The Americans were almost as slow.

Sometime around the year 1779 Jean Baptiste Point du Sable, a Negro of French extraction, using squared logs, had built a large cabin on the north bank of the Checagou River not far from the lake. Here he traded with the Indians, and with white travelers who very occasionally visited the region. Although he did a good business, du Sable left the region in 1800, after selling his holdings to another fur trader. He is still honored as Chicago's first citizen.

Three years later, after acquiring the land by treaty with the Indians, the United States sent an army man from Detroit to establish a fort at the mouth of the Checagou River, just south of the present Michigan Avenue where the river made a sharp bend to the south. This captain (later to be unceremoniously called "Whistler's Grandfather"

After the Black Hawk War of 1832, the remaining Indians in Chicago were forced to leave. This oil painting depicts the final meeting of the Potawatomi on their traditional homesite.

Fort Dearborn, erected in 1803, stood on what is now the south side of the Michigan Avenue Bridge. The site is marked by bronze plaques.

because of the fame his grandson, James, achieved for his painting known as *Whistler's Mother*) designed the post, named it Fort Dearborn in honor of Henry Dearborn, the Secretary of War, and commanded it for several years. By 1812 a community of about twelve cabins had grown up around the fort, and news of the war with England was most alarming to these isolated settlers and army men. General William Hull, head of American army forces in the Northwest, ordered the evacuation of Fort Dearborn, "provided it can be effected with a greater prospect of safety than to remain."

However, when the order reached Captain Nathan Heald, then commanding the fort, it did not include General Hull's option for him to remain if he thought it would be safer to do so. Potawatomi Chief Black Partridge, a friend of the settlers, warned that it would be more dangerous to leave than to stay, but rather than disobey the command, Heald ordered the company to abandon the fort on August 15, 1812. The group, consisting of only about 100 soldiers and settlers straggling south along the lakeshore, heading for the safety of Fort Wayne in Indiana, had gone only about two miles when they were massacred. Only the Kinzie family escaped. Kinzie had taken over the du Sable property in 1804 and had become the leading figure in the area.

A new and considerably more elaborate Fort Dearborn was built in 1816, but the community continued to drowse. Before 1825 Chicagoans with county business had to travel clear to Lewiston. In 1831 Chicago became the seat of Cook County. In the year 1833, when Chicago was incorporated as a town, the first of the many major alterations of the land was carried out. Just before reaching the lake, the Chicago River had been turned sharply south by a sandbar, and flowed in a shallow stream for some distance before it emptied into the lake. The sandbar was cut through, permitting the river to flow directly into the lake, and making a small harbor of sorts. The improvement was needed to handle the 20,000 visitors who came through Chicago that year, most of them by boat. Later, of course, the old channel of the river was filled in.

The sharp upturn in activity in the Chicago area beginning in 1833 came as a result of the announcement that Chicago had been chosen as the terminal of the important Illinois and Michigan Canal. Settlement was made possible by the removal of the Indians after the Black Hawk War.

Chicago was incorporated as a city in 1837, the charter coming from the remote capital at Vandalia. One of those who made the tiresome trip westward on a packet boat over the Erie Canal, then over Lakes Erie, Huron and Michigan to Chicago was the soon-to-be-famous actor Joseph Jefferson. "In the year 1838," he wrote, "the new town

(Above) General Henry Dearborn,
in whose honor Fort Dearborn was named.
(Left) William Butler Ogden,
first mayor of Chicago.

Low-lying Chicago wallowed in a sea of mud until 1850 when the streets were raised twelve feet. Some houses and buildings were raised on jacks, but in other instances new entrances were cut at street level.

of Chicago had just turned from an Indian village into a thriving little place . . . Off we go ashore and walk through the busy little town, busy even then, people hurrying to and fro, frame buildings going up, board sidewalks going down, new hotels, new churches, new theaters, everything new. Saw and hammer—saw, saw, bang, bang—look out for the drays!—bright and muddy streets —gaudy-colored calicos—blue and red flannels and striped ticking hanging outside the dry-goods stores — bar-rooms — real-estate offices—attorneys-at-law—oceans of them!"

In the 1850's Chicago raised itself from the mud by lifting the level of the streets. In the period from 1850 to 1870 Chicago is said to have experienced the fastest growth of any city in history, mostly because of the railroads. This was accelerated by the prosperity which the Civil War brought to Chicago, including a vast increase in grain shipments—65,400,000 bushels in 1862—and the

building of the mile-square Chicago Union Stock Yards in 1865. As early as 1860 Chicago had a philharmonic society, and in another field of "culture" the Chicago White Stockings, ancestors of the Chicago Cubs, in 1869 defeated a Memphis team, 157 to 1.

"THE PULSE OF AMERICA"

On the evening of October 8, 1871, conductor Theodore Thomas led his own symphony orchestra in the Crosby Opera House in a concert of symphonic music by Beethoven, Schumann, Gounod, Schubert, Wagner and Chopin. The musicians had scarcely retired to their beds in a North Side hotel when a fire alarm was sounded, and Thomas and his orchestra were forced to flee, along with thousands of others, from the onslaught of the great Chicago Fire.

A strange, somewhat eerie aftermath of the fire came about through the dumping of debris into the lake at Chicago's doorstep, which created a large part of the land later used for Grant Park. The miracle of rebuilding was accomplished, and the depression of 1873 was passed with hardly any difficulty by Chicago's banks, which continued to pay when banks in other parts of the country went into receivership. Manufacturing in the city increased a hundred percent in only three years.

The bustling 1880's were climaxed by an extremely busy year in 1889. Chicago continued to gobble up independent towns and cities at its edge, incorporating the city of Lakeview and the town of Jefferson, along with the town of Hyde Park on the South Side, with its tree-shaded streets.

In that same year Jane Addams opened Hull House, a settlement house, which was to gain world fame and which pioneered an entirely new concept in meeting the diverse needs of people living in a community.

In a different field, President Benjamin Harrison journeyed to Chicago to be the principal figure in the opening ceremonies for the great new Auditorium Theater on December 9, 1889. This brilliantly decorated theater, with the world's finest acoustics, soon came to be known as "the most famous building on the American continent."

With the best concert hall in the nation, leading Chicago people were able to persuade the distinguished Theodore Thomas to establish a permanent symphony orchestra in the city. Under his direction the Chicago Symphony orchestra was organized in 1891. With promotional help from Thomas, Orchestra Hall was completed in 1904. Today the Chicago Symphony is one of the finest orchestras in the world.

History of a different kind was made at the Democratic National Convention at Chicago in 1896. William Jennings Bryan stirred the nation when he addressed the convention in what has come to be known as his "Cross of Gold Speech." This address won him the Presidential nomination and helped to keep him in the forefront of Democratic politics for sixteen years. The speech is generally considered one of the best-known orations of all time.

The elevated lines of Chicago were combined in 1897 so that the downtown area was completely encircled by tracks. This loop of rail gave the downtown Chicago area its famous nickname—the "Loop."

In 1897 the Chicago Art Institute held the first of its famous exhibitions of Chicago area artists. Additions have been added to the original building, which was constructed for the Columbian Exposition. Collections range from primitive cultures to modern. The most famous works cover the French Impressionists and Post-Impressionists.

One of the strangest episodes in the city's history began in 1886 when a small boat owned by Captain George Wellington Streeter went aground about where Superior and St. Clair streets meet today. Instead of trying to float his boat, Streeter decided to leave it there and live in it. Before this time, the area east of St. Clair and south of Oak Street was part of the lake. As time went by, sand and debris piled up around Streeter's boat, and a large area of new land resulted.

Captain Streeter not only claimed the land, but also declared that it was a part of the "District of Lake Michigan," and not to be considered a part of Illinois. For years Streeter fought in the courts to keep title to "his" land. He also stood off numerous attempts to evict him. Finally, the matter was settled and the area became one of the most valuable sections of the North Side,

still known to some as Streeterville.

In 1900 the famed actress Sarah Bernhardt visited Chicago and gave the city a remarkably descriptive tribute, "I adore Chicago. It is the pulse of America."

THE PULSE QUICKENS

Chicago took a great step forward in 1908 when it adopted the famous plan for the city on which noted designer Daniel H. Burnham had been working since 1905. Burnham, as chief designer of the World's Columbian Exposition, had received much of his inspiration for the "plan" from the great fair. This plan provided a blueprint for the development of the city along carefully thought out lines rather than on a hit-or-miss basis. It was Daniel Burnham who admonished Chicago to "Make no little plans; they have no magic to stir men's blood. . . . Make big plans; aim high in hope and work. . . . Remember that our sons and grandsons are going to do things that would stagger us. . . ."

This advice, combined with the Chicago motto, "I Will," have kept the city plunging ahead at a fast pace throughout the twentieth century, in spite of such disasters as that of December 30, 1903. A large crowd had gathered that evening at the Iroquois Theater, which stood about where the Oriental Theater stands today. While a bloodthirsty performance of *Mr. Bluebeard* was going on, the stage curtain suddenly burst into flames; the stage setting flared up; flames billowed out over the audience which fled to the doors in panic. Since the doors opened in, not out, hundreds piled up behind the unyielding doors, and an incredible total of 575 lost their lives in one of the worst disasters in the country's history. The result of the fire was the establishment of fire prevention laws in all United States theaters.

As the second decade of the century began, Chicago had surged ahead to become the greatest buyer and slaughterer of meat animals in the world, had taken first in the manufacture of farm implements and second in printing, along with a growing list of other accomplishments.

On July 24, 1915, Western Electric Company workers from the Cicero plant chartered the steamer *Eastland* for a lake excursion. A happy and excited group of excursionists got on board the boat as it lay docked at the Chicago riverside. When many of them crowded to one side of the boat, the *Eastland* turned over on its side and lay helplessly in the water. Horrified observers on the shore did all they could do, but 812 persons, mostly from Berwyn, lost their lives.

The depression of the 1930's brought the collapse of the utility empire built up by Samuel Insull, who at one time was considered to be—justifiably—one of the most important figures of the city and the nation.

Chicago again demonstrated its "I Will" spirit by risking a large investment in a great world's fair in the midst of the depression. The crowds and extra spending brought by the Century of Progress fair in 1933 and 1934 did much to relieve the depression.

In 1933 Chicago was saddened by a strange tragedy. Mayor Anton Cermak of Chicago was riding with President-elect Franklin D. Roosevelt on the streets of Miami, Florida, on February 15, when Joseph Zangara, an anarchist, leaped from the crowd, pulled a gun and aimed it at the President. A woman from the crowd managed to seize the man's arm, deflecting the shot which struck Mayor Cermak, who died later.

Chicago gave its attention so thoroughly to the winning of World War II that even the foundry of the Museum of Science and Industry was turning out metal parts for the war, as interested crowds watched the demonstration. Of course, the vast wartime industry of the city was a critical part of the total wartime effort.

"BOOMTOWN, U.S.A."

Modern Chicago is growing so rapidly that even its residents cannot keep up. The city watches as the 100-story John Hancock Center rises, the 70-story Lake Point Tower becomes the world's tallest apartment building, and the First National Bank pyramids to a 60-story height, all dramatic evidence of a tremendous construction which is transforming Chicago.

The round towers of Chicago's Marina City, looking like two enormous corncobs set on end, follow the core-and-cantilever construction used by Frank Lloyd Wright. Residents with boats can cruise right into the building from the Chicago River. The bottom floors of the building are parking spaces reached by a seemingly endless spiral ramp. A bank, restaurants, stores, television station and offices as well as apartments, make the Marina complex a true city in itself. Other cities all over the country are now imitating Chicago's Marina City.

Even the exterior of Chicago's new $70,-000,000 Civic Center is an innovation. The special steel construction was designed to take on a rusted, antique looking appearance and will never need further attention. This masterpiece of civic architecture houses some of the country's most modern courtrooms as well as other city offices.

Carl Sandburg called Chicago "Hog butcher of the world, Tool Maker, Stacker of Wheat, Player with Railroads and the Nation's Freight Handler." It is no longer butcher of the world, since most of the major packers have moved their plants elsewhere, but it is still all the rest and much more.

Its 14,000 factories pay their workers, $8,000,000,000 a year in salaries; those factories bring the city first rank in producing

Wacker Drive, completed in 1926 as part of a program of civic improvement, is a two-level road skirting the south and east banks of the Chicago River.

food products, electronic equipment, television sets and radios, machinery, railroad equipment, petroleum products, packaging materials, telephones, housewares, candy and confections, cosmetics, and athletic goods, to say nothing of snuff. It is easy to see why the city that leads the world in all those fields might be called the "Windy City," from bragging if for no other reason!

The boasts of Chicago can be almost endless—the busiest airport in the world (O'Hare International), the mightiest exchange for grain (Board of Trade), the world's largest commercial building (Merchandise Mart), the greatest concentration of conventions and trade shows in the world, 58 institutions of higher learning and 200 technical schools (forming the largest single concentration of such places of learning anywhere in a similar area) and many others.

On January 16, 1967, Chicago's supremacy

in the convention field appeared shaken. The largest trade show in the nation, the Housewares Convention, was to open in the morning, and workmen were putting the finishing touches on the exhibits when a flash of flame sent them scurrying. Before the fire could be controlled, McCormick Place, largest convention hall in the nation, was a complete ruin. The enormous girders had buckled under the intense heat; the massive concrete walls had shriveled and collapsed; even the 5,000 seat Arie Crown Theater at the far end of the building from where the fire started, was left unfit for use.

But Chicago has never succumbed to disaster, and the city sprang into action to find alternative places for coming conventions, and plans were made to build a newer and larger convention hall at a record pace.

Admirers of the city simply call this another demonstration of the "I Will" spirit.

Rings Around Chicago

THE INNER RING

Largest of the suburbs of Chicago is tree-shaded Evanston. Father Marquette is said to have beached his fleet of ten canoes on the shore of what is now Evanston in 1674. The area later took on some importance as a lake port. The first house in the region was built as early as 1826, but the town was not laid out until 1854. Northwestern University opened a year later, and the community was named Evanston in honor of John Evans, one of the university founders.

Today, a city of more than 80,000, Evanston provides a bustling commercial center for its residents, large numbers of whom make their living in Chicago. One of the country's leading institutions of its kind is the Traffic Institute of Northwestern University, which has helped to keep Evanston one of the safest cities in the country, and which is consulted by traffic authorities from all over the world.

Other communities along the lakeshore north of Evanston provide the finest possible residential atmosphere for the thousands who occupy the fine homes and estates of Wilmette, Kenilworth, Winnetka, Glencoe, Highland Park, Lake Forest and Lake Bluff, lying like elegant jewels along the shore of Lake Michigan.

One of the fastest-growing communities of the country during the 1950's and 1960's was Skokie, which likes to be called the world's largest village, since it has never been incorporated as a city. Other residential suburbs of this area are Morton Grove, Glenview, Niles, Des Plaines and Park Ridge. Farther north and west are Mt. Prospect, Arlington Heights, Mundelein and Libertyville.

Oldest and most sedate of the western Chicago suburbs is Oak Park, settled in 1837 and known as Kettlestring's Grove in honor of its pioneer settler. It has recently lost its title of "world's largest village" to Skokie, but it still keeps its village government.

Most controversial of Chicago suburbs is Cicero, which has been forced on many occasions to live down its reputation of being in the control of gangsters. Founded in 1867, Cicero today is a major industrial center, with more than 150 factories.

Other west and south suburbs include Berwyn, Oak Lawn, Evergreen Park, Blue Island, Harvey, Homewood, Chicago Heights, Park Forest, Calumet City and Lansing.

Elmhurst, a western suburb, was first known as Cottage Hill because of its first house, called Hill Cottage, built in 1843 by J. L. Hovey. Downers Grove, to the west, takes its name from Pierce Downer who built the first home there in 1832. Maple Avenue in Downers Grove was laid out in 1838 by two pioneers who cleared the way by dragging a heavy log along the prairie between two oxen. Land where Wheaton now stands, northwest of Chicago, was first claimed by Warren and Jesse Wheaton. Today it looks forward to renewed growth through the forthcoming Weston Nuclear Accelerator to be built nearby.

Among other suburbs on the Chicago fringe are Lombard, Glen Ellyn, Naperville, La Grange, Maywood, Brookfield, Riverside, Lyons and Palos Hills.

Morton Arboretum, pictured here in all the glory of autumn, provides nature lovers with one of the finest collections of trees and shrubs ever assembled.

THE OUTER RING

Chicago's tremendous metropolitan area, now almost solidly built up, is encircled by an outlying ring of "satellite cities" from Waukegan on the north to Kankakee on the south, including the arc of cities along the placid Fox River to the west. Within this tremendous semicircle, new homes, communities and industries are being rapidly added to the great Chicago complex, with the expectation that the entire enormous region will be almost completely populated and built-up—hopefully with enough space saved for parks and recreation.

The name Waukegan is Indian for fort or trading post. La Salle is said to have considered placing a trading post at the Indian village there and the French did maintain an insignificant trading station. The trading post of Thomas Jenkins in 1835 was the modern beginning of settlement.

Waukegan prospered in the boom that brought Chicago's rise, and today it is the strongest industrial community in Illinois north of Chicago. Over the years in radio and television, Waukegan became one of the best-known of the nation's smaller cities as the much publicized birthplace of comedian Jack Benny.

Barrington, Grayslake, Fox Lake, Carpentersville and Dundee are all communities on the outer fringe. Angelo Carpenter built Carpentersville almost by himself, being responsible for a grocery store, sawmill, woolen mill and gristmill. He platted the town in 1851, and was known for giving houses or lots to needy people of the community, as did his widow after his death.

After the end of the Black Hawk War, James and Hezekiah Gifford began a settlement on the Fox River in 1835. When Gifford plotted a road to Belvidere, his wife joked, "Anyone would think that you expected this farm to become a city, with stagecoaches going through." Before the year ended two stages came by each week, with a flurry of horns. The city of Elgin gradually took form.

Small industry, dairying and the establishment of the Elgin National Watch Company in 1866 brought prosperity. Elgin soon was the center of the entire dairying industry of the Midwest and its markets established the price of butter and cheese over a wide area. Modern Elgin continues to diversify its industries.

There was a sizable Potawatomi village on the site of Aurora when the earliest settler, Joseph McCarty, came there in 1834. Soon after he established Aurora, McCarty came east to look at the site of Chicago, but he dismissed it as "more promising for the raising of bullfrogs than humans." Two towns grew up opposite each other along the Fox River, each trying to remain separate and with great rivalry between them. When the residents finally decided to establish a joint civic center on Stolp's Island in the middle of the river, the rivalry stopped enough to permit the combining of the settlements as Aurora.

Aurora was the Illinois pioneer in electric street lighting, placing its light fixtures on high steel towers in 1881. Today the city is the heart of a farm and industrial complex, with important railroad yards. Leading products include road machinery and heavy steel products.

Charles Reed, the first settler, founded Joliet in 1831, but the settlement was abandoned until after the Black Hawk War. First called Juliet, the name was changed to Joliet in 1845. The arrival of the first boat on the Illinois and Michigan Canal was wildly hailed, and canal traffic brought an industrial boom to the town. The first railroad, in 1852, was followed by five additional railroads. Steel manufacturing sprang up. One wallpaper manufacturing plant was followed by another until the six plants of the Joliet region were producing a third of all the wallpaper made in the country. Today Joliet is still the leading manufacturing center of wallpaper in the United States.

The city is one of the principal industrial centers of the state with oil and limestone processing, earth-moving equipment, chemicals and electronic parts being added to steel and wallpaper and almost 1,000 other manufactured products. It is also known throughout the state as the location of a state penitentiary. The Illinois waterway makes it a busy traffic point.

When the Illinois Central Railroad missed the old French town of Bourbonnais, a new adjoining town named Kankakee was begun around the railroad depot in 1855, and soon the new community had far outdistanced the old. The Indian name Kyankeakee means "beautiful land."

City, Town, and Country

WHERE THE ROCK WAS FORDED

Galena was thriving and populous; Chicago had just begun to receive the throngs of traffic that was to make it a transportation center, and the Galena to Chicago stagecoach was setting up its run in the early 1830's. Since there were no bridges, a suitable place had to be found to ford the Rock River. A shallow spot with a hard rocky bed was found for the stage to cross. An early traveler admired the location, saying, "I've lived in nineteen states and three territories and been whipped a thousand times, but I'm damned if I ever see so pretty a country as that."

Soon a sawmill had been set up by Germanicus Kent near the Rock ford to take advantage of the waterpower. A small settlement grew up, followed soon after by another on the opposite side of the river. In 1839 the two settlements combined and were incorporated as Rockford, named in honor of the pioneer ford across the Rock River. In 1836 Winnebago County was formed, and the county seat was placed at Rockford in 1839.

In the 1850's the Chicago and Galena Union Railroad arrived, and sizable factories were set up to take advantage of the waterpower provided by a new dam and millrace. John H. Manny came to Rockford in 1853 and began to build quantities of his new reaper-mower combination. He was sued by Cyrus H. McCormick for patent infringement, but Manny won the suit. One of his lawyers was Abraham Lincoln.

Among the interesting sidelights of Rockford history was Rockford's amateur baseball team which hit its peak in the year 1870.

A Chicago newspaper wrote, "If Chicago has no cause for local rejoicing over the achievements of her professional baseball representatives she can at least join heartily in the State pride resulting from the remarkable record made by the club of amateurs residing in the flourishing town of Rockford.... We consider the Forest City Nine the champion club of America." The team soon turned professional and joined the newly formed National League, so that Rockford for a time had big league baseball. Adrian "Pop" Anson, later famous in Chicago baseball, was a member of the Rockford team.

Today Rockford is the second largest city in Illinois, one of the leading manufacturing centers of the country—first city of the nation in the production of screw products and fasteners, and second in the tremendously important field of the production of machine tools—and a leader in many other fields.

CITY OF THE PEOUREA TRIBE

Peoria likes to think of itself as the oldest city in Illinois, tracing its founding back to the establishment of Fort Crèvecoeur in 1680. Although there were a number of breaks in the continuity of settlement, Peoria can certainly claim to be the oldest Illinois settlement to have developed into a major city.

The Peourea Indians of the region (as Father Marquette called them) were friendly to European settlers, which made even more tragic a mistake that occurred during the War of 1812. Governor Ninian Edwards, disturbed by the constant harassment by the Indians during the war, took a force of troops

*By 1858 smokestacks filled Peoria's skyline
and steamboat traffic made the city a busy port.*

upstate and destroyed the Indian village of Au Pe on the site of Peoria. He did not know what Chief Black Partridge of Au Pe, far from being an enemy, actually had been aiding the Americans in ransoming the captives from the Fort Dearborn Massacre.

In 1813 the Americans built Fort Clark where the village of Au Pe had stood, and this can be considered the beginning of modern Peoria. Peoria County was established in 1825, the community around Fort Clark was named as county seat, and the French name of Peoria was restored. For some time, the business of Putnam County, then including Chicago, was carried on in Peoria.

In 1854 both Stephen Douglas and Abraham Lincoln spoke at Peoria, four years earlier than their famous series of debates. According to historian Albert Beveridge, it was here that Lincoln ". . . for the first time in his life, publicly and in forthright words denounced slavery, and asserted that it was incompatible with American institutions."

Because of its location on the Illinois River, Peoria was first known as a transportation center. Meat packing soon grew to large proportions. Another early industry was the distilling of whiskey. Today the city is a leading distilling center.

The Caterpillar Tractor Company of Peoria is the largest single employer in all of Illinois, and this company, with others, gives Peoria the lead in production of major equipment items, as well as many other lines.

CITY ON THE SANGAMON

When Illinois became a state, the present capital site was a beautiful valley of the Sangamon River, swarming with wild turkeys, deer and other game. In the year of statehood, 1818, a North Carolina man, Elisha Kelly, wandered into this lush region, sampled its game and was so impressed that he returned to his home and persuaded his father and four brothers to return to his paradise on the Sangamon River. Here the Kellys built a substantial log cabin, enjoyed the fish almost at their doorstep and planted a garden for vegetables.

Before long the Kelly household was the nucleus of a slowly growing settlement. Although not yet deserving to be called a town in 1821 when Sangamon County was formed, the Kelly settlement was the only one large enough to house county officials, and so the community was chosen as county seat. Nearby Spring Creek and one of the Kelly's fields gave the new name to the sprouting city—Springfield. John Kelly was given a contract to build a county courthouse out of "logs twenty feet long . . . a door and a window cut out" for a price to "the said Kelly of forty-two dollars and fifty cents."

Later a rivalry grew up for the county seat between Springfield and Sangamo Town. When the committee decided to look at Sangamo Town, they asked Andrew Elliott to guide them there. He took such a roundabout road through thickets and swamps, across creeks and through brambles that the committee declared Sangamo Town was almost impossible to reach and gave Springfield the permanent county seat. Sangamo Town soon withered and died.

Robert Thompson was paid $2.25 for designing the "magnificent frame structure" which provided the new courthouse. In 1832 the shallow and treacherous Sangamon River was negotiated by the fearless steamboat *Talisman*. The excited Springfield *Journal* exulted, "Springfield can no longer be considered an inland town. We congratulate our farmers, our mechanics, our merchants and professional men, for the rich harvest in prospect, and we cordially invite emigrating citizens from other states, whether they be poor or rich, if so be they are industrious and honest, to come thither and partake of the good things of Sangamo."

While the *Talisman* went farther upriver, the level of the river dropped, and the proud boat was humiliated by having to back downstream. Springfield was not destined to be a busy port, but destiny held other things.

As the northern part of the state became settled with surprising speed, pressure grew to choose a state capital at a more central location than Vandalia. Led by Abraham Lincoln, on February 25, 1837, the legislature chose Springfield to be the capital, and Lincoln moved there the following April. For twenty-five years this man, for whom the future held such great accomplishments, was content to practice law in Springfield, with a short time in Washington as a Congressman. The reputation which he had earned in the state legislature grew with the new capital.

Springfield was incorporated as a city in 1853; the first of the series of increasingly great state fairs was held there that year.

On February 11, 1861, Abraham Lincoln boarded the train that would take him to Washington and the Presidency of the United States. Most of Springfield had gathered at the Great Western passenger station and they heard his brief and moving words of farewell from the observation platform of the train. This address is considered one of

Weeping mourners filed by in silent tribute as the body of Lincoln lay in state in the old capitol on May 3 and 4, 1865.

his most impressive. Those who heard him said he appeared to know he would never return alive to the Springfield he loved so much.

In early May, 1865, they brought his body home to Springfield where it was laid to rest in Oak Ridge Cemetery. Both the Lincolns had often admired the beauty of that place.

It is ironic that in that same year another legislator, perhaps an aspiring Lincoln, introduced a bill in the legislature to move the capital from Springfield to Peoria. Nothing came of this movement, but Springfield sprang into action, and bolstered the city's standing as state capital with an offer to buy the state capitol building for $200,000, which was then used to start a new capitol. The cornerstone for the new one was laid in 1868. Some state departments moved to the new

building in 1875, but the legislature argued over appropriating funds to finish the work, which was not completed until 1887.

In recent years, rich surrounding farmlands, coal mining and a variety of industries have added to the business of state government to give Springfield a stable economy.

In 1924 the city approved a plan for developing Springfield in a manner worthy of a capital of a great state. Work on this plan has progressed sporadically since that time. In 1930, the voters approved the creation of Lake Springfield to be built with the help of Federal funds.

Today Springfield is not only the capital of the great state of Illinois but also the capital of an even greater state of the spirit— The Land of Lincoln.

THREE OF THE "QUAD"

When Marquette and Jolliet glided down the Mississippi, they found that at one point it took a mammoth curve and turned almost directly west. Later it was found that this particular stretch of the river was its longest portion flowing in a westerly direction. At the time the explorers visited this region it was occupied by the Illini Indians, but they were driven out by the Sauk and Fox tribes in 1680.

When Zebulon Pike visited the area in 1805, the Indians still considered themselves under British control. Young Sauk warrior Black Hawk told of the Pike expedition, "A boat came up the river with a young American chief and a small party of soldiers. . . . He gave us good advice; said our American father would treat us well. He then requested us to pull down our British flag . . . This we declined, as we wished to have two fathers."

In 1816 the American government built Fort Armstrong on the island of rock which gives Rock Island its name. Colonel George Davenport, who gave his name to the city later founded in Iowa across the river, was the first permanent settler of the region. After 1828 many settlers followed.

The area, swept by the Black Hawk War in 1832, was established as Rock Island County in that same year, but another year went by before county organization really came into being.

River shipping grew, and in the height of the steamboat era as many as 1,900 steamboats docked in the area. Tremendous quantities of timber were rafted down the Mississippi from the timberlands of the north, and the lumber mills of the region boomed. The Mississippi's first railroad bridge in 1855 brought new business to the area.

An interesting incident is connected with this bridge, which was partially destroyed in 1856 when the steamer *Effie Afton* hit a bridge pier and burned much of the structure. A local paper reported that "A distinguished lawyer who is employed by the bridge company to defend that mammoth nuisance is expected in Davenport in a few days, for the purpose of examining that huge obstruction to the free navigation of the river."

That lawyer was Abraham Lincoln; his investigation disclosed that the boat had experienced a mechanical failure before the crash, and so the boat was responsible for the accident. Lincoln and his associates won the case.

The Rock Island Arsenal, established on the island of Rock Island during the Civil War, has boomed in wartime and declined in peace. More than 12,000 Confederate prisoners were held on the island in the Civil War, and during two world wars the Arsenal employed thousands. Today missile research is the principal activity, and the Arsenal is the largest manufacturing arsenal in the country.

As the steamboat traffic and lumber industries declined, other industries came to take their place. Today the region has one of the largest concentrations of agricultural implement manufacturers anywhere. Rock Island boasts a mammoth International Harvester operation, along with many others, and Moline is headquarters for the vast John Deere Company complex of farm equipment manufacturing. Moline also produces a wide variety of other items, including toys.

Now the four cities that make up the so-called Quad City region—Rock Island, Moline, and East Moline in Illinois, and Davenport in Iowa—are grouped together into one large metropolitan area.

FERRY TOWN

Illinois' pioneer community, Cahokia, found that it could not compete with St. Louis, Missouri, after that city was established on the west bank of the Mississippi River not far to the north. But when Captain James Piggott set up a ferry service from St. Louis to the east riverbank near Cahokia in 1795, a settlement soon grew up there.

As the region grew with the settling of pioneers and the development of nearby coal deposits, the settlement near Cahokia took the name of Illinoistown. Because there was no bridge, the numerous railroads which soon came into Illinoistown terminated there, and the trains had to be ferried across the river. Illinoistown was incorporated in 1859, and not long afterward a new town was laid out nearby, known as East St. Louis. In 1861 the merging of the two towns was accepted in a vote of the residents of the area. Illinoistown became East St. Louis, although many wanted to preserve the older name.

Floods were the worst danger to the safety of East St. Louis. In 1844 the entire lowland area had been flooded so extensively that steamboats could load coal at the foot of the bluffs. In 1875, after bitter arguments by "high graders" and "low graders," the grade level of the main streets of the city was raised in height varying from 8 to 15 feet, leaving some old buildings with only their tops showing above the street. A great system of levees also helps protect the region.

The Eads Bridge, built in 1874, was one of the greatest engineering accomplishments of the time. It took certain railroads across the river, but other roads still had their terminals in East St. Louis to avoid bridge tolls. Although steamboating declined, industry grew in the region. At the turn of the century there were so many new jobs that housing could not be built fast enough to accommodate the new workers.

Today East St. Louis is a prosperous industrial city, with large concentrations of stockyards, meat packing, rubber manufacturing, quarrying, oil refining and steel mills.

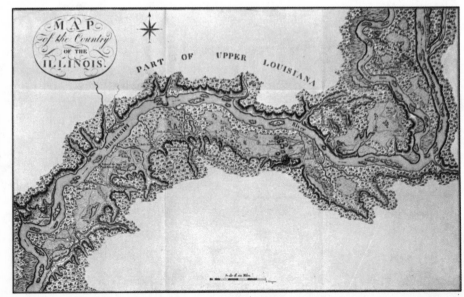

Early map of the area around Cahokia and East St. Louis.

PRAIRIE TOWN

In 1829 Macon County chose as its county seat an entirely vacant stretch of prairie without even a road or footpath. This unpopulated town was named Decatur. Soon James Renshaw erected the first cabin in the area set aside for the coming city.

By the following year, when Abraham Lincoln came through the settlement to live with his family on a nearby farm, a few other buildings had been erected. In this region he worked for farmers, practiced his famous rail-splitting, borrowed books from Major Warnick, a county official, and otherwise worked, studied and matured. He made his first public speech in what is now Lincoln Park in Decatur.

The early development of Decatur was based on the farming region around it. Railroads, arriving in 1854, stimulated manufacturing, and the Civil War called for increased production. The first coal mines of the area in 1874 brought new activities.

One of the leaders of the region was James Millikin, who was able to earn a fortune as a banker and industrialist. He used part of his wealth to endow a university at Decatur which now bears his name and was dedicated by President Theodore Roosevelt in 1903.

In 1923, in order to have an adequate water supply, the city built a new dam which formed the present Lake Decatur with its 12-mile shoreline.

World War II caused a great expansion in Decatur's manufacturing, including a United States factory which worked on a part of the atomic bomb. The tremendous expansion of the soybean crop brought about an entirely new industry of bean milling and processing. Now the city likes to think of itself as the world's soybean capital.

OTHER CITIES

Alton was founded between 1815 and 1818 when three different towns developed in the region now occupied by the single city. The town named Alton had the best location on the river, and it eventually absorbed the other two towns.

Alton was the scene in 1842 of a strange affair involving Abraham Lincoln. Mary Todd, later Lincoln's wife, had written an article critical of State Auditor James Shields. Lincoln accepted the responsibility for this and was challenged by Shields to fight a duel. He selected broadswords as the weapons and Alton as the location. The duelists and their seconds rowed out to an island in the river. While Lincoln swung his sword in practice the seconds conferred and after a long time agreed that Shields would accept a formal statement from Lincoln, which read in part that although he "did not think . . . that said article could produce said effect . . ." he had no intention of "injuring the personal or private character or standing of Mr. Shields."

Bloomington was founded in 1843 and drowsed along for some years until three events gave it more rapid growth; the founding of Illinois Wesleyan University, the coming of the Illinois Central and Chicago and Mississippi railroads, and the coming of Illinois State Normal University to North Bloomington (Normal). The Illinois Republican party was founded at Bloomington in 1856.

John G. Comegys made an attempt to settle the Cairo region in 1818, but when he died two years later his plans failed. However, he had given his new community the name Cairo because of his belief that the delta resembled the Nile delta near Cairo,

A view of the village of Alton from the book The Valley of the Mississippi.

Egypt, and this region has kept the nickname of Egypt ever since. The Cairo City and Canal Company began a settlement in 1837, under the leadership of Darius B. Holbrook, but it slumped with the decline in the company stock. Greatest prosperity of the community came in 1855 with the completion of the Illinois Central Railroad between Cairo and Chicago.

During the Civil War, Cairo was a center for the Union Army, and at the end of the war the city had a population of about 8,000. Mark Twain wrote, "Cairo is a brisk town now and is substantially built and has a city look about it. . . ."

Modern Cairo, farther south than Richmond, Virginia, has fine magnolia trees and something of the elegance of the South.

Urbana was settled in 1822, more than 30 years before Champaign. In 1833 Urbana became the seat of Champaign County, but the Illinois Central Railroad placed its roadway about two miles from Urbana, and a new town of West Urbana (now Champaign) sprang up. Urbana tried to absorb the new town in 1855, but the residents defeated this move, and the new town was incorporated as Champaign in 1860. The two communities have grown up side by side ever since.

When plans were made for Illinois to have an industrial college, Champaign and Urbana buried their differences and made a strong appeal for the new college which was finally located there and became the University of Illinois, described in more detail in a later section. Today Champaign is the trade and industrial center and Urbana principally the residential area, in which is the larger part of the University of Illinois campus.

If the legend concerning Freeport's name

River transportation around Cairo about the middle of the nineteenth century.

is true, the origin of that name is one of the most unique in the country. William Baker was so generous to all who came along the Chicago to Galena trail that his wife finally said in exasperation, "This place is getting to be a regular free port for everybody coming along the trail. You'd best call your new town 'Freeport' because that is exactly what it will be." The story goes that the name stuck, and Freeport it is today.

Many miners left the Galena region to the west and settled in Freeport which became an industrial area with the coming of the Galena and Chicago Union Railroad in 1853. Today the city is a center for both industry and farm produce.

Granite City came into being in 1892 with the establishment of the National Enameling and Stamping Company of William F. Niedringhaus. The city's name came from the fact that the company's main product was pots and pans of a ware known as granite. The city was incorporated in 1896 and boomed and spread with astonishing speed. Steel-rolling mills and a steel foundry added to the city's industry.

Two young men from the East, Willard Keyes and John Wood, took claims on the present location of Quincy in 1822 and built their cabins there. Several other pioneers soon followed their lead, calling their settlement The Bluffs. Wood quickly became a leader of the area and later of the state. At his request the legislature established Adams County in 1825. A committee to select the county seat was led by Willard Keyes to inspect the city; although their way led over "bogs, quicksands, and quagmires," they chose The Bluffs as county seat, and the name was changed to Quincy, both county and city being named in honor of President John Quincy Adams.

Beginning about 1850 and continuing for 20 years, Quincy was the second largest city in Illinois. It shipped large numbers of hogs and other livestock from its port on the Mississippi and had many factories with a wide range of products, including wagons and carriages, organs, corn planters and plows, steam engines, shoes and stoves.

The decline of steamboating brought some diminishing of Quincy's importance, but it still has many large and healthy industries.

TOWN AND COUNTRY

Illinois is dotted with small communities, some only slumbering crossroad hamlets; others, though relatively small in population, are flourishing centers. Most of them have fascinating stories of their growth and development, poignant memories of their founders and other personalities, and other records of the past which should be studied and preserved but for reasons of space cannot be treated here.

The question, of course, comes to mind why these communities and even larger ones came into being in the first place. The simplest and most frequent answer is that they just happened. A pioneer settler, perhaps unable to continue farther, chose a spot for settlement; others joined him. If there was sufficient water and wood and a means of making a living, probably the community continued. If the leaders had enough imagination or vision, they brought industry or other means of growth into the community.

In Illinois the rivers were a principal reason for establishing communities. Later on, roads and railroads provided a reason for community settlement. Many towns which found themselves bypassed by the railroads, either picked themselves up and moved to the railroad or slowly declined.

Minerals and other natural resources in a region often brought mushroom growth in communities established to exploit these resources. Galena and its lead mines are the best example of this. Other communities owe their existence to coal and oil and other minerals.

Some communities were established for specific reasons. The town of Zion is a good example of a religious-centered community. In 1899 John Alexander Dowie bought a large tract of land along Lake Michigan as a home for his newly established Christian Catholic Apostolic Church, a community to be called Zion. The population reached 10,000 within a few years as followers of Dowie flocked in. Over the years, Zion has had many ups and downs.

Establishment of a single large industry has often resulted in a community springing up about it, such as the town of Pullman. In 1881 George M. Pullman, whose invention of the railroad sleeping car brought him a fortune, hired the country's leading experts to plan a model town for the workers in his plant. The size of the project attracted world attention. The town became part of Chicago in 1889.

Some communities have been planned solely for residences. The town of Riverside was one of the earliest planned residential communities in the country. Park Forest following World War II, and a host of others have sprung up in modern times. Such planned communities often offer clubs, swimming pools, golf courses, shopping centers, parking and other attractions.

Politics also plays an important part in the life of many cities. Gaining or losing the

*Salmon Rutherford's tavern in Dresden, now the
site of a nuclear power plant.*

county seat has brought life or death to several communities, and the city or village with important political leaders either as residents or natives often has considerable advantage.

Many Illinois communities were founded either as havens for or to attract persons of various ethnic backgrounds, and these are discussed in more detail in a later section.

GHOSTS OF THE PAST

Communities which come into being based on a single activity are apt to suffer greatly when that activity declines. Galena, Nauvoo and Shawneetown are examples of this.

At one time Galena was Illinois' leading city—the thriving center of lead mining, a bustling port on the Galena River, a city of fine homes, thriving hotels, stores and an important newspaper. It appeared to be a permanent success. Then the lead supply gave out; the railroad brought greater success to other communities; the river silted up and closed the port, and today Galena is a fascinating, successful small community, but not the leading city of Illinois.

Nauvoo, in its turn, was also once the largest city of the state. After its skyrocket rise and dizzy decline, the deserted town was taken over by a group of French followers of Etienne Cabet, who hoped to found a community based on Christ's moral principles. Set up as a communal society, based mainly on the growing of grapes and making of wine, the group flourished for a while, but quarrels divided the people, and failure resulted.

Shawneetown was settled soon after the nineteenth century began; a government land office dealing with much of Illinois was set up there. As the easternmost Illinois port on the Ohio River, it received a constant

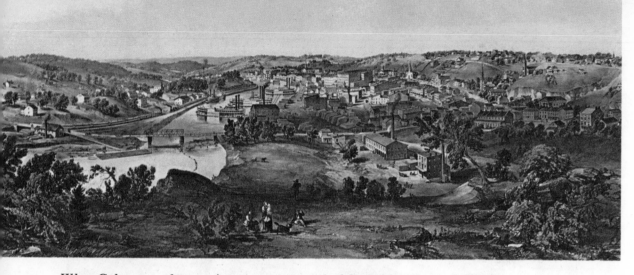

When Galena was the most important port north of St. Louis, steamboats lined the docks and the chimneys of mine buildings dotted the skyline.

flood of newcomers and goods and equipment from the East. Nearby salt mines furnished another source of income for the region.

When much of the state was a wilderness, Shawneetown was an established community. It was especially known as a banking and financial center. When the tiny community of Chicago was getting started 300 miles to the north, legend says a delegation of its people came to Shawneetown asking for financing. The Shawneetown banks refused a $1,000 loan because Chicago was too far away to have a bright future.

Almost every year the floods of the Ohio submerged Shawneetown, but the river was the principal life of the community and it clung to the river. Levees were constructed after the flood of 1884 and raised five feet above the 1913 high-water mark. The flood of 1937 almost completely destroyed the old town, and a new and much more modest town was relocated on higher ground.

The way of life in village and country has changed tremendously in modern times. Early settlers were compelled to spend most of their time securing a minimum of food, clothing and other necessities to survive. For the most part they could not use labor-saving machinery because it was either too expensive or unavailable. Recreation was generally "homemade," consisting of house-raising parties, hayrides, square dances and other simple pleasures. The church was often the center of community life.

Today the gulf between the small town and the farm on the one hand and the city on the other has narrowed. The whole country-side has become in effect one vast city. Trains, the automobile, commercial airlines, and the increasingly common operation of private airplanes gives the rural Illinoisan complete access to both rural and urban ways of life. No longer need there be any distinction between a "country boy" and a "city slicker." Television, radio, motion pictures and newspapers have brought the same knowledge of the world to the people of the country as to those of Chicago. Rural people have, in fact, a broader outlook since they enjoy the "best of both worlds."

The People of Illinois

Illinois was French before it was American, and a few descendants of these first settlers may still be found. Early American settlement of Illinois was mostly of native stock, particularly from the South. As the waves of immigration from Europe increased, Illinois proved particularly attractive, both on farms and in cities.

By the twentieth century, Chicago counted more Dutch, Scandinavians, Poles, Lithuanians, Bohemians, Croatians and Greeks than any other city in the United States. There were large colonies of Germans, Italians and Chinese. It was said at one time that more nationalities lived on Halsted Street than on any other one street in the world.

Other large cities have a wide ethnic mixture, but some are noted particularly for large groups of one nationality, such as the Swedish people in Rockford, Moline and Galesburg, and the Portuguese of Springfield and Jacksonville.

Smaller communities were founded by particular ethnic groups or at one time or another have been dominated by one group.

Bishop Hill was founded by Erik Jansson, who had left his native Sweden because he disagreed with the state religion. He and his followers set up a communal society in Henry County. They dug out caves and lived in these the first winter. Then they built their homes. They lived separately but worked to-

A primitive painting by Olaf Haus of one of the farms that was part of the Swedish community of Bishop Hill.

Park House, the home George Flower built for his parents in the English community that is now the town of Albion. When he inherited the estate, George Flower painted this primitive watercolor. The paintings of Mr. and Mrs. George Flower were done by D. Roster in 1855.

gether, often as long as 18 hours a day. With a population of 1,500, Bishop Hill at one time was the principal settlement between Rock Island and Peoria, but dissension eventually split the group; Jansson was murdered, and the colony broke up.

Norway, according to some authorities, was the earliest permanent Norwegian settlement in America. It was established in 1834 under the leadership of Cleng Peerson, an unusual pioneer who was responsible for establishing more than 30 Norwegian settlements from Texas to northern Wisconsin.

One of the most interesting settlements was the English community around what is now the town of Albion. This was founded in 1818 by George Flower and Morris Birkbeck. They hoped to establish a community where conditions would be better for the average Englishman. They pooled their resources and covered several states looking for a site. "Bruised by the brushwood and exhausted by the extreme heat we almost despaired," Flower described the search,

"when . . . a few steps more, and a beautiful prairie suddenly opened to our view . . . lying in profound repose under the warm light . . . the whole presenting a magnificence of park-scenery, complete from the hand of Nature . . . we gazed long and steadily, drinking in the beauties of the scene which had been so long the object of our search."

Birkbeck stayed to complete arrangements, such as filing land claims in Shawneetown, and Flower returned to England to sell his holdings, assemble seeds, livestock and other necessities and persuade settlers to accompany him. About 50 people came with Flower from England, and by October, 1818, there were 200. Before long the town of Albion had been founded, and the "English Prairies" blossomed as a center of unusual wealth and culture in the wilderness.

Whether they founded their own communities, went to the farm or settled in the city ghettos, life was hard for first-generation immigrants. Most of them had left their homeland to seek greater freedom or economic opportunity. Because their dress and customs often set them apart, they generally had difficulty being accepted. They often lived in groups in the same neighborhoods, and frequently their native language was heard more often than English.

However, the succeeding generations usually were able to break away, and the process of "Americanization" was accelerated. Today Illinois boasts representatives of almost every known ethnic group; many of them rightly take pride in their background and preserve as much of the old traditions as they can, but most just as emphatically consider that they are truly Americans.

The process of the "melting pot" is still continuing in the state. In 1960 the census listed 686,093 foreign-born residents of Illinois. The origins of these are listed in the order of their numbers: Poland, 94,132; Germany, 87,707; Italy, 72,139; Russia, 45,522; England, 37,179; Sweden, 34,606; Czechoslovakia, 30,345; Lithuania, 27,977; Ireland, 26,880; Mexico, 25,477; Canada, 25,268; Yugoslavia, 24,570; Austria, 23,288; Greece, 16,600; Hungary, 15,652; Norway, 11,524; The Netherlands, 7,734; Rumania, 7,194; Denmark, 7,087; ·Belgium, 6,495; France, 5,684; Northern Ireland, 3,554; Japan, 3,551; China, 3,520; Switzerland, 2,940; The Philippines, 2,534; Finland, 2,297; Spain, 735; Portugal, 136.

IN THE STEPS OF THE FIRST CHICAGOAN—NEGROES IN ILLINOIS

The history of the Negro people in Illinois is covered in other sections of this book. It might be said, however, that the true history of the Negro in Illinois did not begin in 1720 with the importation of the first slaves by Philippe Renault, but rather in 1779 when a very remarkable man who was to become the first prominent Negro in Illinois history came to the territory.

This was Jean Baptiste Point du Sable, who in a very real sense may be considered as the true founder of the city of Chicago. The "Father of Chicago," according to Thomas A. Meehan in the *Journal of the Illinois State Historical Society*, was "a man whose claim can be substantiated by at least three con-

An early lithograph of an Illinois farm.

temporary documents. He resided in Chicago for almost twenty years, reared two children there, and even in the last years of his residence, saw a grandchild born in almost the heart of the present-day city.

"At the close of the eighteenth century and at the very dawn of the nineteenth du Sable, a Negro or mulatto, had a spacious, cultivated, and well-stocked farm together with a mill and an Indian trading post, on the very site that today is studded with skyscrapers and ribboned with drives, streets and boulevards. From this ingenious, resourceful, and seemingly well-educated Negro, Chicago draws her permanency."

Some have said du Sable was from Santo Domingo, but others now think that he was descended from the famous Dandonneau family of Canada, whose son Pierre was Sieur du Sable. The first exact report about Jean Baptiste Point du Sable was made by the British commandant at Mackinac, who in a report of July 4, 1779, writes of "Baptiste Point De Saible, a handsome Negro, well educated, and settled at Eschikagou (Chicago), but much in the French interest."

In 1790 a traveler wrote that he and three others stopped at Point du Sable's place and purchased flour, bread and pork. As Meehan points out, ". . . a man some two hundred miles from the nearest center of civilization, who could supply flour, pork, and bread to a party of at least four, evidently had hogs, fields under cultivation, his own flour mill, and also someone to bake bread. Du Sable had all of these things and many other accommodations—which makes one wonder at the ingenuity of a man who could have such a fine establishment in the midst of the wilderness. . . . It is remarkable that every contemporary report about du Sable describes him as a man of substance. Undoubtedly he owned one of the most complete establishments in the Middle West outside of Detroit and St. Louis."

Du Sable married a Potawatomi woman, journeying 280 miles to Cahokia for a marriage ceremony by a Catholic priest. In 1800 Du Sable sold his Chicago holdings. He later lived in St. Charles, Missouri, where he signed over all his properties and holdings to ". . . granddaughter, Eulalia, in exchange for her promise to care for him in his old age and to bury him in the Catholic cemetery there." He died at St. Charles in 1814.

Another early Negro of prominence was George Washington who farmed and built an estate. Through his will, 150 Negro students have received assistance of about $30,000 for their higher education.

Manufacturing saltpeter, Frank McWorter earned enough money to purchase his freedom and that of his wife, Lucy. With three of their free-born children they moved to Illinois, where among other accomplishments he laid out the site for the town of New Philadelphia. He also was successful at farming and raising stock. With the sizable fortune he gathered, McWorter purchased freedom for all of his children and two grandchildren.

William de Fleurville opened the first barbershop in Springfield, and he became Abraham Lincoln's barber. His business place also served as a meetinghouse for most of Springfield, and was almost a second home to Lincoln. De Fleurville saved his money and invested in real estate. When Lincoln left for Washington, he said a personal good-bye to de Fleurville. When the barber died, according to John E. Washington, "His funeral was one of the largest ever held in Springfield and was attended by the most distinguished

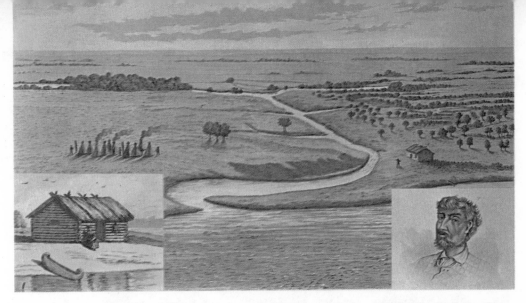

The site of Chicago as it probably appeared about 1779. The Chicago River takes its familiar fork out on the prairie. The insets show Jean Baptiste Point du Sable and the cabin he built at the mouth of the river.

people of the city which he had helped to develop and which he loved so much."

John Jones came to Chicago in 1845 with only $3.50. He established a tailoring business and prospered. He served as vice-president of the Colored National Convention at Rochester, New York, in 1853, and devoted himself to the repeal of Illinois' repressive "Black Laws." He was the first Negro to hold elective public office in Cook County, as county commissioner. On his death in 1879 he left an estate worth $55,000 and a legacy of leadership in the community.

During the Civil War the Twenty-ninth United States Colored Infantry became the first full Civil War regiment composed almost entirely of Illinois Negroes. Of course many other Negroes from Illinois also served.

After the war, the number of Negroes in Illinois increased slowly. As early as 1874 the Illinois General Assembly passed a law forbidding segregation in public schools. Two years later John W. E. Thomas of Chicago became the first Negro elected as a state rep-

resentative. In 1885 the Illinois General Assembly passed a civil rights act forbidding racial discrimination in restaurants, hotels, theaters, railroads, streetcars and places of public accommodation and amusement.

In 1891 Dr. Daniel Hale Williams of Chicago performed the first successful heart operation. The patient was a fellow Negro who had been stabbed in the heart; the operation took place in Provident Hospital.

The Spanish-American War saw the formation of the volunteer Eighth Illinois National Guard Regiment, composed of Negroes, mostly from Chicago.

The earliest Negro Illinois newspaper of record, the *Conservator*, was established in Chicago in 1878. The largest Illinois Negro newspaper, the Chicago *Daily Defender*, was founded in 1905.

The job opportunities afforded by the two world wars brought large numbers of Negroes to the North, and problems of adjustment and housing became acute in many areas.

In 1924 Albert B. George of Chicago became the first Negro elected to a judgeship in Illinois, and in the same year Adelbert H. Roberts was the first Negro elected to the Illinois Senate.

Governmental history was made in 1929 when Oscar De Priest of Chicago was seated in the United States House of Representatives. He was the first Negro Congressman ever seated from the North. In 1934 Arthur W. Mitchell of Chicago became the first Negro of the Democratic party in Congress.

Improvement of relations between the races became a subject of governmental action when Governor Dwight H. Green established an Illinois Interracial Commission, with advisory functions. In the same year the Chicago Mayor's Commission on Human Relations (its present title) became the first such municipal commission in the United States.

The year 1953 found Joseph D. Bibb heading the Department of Public Safety, the first Negro to hold a rank of this kind in the executive branch of Illinois government.

In 1961 the Illinois General Assembly passed a law forbidding discrimination in employment in Illinois and setting up the Fair Employment Practices Commission with power to investigate and initiate judicial action against violators of the act.

The University of Chicago in 1967 named the distinguished Negro scholar John Hope Franklin to be chairman of the history department of the university, one of the first appointments of a Negro department head in any institution of this caliber.

That same year saw many, both Negro and white, who were not satisfied with the progress of the Negro people to that date. Those who advocated laws for compelling integrated housing or those who were for the more moderate position of providing fair treatment in the sale of real estate, were disappointed when the legislature failed to pass open-housing legislation in 1967. However, Chicago and other cities had passed or were passing such legislation, such as that of Wheaton which was hailed by some as a model open-housing law.

Outstanding Illinois Negro citizens today are not only leaders of the Negro community but have earned national and international reputations in world affairs. Some of these include renowned singer Mahalia Jackson; Pulitzer Prize winning poet and playwright Gwendolyn Brooks; distinguished scientist Percy Julian; John Johnson, founder and developer of one of the country's leading publishing operations, including the magazines *Ebony* and *Negro Digest*, as well as many books; Archibald Carey, distinguished attorney and alternate delegate to the United Nations; Dr. Theodore K. Lawless; Judge James B. Parsons; and Chicago Cubs' baseball star, Ernie Banks, who has been given the title, "Mr. Cub."

THE GROWING SUCCESS OF LABOR

The organized labor movement of Illinois is usually considered to date from about 1850. The thousands of workers who came into the state to build canals and railroads had been familiar with labor unions in Europe and wanted them in Illinois, also. One of the early unions was the American Miners' Association. After the Civil War, labor organizations were discouraged by the "Black Law," which almost had the effect of outlawing unions.

The passage of the eight-hour day law of 1867 was offset by the fact that special contracts or agreements could be made by workers and employers for longer hours. Child labor laws were passed in 1872 and 1877 but they had comparatively little effect. However, in 1877, local groups of the Knights of Labor were founded in Chicago, Peoria and Springfield. In the years that followed, the labor movement grew rapidly in the state.

The Haymarket Riot had a serious effect on labor organizations, but labor and its problems received new consideration from state government under the administration of Governor John Peter Altgeld. A law of 1893 prohibited employers from keeping their workers from forming, joining or belonging to legitimate labor unions, but this was declared unconstitutional in 1900. A State Board of Arbitration, formed in 1895, adjusted 75 strikes in 21 years of operation.

Child labor was first successfully controlled by law in 1893, but this law was declared unconstitutional in 1895. However, by 1903 children under 14 could not be employed. An Illinois Department of Labor was established in 1927, and an Unemployment Compensation Act was passed in the same year.

In Illinois today, both through law and common understanding, the rights of labor are respected and the welfare of the workingman protected. The labor force in the state now stands at 4,595,000 men and women, and, by comparison with other states, this is a skilled and productive group.

EVER SINCE MARQUETTE

Ever since Father Marquette held the first-known church services near Starved Rock, religion has played an important part in the life of the state. Catholic missionaries were among the earliest of the French settlers and early Illinois was entirely Catholic. The Catholic diocese of Chicago, now the archdiocese, was not founded until 1843. Today the Catholic church ranks as the largest of all church units, with an Illinois membership of 2,340,000 for 1966.

The first Methodist arrived in Illinois in 1785, at New Design, and Methodists held the first religious services in modern Chicago. Baptist preachers have been in Illinois since 1787, and the first Baptist church began services in 1796 at New Design.

The Presbyterians arrived in Illinois in 1797, and the first Presbyterian church was put up in Sharon, in 1816. Congregational worship started in Illinois in 1833, and the Lutherans came in the 1840's.

The large number of the Jewish faith in Chicago have made that city one of the world's principal centers of Jewish worship, with some of the finest synagogues in the country. Other leading Jewish communities include East St. Louis, Waukegan, Springfield, Maywood and Peoria.

The Chicago area is the world center of a more recently founded religion, the Baha'i faith, conducted in the lofty, domed temple of Baha'i at Wilmette. The principal theme of this religion is universal brotherhood. The temple was more than twenty years in building because members of the faith would not permit any debt and only proceeded when they had funds on hand.

Growing to Greatness

The journey had not been an easy one for the 13 members of the Lincoln party. They entered Illinois for the first time in March, 1830; the ground had partly thawed, and the wagon wheels sank deep into the icy mud. All the household goods they possessed were piled on the wagons. Thomas Lincoln, father of Abraham, led the way on his horse as he brought his family and relatives from a not very successful life in Indiana, just as he had earlier led his then smaller family from Kentucky into the Hoosier State.

There was considerable difference between the two journeys. On the first, Abraham had been a boy of seven; on February 12, 1830, he had just turned twenty-one. Now, in his untanned skin moccasins, he towered six feet four inches. It is probable that Abraham led the oxteam drawing one of the wagons. Not generally remembered is the fact that he had a small stock of peddler's goods and sold knives, thread, needles, buttons and other items to occasional settlers and other travelers. Fifteen miles was the most that the little company ever managed to travel in a day, but they finally reached Decatur, where they located their relative John Hanks, who had selected a homesite for them on the open prairie. Hanks had dry timber waiting to build their log cabin. The family was able to clear ten acres of land, plant and harvest a corn crop and fence some of the land with rails, the splitting of which would later give Abraham Lincoln his best-loved nickname, the rail-splitter.

The winter of "The Big Snow" was one of the worst in memory; snow piled into 15-foot drifts. Game was almost impossible to find, and for much of the time the corn from their first crop was the only thing they had to eat. Most of the winter it was nearly impossible even to visit the neighbors. Then came spring floods. Thomas Lincoln decided to make another move, but this time Abraham Lincoln did not go with his father and stepmother; he had decided it was time for him to be on his own.

A year after he had arrived in Illinois, Abraham Lincoln faced the problem all men must face—what to make of his life. The prospects did not seem bright for the son of a poor family with only about a year of what passed for "formal" schooling in those days, but this man was different—how different the whole world someday would know.

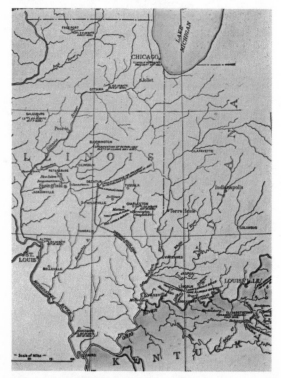

Route of the Lincoln family to Decatur.

Lincoln might have anticipated living for 30 years in Illinois, but he could never have foreseen how those years of intimate association with the state were going to mold him into the man who would one day be honored by having his state adopt the cherished nickname, Land of Lincoln.

NEW SALEM SAGA

In 1831 Abraham Lincoln and his two stepbrothers helped build a flatboat and pilot its load of produce down the Mississippi River all the way to New Orleans. On the way down the Sangamon River, their flatboat stuck on the milldam at New Salem, where the bow turned up toward the sky and water began to flow in. While spectators gave a number of suggestions about getting the boat free, Lincoln calmly took off some of the cargo and borrowed an auger. After he drilled a hole in the bow and let the water out, he filled the hole with a plug, and they were able to float the boat off the dam and continue the journey.

The things Lincoln saw and his experiences on this trip are not very well known, but they must have given this brilliant young man a new idea of what life could be like beyond the rough, pioneer country which was all he had known up to this time.

The flatboat project had been one of the ventures of a strange character, Denton Offut. He was noted for his many ideas and for his general inability to make a success of any of them. When Lincoln came back north, Offut hired him to run a store he had established at the town of New Salem, then only two years old.

Lincoln's first day in town was election day, and as he seemed to have nothing else to do, the clerk asked Lincoln to help him with the polling. It is said that in this way Lincoln met every man in the village on his first afternoon in New Salem. At the store he served his customers with great conscientiousness and charm, and soon became well liked by everyone. The tales of his devotion to learning are no legend. Every spare moment he read any book available that would improve him—such as Kirkham's *Grammar*. Customers who came to the store often found him in his favorite reading position, lying outside the store on his back under a tree, with his long legs extended far up the trunk.

Frontier amusements were rough and ready—cock fighting, horse racing and wrestling. Denton Offut had bragged so much about his new clerk's great strength that the boys from Clary's Grove came over to New Salem with their champion, Jack Armstrong, and challenged Lincoln to a wrestling match. Just when Armstrong was about to give in, his friends rushed in to help him, and the enraged Lincoln flung out a challenge to any of them to wrestle, but no one dared. Later Lincoln and Armstrong became good friends.

The Offut store was closed in 1832, and Lincoln volunteered to serve in the Black Hawk War. The local militia promptly elected him their captain. Mustered out after 30 days in service, Lincoln enlisted as a private in Captain Elijah Iles' company of Independent Rangers. Again mustered out, Lincoln reenlisted for another 30 days in the militia company called the Independent Spy Corps, led by Jacob M. Early, a Methodist preacher and physician from Springfield. They spent the last two weeks of their enlistment vainly trying to find Black Hawk in the swamps of southern Wisconsin.

When Lincoln later spoke about the leadership of General Lewis Cass in the war he could not refrain from poking fun both at

Abraham Lincoln in his familiar role of rail-splitter.

the general and at himself. "If General Cass went in advance of me picking huckleberries, I guess I surpassed him in charges upon the wild onions. If he saw any living fighting indians (sic), it was more than I did; but I had a good many bloody struggles with the musquetoes (sic), and I can truly say I was often hungry."

Returning to New Salem he went into partnership in another store, which failed and left him in debt. His appointment as postmaster did not give him enough income and he took up surveying. Defeated in a try for the state legislature in 1832, Lincoln tried again in 1834 and won, then was reelected in 1836, 1838, and 1840.

A. LINCOLN—ATTORNEY AT LAW

Lincoln's service in the legislature increased his interest in the law, and he continued his law studies with the help of his friend John T. Stuart of Springfield. In 1837 Abraham Lincoln was admitted to the bar. In New Salem he borrowed a horse, stuffed his few belongings in his saddlebags and rode off to a new life in Springfield. His six years in New Salem, are generally considered to have been the turning point of his life.

In Springfield, he became a partner of John Stuart. Then in 1841 joined one of Illinois' most notable lawyers, Stephen T. Logan. In 1844 Lincoln was able to form his own law firm, taking William H. Herndon for a junior partner, and this firm continued until Lincoln's death.

In 1842, Lincoln married Mary Todd, a rather aristocratic girl from Kentucky whom he had met when she was visiting her sister in Springfield. The first of their four sons, Robert Todd, was born in 1843.

By this time Abraham Lincoln was ranked among the best lawyers of Illinois. The eighth Illinois judicial circuit had been organized in 1839. The judges went from one county seat to another holding court in a circuit. Most lawyers stayed in their own and adjoining counties, but Lincoln loved to travel and went all over the eighth circuit, gaining a wide reputation in courthouses at Mt. Pulaski in Logan County; Metamora Court House in Woodford County; Postville Courthouse in Lincoln, and many others. He also came to know thousands of people and the problems they faced. In 24 years of practice Lincoln represented clients in hundreds of law cases. Many of these were famous and important cases, such as the Rock Island-Davenport bridge case. Others are remembered for their human interest.

In 1846 Lincoln was elected for his first and only term in the House of Representatives. The first years in Washington were not indicative of his later life there. He made little impression in the capital, and his opposition to the war with Mexico brought him into temporary disfavor with the voters of his district who refused to return him to Congress. This backwoods lawyer had been admitted to practice law before the Supreme Court of the United States in 1849, although it is somewhat ironic that he lost the only case he took before the Supreme Court— Lewis vs. Lewis.

Joseph Jefferson, the actor, has an interesting account in his autobiography. He tells of the high license fee which the city of Springfield demanded before actors could perform: "In the midst of our trouble, a young lawyer called on the managers. He had heard of the injustice, and offered, if they would place the matter in his hands, to have the license taken off, declaring that he only wished to see fair play, and he would accept no fee whether he failed or succeeded. The case was brought up before the council. The young lawyer began his harangue. He handled the subject with tact, skill, and humor, tracing the history of the drama from the time when Thespis acted in a cart to the stage of today. He illustrated his speech with a number of anecdotes and kept the council in a roar of laughter; his good-humor prevailed, and the exorbitant tax was taken off. This young lawyer was very popular in Springfield, and was honored and beloved by all who knew him . . . his name was Abraham Lincoln!"

GREATNESS FULFILLED

Lincoln's growing prominence brought him an offer from Zachary Taylor, President of the United States, to become the secretary of the newly formed Oregon Territory and later the position of governor, but he refused both appointments. How the course of history might have been changed had Lincoln accepted either of those two appointments in a then remote region!

One of the saddest days for the Lincolns came in 1850 when their second son, Edward Baker, died after being "sick for fifty-two days." To Lincoln he was one of his "dear codgers." It is said that neither of the Lincolns was ever quite the same after this loss. However, there was the happiness of the birth of their third son, William Wallace the same year as Edward's death.

Not until he was elected President did Lincoln change his appearance to add the most familiar feature we know today. A young girl, eleven-year-old Grace Bedell of Westfield, New York, wrote Lincoln suggesting that he would look better if he wore a beard. He replied, "As to the whiskers, having never worn any, do you not think people would call it a piece of silly affectation if I were to begin it now?" But when he took the oath of office, he became not only the first Republican President, but also the first President of the United States to wear a beard.

The story of those years as President is known to everyone and does not have special application to Illinois. Many tragedies came to the Lincolns during his term as President. Among the worst was the death in the White House in 1862 of William Wallace Lincoln, just eleven years old. There were also the defeats in battles, the bitter words of people who did not like his actions and the treachery of several friends and associates.

But through all defeats and adversity the quiet man from Illinois dominated his time— "The gaunt figure of one man stands above all the rest. The prairie son gave his life so that 'government of the people, by the people, for the people, shall not perish from the earth.' The bullet which silenced his words could not silence the spirit of them—'with malice toward none; with charity for all.'"

Although very poor as a youngster, Lincoln was financially successful in his law practice. It is not generally known that when he died he left a net estate of $110,296.80, and this did not include his real estate. In 1870 Congress gave Mary Todd Lincoln an annual pension of $3,000. Just before she died in Springfield in 1882, Congress increased the pension to $5,000 plus a gift of $15,000.

Thomas (Tad) Lincoln, who was born in 1853, died in 1871, but the Lincolns' oldest son, Robert Todd Lincoln, lived until 1926. His career might have received greater prominence if it had not been so greatly overshadowed by his famous father. He served as Secretary of War, United States Minister to Britain and had a successful career in business.

The Lincoln family's cabin near Decatur.

Personality Parade

*General Ulysses S. Grant
as photographed by the famous Civil War
photographer, Mathew Brady.*

MR. PRESIDENT

Ulysses S. Grant left his home in Galena to fight in the Civil War, and he came back to Galena after the war; but Grant had been born in Ohio and had lived most of his life outside of Illinois. Although he had tried many types of work after he resigned from the regular army in 1854, he had not been successful. A short time before the start of the Civil War, he went to work for his father who owned a leather store in Galena, at a salary of $600 a year. When war broke out he obtained a commission as colonel of the 21st Illinois volunteers. Shortly afterward he was promoted to the rank of brigadier general and put in command of the Cairo district.

Successful in protecting Illinois from Southern invasion, Grant was made a major general of volunteers. He then began to sweep southward, and won a great victory to climax the long and bitter siege of Vicksburg. These accomplishments earned for Grant President Lincoln's appointment as commander-in-chief of the Union armies. Finally, on April 9, 1865, the famous surrender of General Lee took place at Appomattox. Grant's treatment of Lee and the Southern troops was as generous as was ever given to defeated armies. Grant even permitted the Southern men to take their horses with them because they would be needed for spring plowing.

In 1869 Ulysses Simpson Grant responded once again to his country's call and became the 18th President of the United States. Everyone respected the President for his honesty, but he had a difficult time in office, with many taking advantage of his lack of experience in politics. At the end of two troubled terms he returned to Galena and the home there that had been given him after the Civil War by grateful residents of the town. Plagued by financial troubles, and dying of cancer, he pushed forward to write his memoirs in order to meet his debts and provide for his wife and family.

It appeared that his country had almost forgotten the General-President. If it had not been for the strange and complicated story of James (Tama Jim) Wilson, the Congressman from Iowa, who gave up his seat in Congress so that Grant would have a government pension, the great man from Galena might have died without any further recognition from his country during his lifetime. Wilson's seat had been disputed. He deferred consideration of his appeal so that Grant's pension might be voted on, leaving Congress no time to act on the Wilson matter. Today the tomb in which lie the bodies of President and Mrs. Grant is one of the most visited shrines in the city of New York.

THE LITTLE GIANT

He was only five feet four inches tall, but his size could not keep him from becoming a "giant" in politics, and so they nicknamed Stephen Arnold Douglas the "Little Giant." Like Lincoln, Douglas had come to Illinois as a young man of 21. The Douglas monument at Winchester records that he "taught his first school and began his legal career here in 1833-34."

Only a year after he was licensed to practice law, Douglas became prosecuting attorney for the first judicial circuit, in 1835. He served in the state legislature, as register of the Federal Land Office at Springfield and as secretary of state of Illinois and as a justice of the state supreme court, the youngest supreme court judge in the history of the state—all before the age of 28.

When Douglas ran as the Democratic candidate for Congress in 1837, his opponents laughed, but Douglas campaigned so hard that he lost by only thirty-five votes! He ran again in 1843, and this time he won. Four years later he won election to the United States Senate, where he served until his death. His service in Congress coincided with one of the most critical periods in the history of the United States, the period just preceding the Civil War.

The greatest ambition of Stephen A. Douglas was to win the Presidency. His friends tried to get the Democratic nomination for him in 1852, but many people felt that at 39 he was too young. In 1856 he lost to James Buchanan. When he won the Senate seat over Abraham Lincoln in 1858, it was certain that he would become the Democratic candidate in 1860, but by that time it was too late. Douglas had angered the Democrats of the South because he opposed slavery; they split away from the party. The Northern Democrats nominated him, but he won only 12 electoral votes.

At the beginning of the Civil War, Douglas saw clearly that the United States must be preserved. He toured the old Northwest Territory rallying the undecided people of his party to support Lincoln and the Federal government. Possibly he did more than any other one person to keep many parts of the country from turning to the South. But Stephen A. Douglas had broken his health in the election and in his unstinting work for the Union. He died in 1861, and his last message was, "Tell my children to obey the laws and uphold the Constitution."

Senator Stephen A. Douglas, the "Little Giant."

OTHER PUBLIC FIGURES

Early Illinois governors had little real authority, although the second governor, Edward Coles, led and won the fight to keep slavery from being recognized in Illinois. Later governors have made distinguished contributions to the state and to the nation.

No governor of Illinois has become President, but Adlai E. Stevenson, the 31st governor of Illinois, was twice Democratic candidate for President, running against Dwight D. Eisenhower. Stevenson later became United States ambassador to the United Nations. He is remembered for his urbanity, humor and popularity.

The first Adlai E. Stevenson, a grandfather of the ambassador, was also prominent in politics and served as Vice-President of the United States under Grover Cleveland. Adlai E. Stevenson III continues the family's tradition of public service, beginning a term as Illinois state treasurer in 1967; he had previously served in the legislature.

Other family names appear more than once in Illinois politics. Richard Yates was the state's Civil War governor, from 1861 to 1865. His son, Richard Yates, Jr., was governor from 1901 to 1905.

The only man in Illinois history to be elected governor three times was Richard J. Oglesby, who succeeded the first Yates as governor. Oglesby's terms were scattered. After his first term, he was followed by John M. Palmer. Then in 1873 Palmer was succeeded by Oglesby. Ten days after he took office, Oglesby resigned to become a United States Senator. Twelve years later, in 1885, Richard Oglesby again became governor of Illinois. His unusual career included work as a rope maker and forty-niner, practice as a lawyer and service in the Mexican and Civil wars, rising to the rank of general.

When John P. Altgeld was elected, he became the first Democratic governor of Illinois in 36 years. He has been called by some "the greatest of all Illinois governors." He is best remembered for deliberately endangering his political career by pardoning three of the men who had been convicted following the Haymarket Riot, because he thought they had not received justice. His belief that this would damage his career proved to be correct, for he was not reelected.

One unusual record in connection with the governorship has been set by the community of Edwardsville, which can boast of being the home of eight Illinois governors.

Among the most notable of native-born Illinoisans was William Jennings Bryan, a persistent candidate for President on the Democratic ticket, and one of the leaders of American thought in this period. He was born at Salem, March 19, 1860.

Of the many Illinois leaders in Congress, perhaps none could match the career of Joseph Gurney (Uncle Joe) Cannon of Danville, who served in the House of Representatives for 46 years, and was Speaker of the House from 1901 to 1911.

Political leaders of the present day include the senior Senator from Illinois, Everett M. Dirksen, of Pekin, who served both as majority and minority leader of the Senate, and who has long been considered as one of the most effective and influential men in the Senate. Illinois' junior Senator, Charles H. Percy, of Kenilworth, although only seated in 1967, has been one of those given considerable publicity as a potential Republican candidate for the Presidency.

Among modern political figures, few have wielded the power or enjoyed the prestige of Richard J. Daley, who in 1967 was elected to an unprecedented fourth term as mayor of the City of Chicago. Among modern governors, Otto Kerner has achieved a favorable national reputation.

BUSINESS LEADERS

Much of the supremacy of Illinois in business and industry has been due to the imagination, courage and drive of the business leaders of the state. A roll call of their names sounds like a who's who of free enterprise.

One of the earliest was Cyrus Hall McCormick, inventor of the reaper, who in 1847 built his first plant in Chicago on the north side of the river just east of the present

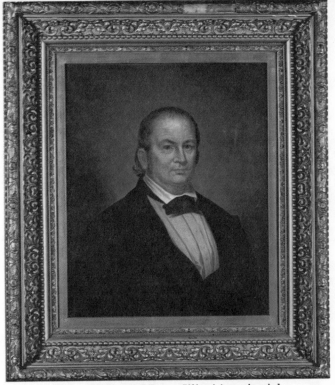

Nathaniel Pope, Illinois' territorial delegate in Congress, who was instrumental in setting the northern boundary of the new state.

Michigan Avenue Bridge. When this plant was destroyed in the great fire, another was built at 2600 south on Western Avenue. The McCormick Company eventually became the International Harvester Company.

The many McCormick family branches in Chicago have provided the city with one of its leading families over the generations, including the branch which controlled the Chicago Tribune Company for many years. The editor and publisher of the *Chicago Tribune* from 1855 to 1874 was Joseph Medill. He supported Lincoln's nomination for President and was very active in the Republican party. The journalism school of Northwestern University is named after him. His grandson, Robert R. McCormick, controlled the *Tribune* from 1925 to 1955.

George M. Pullman, with his Pullman railroad sleeping car; Joseph Glidden, who invented barbed wire; Gail Borden, who developed the concept of condensed milk at Elgin; and John Deere can be listed among the many Illinois men who have helped to change our way of life with their inventions and new industries.

John Deere settled at Grand Detour in 1837, where he opened a blacksmith shop and experimented with plow making. In 1837 he had hit upon the design of a new kind of steel plow. This was far more effective in moving through the sticky prairie soil than any other plow had been. Deere began to make these plows at Grand Detour. Later, Deere set up a plow-making plant at Moline. From that time on the John Deere Company's operations have expanded to become the vast farm machinery and equipment-making firm of today, with branches in several cities.

Gustavus F. Swift and Philip D. Armour both opened their meat-packing operations in Chicago in 1875. Thomas Wilson established his packing business at a later date. These three firms continue as the largest packing companies in the country and also rank among the leading corporations in total volume of business. Other famous Chicago meat-packers were the Cudahys and Oscar Mayer. Of these packers, only Oscar Mayer has retained operations in Chicago.

Chicago is also ranked as the greatest merchandising center of the world. It owes much of this stature to such merchandising giants as Marshall Field, Richard W. Sears, Julius Rosenwald, Samuel Carson, John T. Pirie, J. E. Scott and A. Montgomery Ward.

Marshall Field built his department store into one of the greatest merchandising establishments of the world. His descendants have entered publishing. Under the guidance

Potter Palmer, the man who made State Street Chicago's main thoroughfare.

of successive bearers of the Field name, their firms have become leading publishers of reference books and newspapers.

The businesses founded by Richard W. Sears, now Sears, Roebuck and Company and A. Montgomery Ward, now Montgomery Ward and Company, still maintain their headquarters in Chicago. Sears, with operations throughout the world, is the largest business of its type anywhere, and Wards holds third rank. For many years one of the leading figures in Sears was philanthropist Julius Rosenwald. Montgomery Ward took a particular interest in Chicago's Lake Michigan shoreline. He was instrumental in keeping much of the shoreline unobstructed and for the public use. Because of this he gained the nickname "Watchdog of the Lakefront."

Samuel Carson and John T. Pirie opened a grocery store at Amboy in 1854, a typical country store. Before many years had passed, the partners, along with J. E. Scott, had set up headquarters in Chicago and established several branches. Today the firm is one of the state's leading retail establishments.

One of the most notable names of Illinois is that of Potter Palmer, who began in the retail field but turned most of his attention to real estate and hotels. At the time Palmer purchased a mile of land along State Street, Lake Street was the main street of Chicago. Because of Palmer's promotion, State Street became the leading thoroughfare. The hotel which Palmer built at State and Monroe, where the present Palmer House now stands, helped the development of State Street. For many years Mrs. Potter Palmer was the leader of society in Chicago, and it was said, "She ruled like a queen."

QUILL—BALLPOINT—TYPEWRITER

The Illinois Association of Teachers of English lists 144 "major" authors who have been associated with Illinois.

At one time the Chicago area was considered headquarters for the greatest writers in the country. Critic H. L. Mencken wrote, "In Chicago there is the mysterious something that makes for individuality, personality, charm. . . . Find a writer who is indubitably an American in every pulse beat, an American who has something new and peculiarly American to say and who says it in an unmistakable American way, and nine times out of ten you will find that he has some sort of connection with (Chicago) . . . that he was bred there, or got his start there, or passed through there in the days when he was young and tender."

Carl Sandburg, renowned poet and authority on Lincoln, twice winner of the Pulitzer Prize, was born in Galesburg, but gained his literary fame in Chicago, about which he wrote one of his best-known poems. Novelist Theodore Dreiser worked in Chicago as a young man. Other writers associated with Chicago include Franklin P. Adams (native of Chicago), Sherwood Anderson, Saul Bellow, Gwendolyn Brooks, John Dos Passos, Peter Finley Dunne, James T. Farrell, Edna Ferber, Eugene Field, Hamlin Garland, John Gunther, Ben Hecht, Williard Motley, Donald Culross Peattie, Harry Allen Smith, Charles Vincent Emerson Starrett and Lew Sarett (another Chicago native).

Illinois can claim a number of the nation's top historians and writers in the field of history; in addition to Sandburg there are Paul M. Angle, authority on Lincoln and Illinois history, James Henry Breasted, Walter Havighurst, Lloyd Lewis, Allan Nevins, native of Camp Point and Pulitzer Prize winner in history and Carl Van Doren, native of Hope. His brother Mark Van Doren was also a Pulitzer Prize winner, in poetry.

Chicago has had no monopoly on writers. A literary map of the state shows prominent writers from all sections. Among these are Bernadine Bailey, born in Mattoon; John Bryant, brother of William Cullen, and also a poet, who lived 70 years at Jacksonville; Ernest Hemingway, native of Oak Park, who won the Nobel Prize for literature and became one of the world's best-known writers; Emerson Hough, who wrote *The Covered Wagon* at Elgin; Elbert Hubbard, born in Bloomington, known for his *A Message to Garcia;* Walter Kerr, born in Evanston, renowned drama critic; Vachel Lindsay, born in Springfield, known for his emphasis on the sound of words in poetry; Benjamin P. Thomas of Springfield, biographer of Lincoln and Archibald MacLeish, native of Glencoe, Pulitzer Prize winner for poetry.

One of Illinois' most influential poets was

Father Jacques Marquette, the first European to set foot in what is now Illinois. This painting, by Dr. Harry Wood of Arizona State University, was the result of painstaking research, for there is no known authentic portrait of Marquette. The calumet, or peace pipe, which Marquette described in detail in his journal is seen in the painting.

Edgar Lee Masters, who spent his boyhood in Lewiston, where he absorbed the background for his famous *Spoon River Anthology*, a famous work of regional literature.

Illinois has had unusual leadership in magazines devoted to literature. As early as 1830 James Hall founded a literary magazine at Vandalia and managed to publish it for two years. *The Dial*, established by Francis Fisher Browne in 1880, affected the flowering of Illinois as a literary center. One of the most influential and renowned magazines of verse is Chicago's internationally recognized *Poetry, A Magazine of Verse*, founded and edited by poet Harriet Monroe. She personally was most responsible for keeping *Poetry* alive. Just before her death in 1936 she wrote, "What a printing may mean to a struggling poet in the way of spiritual food and refreshment, hundreds of letters in our files show. It is that realization which has impelled me to continue the effort to finance and run *Poetry* all these years."

OTHER CREATIVE ILLINOISANS

The musician and conductor, Theodore Thomas, was joked about in the East when he planned to bring his symphony orchestra to play for the uncultured people of Chicago, but Dr. Thomas liked the way the people of the Midwest responded to fine music. He founded the Chicago Symphony Orchestra. He and his even more eminent successor, the beloved Frederick Stock, developed the Chicago symphony into one of the world's finest. Dr. Stock was also well known for his symphonic compositions and arrangements.

One of Chicago's best-known composers was businessman John Alden Carpenter; other composers of wide reputation include Leo Sowerby, many years an organist and choral director in Chicago; Eric DeLamarter;

Felix Borowski, a well-known music critic and Alexander Tcherepnin. Dr. Tcherepnin lived in Chicago for many years with little local recognition, while his compositions were being acclaimed throughout the world.

Another Chicago area musician with a world-wide reputation but little heralded in his home region is Dr. Herbert Zipper. Native of Vienna, protégé of Richard Strauss, conductor of many European orchestras and choruses, Dr. Zipper was interned by the Hitler regime. Escaping to the Philippines, he conducted the Manila Symphony until he was interned in Japanese prison camps. As executive director of the National Guild of Community Music Schools, Dr. Zipper is devoting himself to perfecting an entirely new concept of music education.

Easley Blackwood of the University of Chicago faculty, musician-composer-pianist, receives far greater recognition outside his own state. His compositions have been played by major orchestras around the world.

Other prominent Illinois musicians are Maud Powell and Albert Spaulding, violinists; and Fannie Bloomfield Zeisler, Agnes Conover and Robert McDowell, pianists.

In the popular music field, Charles Butterfield of Rochelle wrote *When You and I Were Young, Maggie*, and George F. Root was the composer of *Just Before the Battle, Mother*. Egbert Van Alstyne of Marengo wrote many works which still are heard—*In the Shade of the Old Apple Tree, Memories, Drifting and Dreaming* and others.

One of Illinois' best-known music schools, Chicago Musical College, was founded by Dr. Florenz Ziegfeld, whose more famous son of the same name was known for his Ziegfeld Follies. Rudolph Ganz, pianist-composer-conductor, has been president of Chicago Musical College since 1933. The college is now part of Roosevelt University.

Chicago is credited with popularizing jazz, which had been invented in New Orleans, and it is not likely that jazz, considered America's most original contribution to the field of musical art, would have grown to its present stature if it had not been so carefully and enthusiastically nurtured in Illinois.

In addition to musicians, many well-known artists have been associated with Illinois. Probably the best known was sculptor Lorado Taft, who came to Chicago at an early age and whose prominent works are valued around the world but are particularly prominent in Illinois. Other well-known Illinois sculptors include G. P. A. Healy, Leonard Wells Volk and George Gray Bernard.

Among America's most notable modern families in the arts is that of the Albrights, Adam Emery Albright and his twin sons Ivan Lorraine and Marvin Marr Albright, who maintained studios at Warrenville.

SUCH INTERESTING ILLINOISANS

One of the most famous of Illinois names is that of Jane Addams. Because of her effort, Hull House became probably the most famous settlement house. Jane Addams received the Nobel Peace Prize for her lifetime of service to others, her innovations in dealing with the underprivileged and her writings in the field of the humanities. On the University of Illinois' Chicago Circle Campus is the building Jane Addams moved into when she first came to Chicago. This building, dated 1856, is a national historic landmark.

Another notable Illinois woman was Frances Willard, dean of women at Northwestern University, firm believer in the rights of women and founder of the Women's Christian Temperance Union.

Among Illinois' best-known women phi-

lanthropists was Edith Rockefeller McCormick, who endeared herself to both children and grown-ups by donating the land on which Brookfield Zoo was built.

Donor of another notable cultural institution was Joy Morton of the Morton Salt Company, founder of the Morton Arboretum, an especially appropriate accomplishment for the man whose father was the founder of Arbor Day.

One of the most unusual personalities to call Illinois his home was William Ashley Sunday. "Billy" Sunday had a career as a professional baseball player with Pop Anson's Chicago White Stockings. Disgusted with the life he was living, Sunday resigned from baseball and served as a youth worker in the YMCA of Chicago. Then he became an evangelist. Dramatic methods in the pulpit came naturally to him. He might roll on the floor or tear his hair, but his sermons had such sincere warmth and real message that thousands were converted.

Another athlete who was tempted to quit athletics to become a minister was Amos Alonzo Stagg. Amos Stagg decided that he could be a greater influence by remaining a football coach. He made the University of Chicago teams respected everywhere and continued to coach at other schools until he was past ninety. During the more than one hundred years of his life, Coach Stagg became one of the best-known and best-loved figures in the country.

One of the renowned athletes of all time was Harold (Red) Grange, who skyrocketed to fame playing on the University of Illinois football team of 1925.

Preeminent in an entirely different field is Dr. Charles B. Huggins, of the University of Chicago, renowned for his discoveries of the hormone treatment of cancer. As a win-

*Black Hawk (1767-1838),
the Sauk and Fox
Indian chief, who led
his people in a desperate
and unsuccessful
effort to keep
their lands in Illinois.*

ner of the 1966 Nobel Prize for Medicine, Dr. Huggins was the latest in the long line of Illinois scientists who have won awards for scientific accomplishments.

An unusual family of Galesburg was the Ferris family. Olmsted Ferris concentrated his efforts on developing and promoting popcorn. He introduced popcorn into England, and Prince Albert, husband of Queen Victoria, became so interested in this exploding food that he presented Ferris to the queen. She, in turn, became so intrigued that she called for a "command performance" concert of corn popping. Even more famous in the Ferris family was Olmsted's brother, George Washington Gale Ferris, inventor of the Ferris wheel. The Ferrises were related to the Reverend George Washington Gale, who founded Galesburg in 1835.

Among other well-known personalities

who might be mentioned are James Butler (Wild Bill) Hickok, born at Troy Grove near Mendota; Allan Pinkerton, founder of the United States Secret Service and the prominent detective firm that bears his name; John Alexander Dowie, unusual founder of Zion; Dr. Leslie Keeley of Dwight, renowned for his Keeley Cure for alcoholics; Julian H. Lewis, who helped in the development of blood plasma; George W. Snow, of Chicago, inventor of the balloon-frame type of construction still commonly used for homes and small buildings; Mary (Mother Jones) Harris, beloved figure among union leaders and laborers; Alexander Bradley, union organizer; Ruben Soderstrom, president of the Illinois Federation of Labor, and a labor leader for over 50 years; and, finally, the eccentric, talented inventor and mathematician Francis Park of Kewanee.

Government in Illinois

Today state government in Illinois is so large and complex that a 440-page catalog is needed to describe its structure and various functions. But serving and governing a population of more than 11,000,000 is an immense task, hardly to be compared to the relatively simpler problems faced in 1818 when Illinois, with a population of only 40,000 became the 21st state.

CONSTITUTION

The constitution is the basis of government in the state. It is augmented by statutes adopted by legislative bodies, administrative rules and regulations which carry legal weight, and by the rulings and interpretations of the courts, subject in many cases to final review by the Supreme Court of the United States.

The first state constitution was approved by Congress in 1818 when Illinois was admitted to the Union. But by 1848 it appeared outmoded and another was adopted. In 1862 still another constitution was proposed, but failed to obtain the necessary popular vote. A constitutional convention was organized in 1869 and the resulting constitution was adopted by the voters in July, 1870. It went into effect in August of that year.

This is the constitution under which the state is now operating. Many authorities claim that it is hopelessly out of date, that Illinois is operating with a "horse and buggy" constitution in a Space Age. As early as 1902 the *Chicago Tribune* declared that the constitution "has outlived its usefulness. It is

not the ark of the covenant. It has no sacred qualities. We may touch it without dropping dead." A constitutional convention was held in 1920, but the constitution it proposed was rejected by the voters in 1922.

The requirements for adoption of a new constitution are so difficult to meet that in spite of many calls for change in later years the old constitution still remains. However, one of the actions of the legislature in 1967, which received much praise, was the beginning of the process leading to the possible writing and adopting of a new constitution.

Amending the Illinois constitution is also extremely difficult, and only one other state has made fewer amendments to its constitution over such a period of time. In 1950 however, the provisions for amending the Illinois constitution were slightly eased by the passage of the "Gateway" amendment, which provided that future amendments may be adopted by either a majority of the electors voting at the election or by two-thirds of the electors voting on the proposed amendment.

STATE GOVERNMENT

The governmental organization of Illinois is in most respects similar to that of the United States and the other states. It is, of course, a representative government, and the main operating principle is the separation of powers among the three branches, which are: the executive (the governor); the legislative (the general assembly); and the judicial (the supreme court). The legislative department determines what the state law shall be; the executive department administers the law; and the judicial department interprets and applies it. The powers and authority of each branch are safeguarded to prevent any one branch seizing too much authority. The judicial branch may declare laws of the legislative branch unconstitutional; the legislative branch has the power to impeach and remove from office both judicial and executive officers, and the state senate may refuse to confirm an appointment of the executive; the executive department may veto acts of the legislature and can exercise the right of pardon and reprieve.

EXECUTIVE

The executive branch consists of the governor, lieutenant governor, secretary of state, auditor of public accounts, treasurer, superintendent of public instruction and attorney general. All are chosen every four years in statewide elections. The governor, who receives a salary of $30,000 a year, may serve an unlimited number of terms. Only the treasurer is forbidden to seek a new consecutive term.

Although the governor is the chief executive, his real powers are somewhat more limited than in some other states. He is charged with proposing laws which he considers necessary or desirable and with the responsibility of the welfare of all citizens. He has the power to grant pardons and reprieves to convicted persons or to reduce their sentences, to issue warrants and petitions to other governors for the return of fugitives and to command the state's military and naval forces in order to maintain law and repel invasion.

Other elected officials are required to make biennial reports to the governor and to furnish him other information which he may re-

quire concerning their offices. The governor is responsible for supervision of nineteen "code departments": aeronautics, agriculture, business and economic development, children and family services, conservation, finance, financial institutions, insurance, labor, mental health, mines and minerals, personnel, public aid, public health, public safety, public works and buildings, registration and education, revenue and general services administration. In addition, the governor is responsible for many boards, commissions and other agencies.

He has wide powers of appointment, placing several hundred persons in key administrative positions—including the directors of the code departments—subject to approval by the state senate. He also appoints members to such agencies as the commerce commission, parole and pardon board and youth commission. For just cause, the governor can remove any official he appoints.

LEGISLATIVE

The legislature, which is called the general assembly, consists of two houses: the senate and the house of representatives. There are 58 senators, one from each senatorial district, who are elected for four years. In the house of representatives there are 177 members, three from each of the 59 representative districts, and they are elected for two years. Illinois is the only state that elects its representatives by what is called cumulative voting. In this method each voter has three votes and may split these any way he wishes among the candidates from his district.

The general assembly meets only in odd-numbered years, the session beginning on the Wednesday after the first Monday in

The old Cahokia Courthouse,
thought to be the oldest building in Illinois.
Originally built as a residence about 1737,
it was sold in 1793
for use as a courthouse and jail.
After being displayed
in Chicago for many years it was
brought back to Cahokia in 1939.

January and usually ending June 30. However the governor is empowered to call special sessions, but is required to state the purpose, and discussion is limited to the subjects outlined.

At the beginning of each session of the general assembly the governor delivers a message on conditions in the state and recommends what he considers to be necessary legislation. Later he submits a budget estimating the amount of money required to finance the state's operation for the next two years.

The leaders of the governor's party submit his proposals to the general assembly. The legislature may dispose of these and other proposals by defeating them in committee or by voting them down on the floor of the senate or house. It may pass some or all of the bills, alter them by amendments and defeat or pass amended bills.

Bills which pass are sent to the governor who may approve or veto them. If the governor holds a bill for ten working days without signing it, that bill becomes law without any action on his part. If the governor vetoes a bill, he sends a message to the legislature explaining why he took this action. The legislature may override the governor's veto with a two-thirds vote of both houses, but this seldom occurs because of the number of votes necessary to override.

The legislature's customary adjournment date is June 30; after this time, bills require a two-thirds vote of each house for passage, instead of a simple majority. The governor can dismiss both the house and senate if they cannot agree on a time for adjournment.

JUDICIAL

Illinois courts begin at the level of city and county government. The downstate circuit courts and the Cook County superior and circuit courts are the state's major trial courts. Judges of the several circuit courts throughout the state may interchange with each other, with city court judges and with the judges of the superior court of Cook County when they find it necessary and convenient. The constitution requires that two or more terms of the circuit court be held each year in each county.

Appeals from trial courts are heard by appellate courts in five districts. These appellate courts have been created to remove some of the burden on the supreme court in hearing appeals from trial courts. There is a clerk for each appellate court district, elected for a six-year term.

The highest court of Illinois is the supreme court, for the most part a court of final appeal. However, some cases may originate in the supreme court, which sits in Springfield and is in session five terms a year.

LOCAL GOVERNMENT

The county organization of Illinois is too complex to describe in detail here. The history and variety of county government make an excellent study for a special project. Special units of government not subject to the county jurisdiction also have been created, such as sanitation, drainage, fire protection, forest preservation, mosquito abatement and education. Many of these special units operate independently.

City, town and village government in Illinois still continues to follow the general pattern of mayor and council, although there are many variations throughout the state, such as the city manager plan. Because of its great size, Chicago has many unique features of government, but its system remains essentially that of the mayor and city council.

Rich Profusion

Although Illinois has been blessed with some of the greatest concentrations of natural wealth anywhere, there is general agreement that the most valuable single resource of the state is the thick and fertile layer of soil. It covers most of the state and, in some places, is as much as 500 feet deep.

VEGETABLE

The evidence of the richness of this soil was not recognized by the pioneers, most of whom shunned the prairie. Only a few such as Louis Jolliet and Gurdon S. Hubbard realized that lands rich enough to grow an endless expanse of head-high grasses meant much for the future of agriculture in America. Hubbard wrote, "The waving green, intermingling with a rich profusion of wildflowers, was the most beautiful sight I had ever gazed upon. In the distance the grove of Blue Island loomed up—beyond it the timber on the Des Plaines River."

For there was, and still is, timber. Surprisingly, at the time of settlement, about forty percent of Illinois was forested. "It is hard now to imagine the grandeur of the great eastern hardwood forest of North America—of which our area is a part," writes W. J. Beecher. "From Illinois where the prairie began, to the east coast, was solid forest. And such a forest! Oaks and tulip trees grew with trunks 5 feet through and shook out their leafy canopies high above the forest floor. . . ."

Today only about ten percent of Illinois is forest, covering about four million acres. The most important trees are oak, hickory, mixed hardwoods, white oak and scrub hardwoods. There is a good growth of the forest crop in Illinois, about 400,000,000 board feet added annually. This is considerably more than is used in a year, so the Illinois supply of trees for lumber is increasing annually. Much of the land cleared for crops was not suitable for agriculture, and a large part is now being placed back into forest.

Because of the state's length from north to south, vegetation varies from that typical of northern regions to that usually thought of as southern—from the white pines and tamarack of the north to the bald cypress and mistletoe and azaleas of the south. In addition to trees, Illinois soil and climate combine to produce more than 2,400 other kinds of plants.

ANIMAL

About 300 types of birds regularly nest in Illinois. Each fall as many as a million waterfowl migrate to the south over the route known as the Mississippi Flyway, which makes the state one of the great hunting areas of the country. Bobwhite quail, most abundant in southern Illinois, make up about 20 percent of all the game animals taken by Illinois hunters. The pheasant is also an important game bird.

Fifty kinds of mammals are native to Illinois. It is surprising to many that there are still more than 7,000 licensed trappers in the state, most of them concentrating on mink and muskrat. Raccoon hunting and fox hunting have followers in all sections of the state.

Concerning Illinois' largest mammal, the

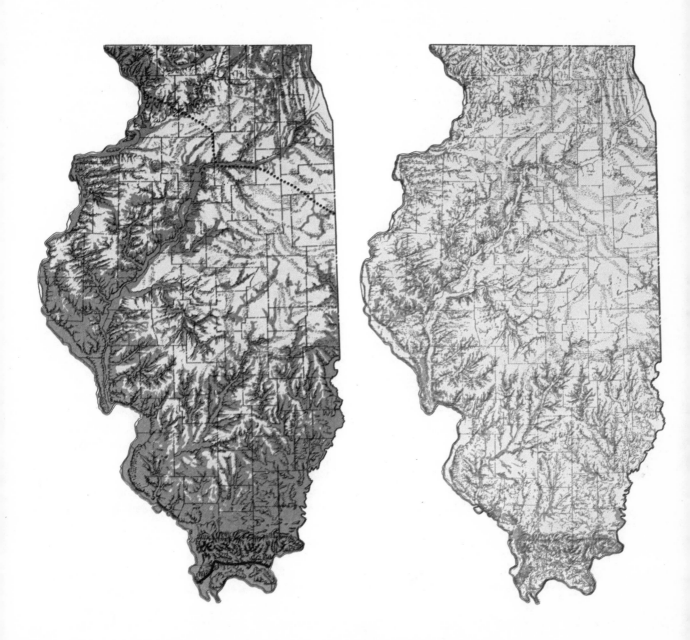

Forest land in Illinois at time of settlement (left) and (right) today

whitetail deer, a writer in the 1830's observed, "Deer are more abundant than at the first settlement of the country." However, by 1855 the Illinois legislature had to establish a closed season, and by 1910 native wild deer had almost entirely disappeared from the state. A closed season was imposed until 1957, when 2,038 deer were bagged. Now the deer population is making a comeback.

One of the most surprising animals in Illinois often makes passing motorists think they have seen a "ghost." These are the famed white squirrels of Olney. Two white squirrels were released in Olney in 1902, and their descendants in the region are now said to number in the thousands. They scamper about over lawns and jump from tree to tree, creating spectacular flashes of white fur.

More than a million people fish in Illinois' 352 natural lakes, reservoirs, innumerable farm ponds and thousands of miles of flowing waters. Popular lake sport fish include large and small mouth bass, crappies, bluegills, warmouths, red-ear sunfish, white bass, and even walleyes, saugers and northern pike. Stream fish include large and small mouth bass, catfishes and a variety of sunfishes.

MINERAL

In the field of minerals, the bituminous coal reserves of Illinois exceed those of every other state! While oil and gas have taken over much of the heating and industrial operations once handled by coal, the importance of coal as a source of chemicals as well as a reserve when other fuels have been exhausted can hardly be overestimated. Although it seems unbelievable, coal-bearing formations lie under more than two thirds of the entire state. Something less than 4,000,000,000 tons of coal has been produced in Illinois since coal mining began. At the present rate there is enough coal in Illinois to last for more than 2,000 years, or enough to supply the needs of the entire country for a century.

The state's major petroleum area is the deep part of the Illinois basin, the southcentral and southeastern parts of the state, but significant petroleum is also found in central and western Illinois.

Limestone, sand and gravel, clay, fluorspar, special sands, such as silica or glass sand, engine and filter sands, grinding and polishing and blasting sand, lead and zinc, tripoli, gypsum, anhydrite, barite, pyrite, oil shales and brines are among the other minerals of Illinois.

Probably the most valuable "mineral" of all is one not usually thought of in this category—water. Illinois' water resources are as large today as they were when this region was a wilderness, and as far as modern science can determine, they will be undiminished and constantly renewed.

Precipitation brings Illinois water from the air in the average amount of 2,000 billion gallons a day. About two billion gallons are used by individuals; 14 billion gallons are used by industry and 23 billion gallons flow down the streams. Most is sent back into the air by evaporation and transpiration. Out of sight, but important as a source of water supply is the groundwater below the land surface. Another vast supply of water at Illinois' doorstep is Lake Michigan.

Hub of the World

No exact comparisons are available, but it is likely that more goods and people pass above, across and along the air routes, waterways, roads and railroads of Illinois than anywhere else in the world.

The water route from Lake Michigan to the Mississippi River has been called "the most important single consideration in the entire history of Illinois." The statement might go even further to say that transportation in general in Illinois has been the most important single activity of the state.

When the opening of the Erie Canal in New York and the choice of Chicago as the terminal of the Illinois and Michigan Canal brought increasing numbers of people and tonnages of goods to Chicago, the business, wealth, population and importance of the city began a growth which has never ceased.

"HALF A LEAGUE OF PRAIRIE"

The two greatest natural transportation routes of the North American continent are the St. Lawrence River-Great Lakes system and the mighty Mississippi River system, with its many navigable branches, such as the Ohio and the Missouri. It was obvious from an early date that any route which could connect these two would be of tremendous importance.

The first Europeans in the Illinois country were quick to observe that the Illinois River system and the Great Lakes system came very close together. Louis Jolliet wrote that the great systems might be connected by means of a canal cut through a mere "half a league of prairie." As La Salle pointed out

not long afterward, this was only partly true. There was a great variation in the water levels in different seasons. Sometimes there was hardly enough water to float a canoe in the Illinois River above Starved Rock and in the Des Plaines and Kankakee rivers.

Realization of the dream of the meeting of the waters was begun in 1836 with work on the Illinois and Michigan Canal. The very difficult work of cutting a canal through the Chicago portage, deepening and enlarging existing passages, constructing a system of locks and towpaths over the 96-mile route from Chicago to La Salle took twelve years.

On the upper part of this system, relatively small canal boats were towed by horses walking the paths along the canals. When the first canal boat arrived at Joliet on April 11, 1848, the entire town turned out in celebration; bands played, cannon boomed and speeches lasted almost all day.

At last a relatively inexpensive way was open to bring the rapidly increasing produce of the Midwest by a more direct route to the markets of the East. Now the products of the area could go through Chicago, over the Great Lakes, the Erie Canal and other routes, carrying the grain and pork that once had to travel laboriously by way of New Orleans. New Orleans began to decline, and by 1860 Chicago handled ten times as much grain as the southern city.

FLOATING PALACES

The importance of the waterways was emphasized by the fantastic growth of steamboat transportation. Steamers had been

GEOGRAPHY

PROVINCES:
- CENTRAL LOWLAND PROVINCE
- OZARK PLATEAUS PROVINCE
- INTERIOR LOW PLATEAU PROVINCE
- COASTAL PLAIN PROVINCE

— Section boundary
⋯⋯ Subsection boundary

WISCONSIN DRIFTLESS SECTION
Rock River Hill Country
Wheaton Morainal Country

Green River Lowland

Galesburg Plain

MISSISSIPPI RIVER

ILLINOIS RIVER

DISSECTED TILL PLAINS SECTION

LINCOLN HILLS SECTION

SALEM PLATEAU SECTION

KASKASKIA RIVER

Chicago Lake Plain
GREAT LAKES SECTION
Kankakee Plain

Bloomington Ridged Plain

TILL PLAINS SECTION

Springfield Plain

WABASH RIVER

Mt. Vernon Hill Country

OHIO RIVER

SHAWNEE HILLS SECTION

HISTORY

GALENA

AMERICAN SETTLEMENTS 1804 to 1830

AMERICAN SETTLEMENTS since 1830

GREAT SAUK TRAIL

NAUVOO

PEORIA
FORT CREVE COEUR

NEW SALEM

AMERICAN SETTLEMENTS after 1800

VANDALIA

CAHOKIA

FRENCH SETTLEMENTS BEGUN 1699

ST. LOUIS TRACE

AMERICAN SETTLEMENTS 1782 to 1818

KASKASKIA

SHAWNEETOWN

— HISTORIC TRAILS
▬ ▬ ▬ ILLINOIS and MICHIGAN CANAL
- - - ILLINOIS RIVER ROUTE
||||||| CHICAGO PORTAGE
⋯⋯⋯ ILLINOIS-MISSISSIPPI CANAL
(now abandoned)

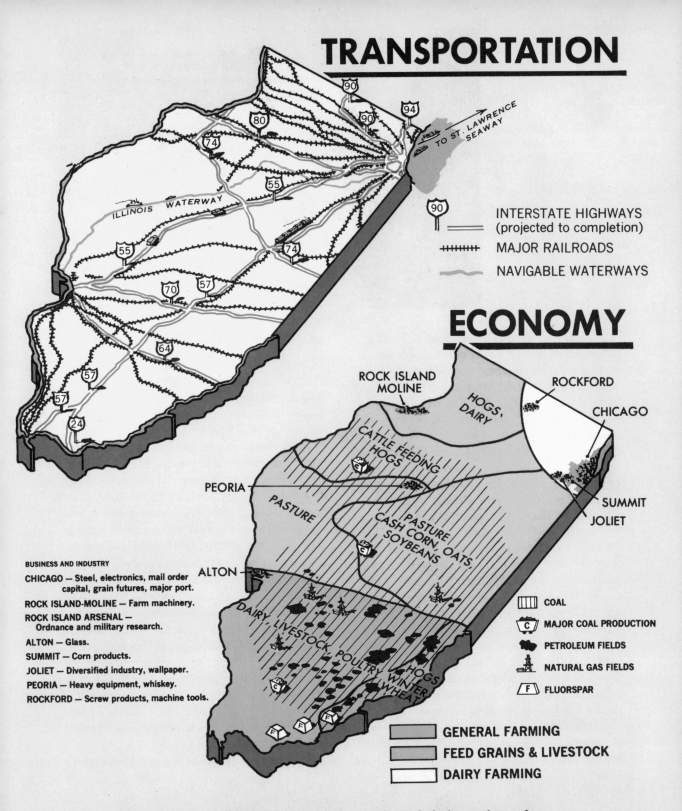

TRANSPORTATION

🛡 90

INTERSTATE HIGHWAYS
(projected to completion)

╫╫╫╫╫ MAJOR RAILROADS

〜〜〜 NAVIGABLE WATERWAYS

ILLINOIS WATERWAY

TO ST. LAWRENCE SEAWAY

ECONOMY

ROCK ISLAND MOLINE

HOGS, DAIRY

ROCKFORD

CHICAGO

CATTLE FEEDING HOGS

PEORIA

PASTURE

PASTURE CASH CORN, OATS, SOYBEANS

SUMMIT
JOLIET

ALTON

DAIRY, LIVESTOCK, POULTRY, WINTER WHEAT

HOGS

BUSINESS AND INDUSTRY

CHICAGO — Steel, electronics, mail order capital, grain futures, major port.

ROCK ISLAND-MOLINE — Farm machinery.

ROCK ISLAND ARSENAL — Ordnance and military research.

ALTON — Glass.

SUMMIT — Corn products.

JOLIET — Diversified industry, wallpaper.

PEORIA — Heavy equipment, whiskey.

ROCKFORD — Screw products, machine tools.

▦ COAL

C MAJOR COAL PRODUCTION

🛢 PETROLEUM FIELDS

⛏ NATURAL GAS FIELDS

F FLUORSPAR

GENERAL FARMING

FEED GRAINS & LIVESTOCK

DAIRY FARMING

Illinois leads in production of heavy metals and their products, farm machinery, fluorspar, corn, soybeans, and food products, also in exports.

*Lock on
the Illinois
and Michigan
Canal.*

created which although huge took only a foot or two of water and could go up rivers which many modern motorboats could not navigate today. The first steamboat, the *New Orleans*, came down the Ohio and the Mississippi in 1811. By 1820, 70 steamboats were chugging along the rivers. Peoria was first reached by steamboat in 1828, and other towns rapidly became ports. La Salle, head of steamboat navigation on the Illinois River, was less than a week from New Orleans. For years Galena was the most important port north of St. Louis, but Galena declined and other Illinois river towns boomed. In 1867 the number of steamboat dockings at Cairo reached the incredible figure of 3,700.

The steamboat period was a colorful one; almost every kind of boat from floating department stores to movable theaters could be found at a riverside. Passenger boats were so luxurious they were called "floating palaces." They had rich wood paneling, thick carpets and every convenience. Steamboat races pitted the fastest boats against one another, and houses in the river cities were built with observation decks so that the boats could be watched in comfort.

MODERN WATER TRANSPORTATION

The coming of the railroads brought a swift decline in use of waterways. The Illinois and Michigan Canal was eventually abandoned, and steamboats have almost disappeared on the rivers. However, the small, efficient diesel powerboat has brought water traffic on rivers and canals to far greater levels than ever before. The sturdy little diesels may easily push as many as 50 giant barges, loaded with bulk cargoes, which can be carried much more economically by water than by other means. Coal, sand and gravel, iron and steel, petroleum products, chemicals—all flow over the rivers and waterways system.

The lower Illinois River was canalized, beginning in 1872, with locks and dams at various points. The Chicago Sanitary and Ship Canal, discussed earlier, once more made part of the old route of the Illinois and Michigan Canal practical for tremendous volumes of freight, and the Illinois Waterway system has been almost constantly improved ever since.

The present Illinois Waterway provides

through navigation from the Mississippi River to Lake Michigan with a minimum channel depth of nine feet. Minimum channel width is 300 feet, except in the Marseilles Canal and the Treats Island cutoff. The Calumet-Sag Channel, completed in 1922, connects the Calumet River with the Chicago Sanitary and Ship Canal near Lemont. It is now being widened to 225 feet.

New waterways planned include improvement of the lower Kaskaskia River, development of the Wabash River, with possible canals to the Illinois River, Lake Michigan and Toledo, Ohio, and a new Illinois and Mississippi Canal, replacing a now almost unused canal between the two rivers.

THE PORT OF CHICAGO

Merchant captains come to the port of Chicago from such faraway places as Japan or Yugoslavia. They often remark that when they tell people they are sailing to Chicago, Illinois, no one believes them.

Strange as it may seem to those who think of Chicago only as a far inland city, this dream of many generations of making Chicago a world port came true in 1959 with the opening of the St. Lawrence Seaway. Now ocean ships belonging to more than 50 scheduled lines enter Chicago's port and dock at either Chicago Harbor or Lake Calumet Harbor. Chicago's overseas imports and exports in the most recent available figures (1964) totaled 1,961,440 tons, and this figure is expected to rise. Imports and exports from Canada were 5,640,945 tons. However, important as the foreign trade is, it is still far below the traffic carried on the Great Lakes from other United States ports to Chicago (18,493,968 tons) and shipments over the Inland Waterways to Chicago (15,617,061 tons). In 1964 the total tonnage for the Port of Chicago stood at 41,713,414.

As steamboat traffic on the rivers increased, collisions, accidents and boiler explosions took a heavy toll of life and property.

ON TRACKS OF STEEL

As early as 1838 a steam engine known as the *Northern Cross* was operating in Illinois. The rails were made of wood with iron straps nailed on top. Among the many dangers of a ride on this road was that the iron strips often came loose and stabbed through the floors of the cars. Farmers who needed sled rails or other iron frequently stole the iron portions of the rails, leaving trains stranded. Passengers were constantly having to stop, get out and load firewood.

Before ten years had passed, "modern" railroading had been established in Illinois. The Galena and Chicago Union Railroad began its successful operation in 1848, and it soon became apparent that the flat lands of Illinois were ideal for railroad construc-

tion. Also it was clear that most of the major overland transportation routes of the country would lead through or into Illinois. The 1850's saw a feverish rush to build railroads throughout the state. When the Illinois Central was finished to Cairo in 1856, it was the longest railroad in the United States.

The coming of the railroads in this period had a decisive effect on Illinois during the Civil War. Earlier the state had been tied to the South by the Ohio-Mississippi river transportation system. Just before the war, the railroads provided more efficient connection with the East, making Illinois' bonds with the North much stronger.

Chicago, located at the tip of Lake Michigan was a natural concentration point for railroads. At first the businessmen of Chicago opposed the railroad because they wanted the merchants to come into the city personally with their produce. Before long, however, the growing concentration of railroads in Chicago brought a great rush of prosperity, as merchants and manufacturers followed the rails to their meeting point. The railroads also gave farmers who were not situated near water transportation a fast and efficient means of bringing their crops to market. Before long, Chicago became the center of the world's greatest concentration of railroads. Now more trains and more railroads operate into and around Chicago than anyplace else. It is the "nation's freight handler," as Carl Sandburg put it.

Many of the advances which have kept the railroads operating at competitive levels have come from Chicago. The first cooled freight cars ran out of Chicago; the Pullman car for people and the Mather car, a humane railroad car for livestock, were centered in Chicago. Chicago also pioneered in the automated freight car sorting yard, and the Chi-

This forerunner of today's huge earthmovers, at work on the
Chicago Sanitary and Ship Canal, was probably a marvel in its time.

cago and North Western Railway's Proviso yards are the largest in the world.

MASTER OF THE AIR

Illinois' mastery of water and rail travel was soon followed by its mastery of the air. Chicago's Midway Airport was known for many years as the world's busiest commercial airport until Chicago's O'Hare International Airport took away the title. The airport was named for Edward (Butch) O'Hare, World War II hero.

Today O'Hare International Airport handles more commercial flights daily than any other airport in the world. However, its facilities are already overtaxed and many airlines are moving certain of their operations back to Midway.

Consequently, plans are now being made for a third major Chicago airport. One of the proposed locations is in the lake several miles offshore. A portion of the lake floor would be encircled by a levee, the water drained out and an airport created on what once was the bottom of Lake Michigan. Air travelers would reach this airport over a combination bridge and tunnel from the shore.

Meigs Field, a single-strip airport, is on Chicago's lakefront. Corporation-owned, commercial and privately-owned planes use this conveniently located field.

Distributed throughout the state are 68 public airports of various sizes and sorts, helping Illinois maintain its lead in aviation.

INDIAN TRAIL TO INTERSTATE

The Indians followed the buffalo in blazing the first overland trails across what is now Illinois. To mark the way, they sometimes tied knots in saplings. These trees grew up bent over with an elbow-like shape, and some of them may still be seen today in residential

The Chicago River became a bustling port as the city continued to grow in size and importance.

sections of the state. Two main Indian trails were the Great Sauk Trail and the St. Louis Trace. The latter ran from the falls of the Ohio (opposite Louisville) to Cahokia. The Sauk Trail began on the Mississippi at Rock Island, swept across to Lake Michigan, skirted the end of the lake and finally reached Canada. There were other trails, such as Green Bay Trail, now followed by Green Bay Road.

Early settlers and traders followed the Indian trails and also made traces of their own, such as Hubbard's Trace, part of which is now Chicago's State Street. Then over these crude roads came regular stagecoach runs for passengers and lighter freight. Heavy freight was carried in huge wagons. In

the 1840's as many as 200 of these wagons might trundle into Chicago in one day carrying grain to the new grain elevators.

The first great highway in the United States was the extraordinary National Road, stretching nearly 600 miles from Cumberland, Maryland, to Vandalia, Illinois. From the time the first section was opened in 1818 it became the great highway of westward migration. This first section, known as the Cumberland Road, reached Wheeling, Ohio. The final section to Vandalia was completed in 1852.

Railroads dominated most overland travel until the automobile became popular; then the rush for hard-surface roads was on. Today, Illinois' magnificent pattern of highways and super roads is climaxed by 1,600 miles of toll and interstate highways.

And so with the greatest pattern of rivers, canals, lakes, railroads, airlines, highways and superhighways ever put together in an area of its size, Illinois continues to hold the key position in the key transportation country of the world—truly the world hub of transport. More than anything else this preeminent position in transportation which makes possible one of Illinois' most important accomplishments—first place in the United States in combined exports of agricultural and industrial products.

COMMUNICATION

The first newspaper published in Illinois was the *Herald*, issued at Kaskaskia beginning in 1814. The history of journalism in Illinois is a stirring one, with many leading newspapers, some of them even coming from among the small town weeklies. Today the metropolitan newspapers of Chicago are among the wealthiest and strongest of the country's major dailies, and some compare Chicago journalism favorably with that of New York for a combination of good reporting and superlative special features.

There is no doubt about Chicago's position

When this photograph was taken, horse-drawn streetcars and cable cars were still common in Chicago. Note the lone automobile in the upper left-hand corner.

Famous cartoonist and artist,
George McCutcheon, designed this cover
for a pioneer Chicago aviation meet.

Chicago's Dan Ryan Expressway
is part of the complex system
of modern highways
throughout Illinois.

*Frink and Walker's stagecoach station, which stood
at the corner of Lake and Dearborn streets in Chicago in 1844.*

as the world's greatest center of printing. Many of the largest magazines of the country are printed in Chicago, along with the catalogs of the largest mail order firms—a mountain of print in itself. In addition, Chicago is the home of *Encyclopaedia Britannica* and the *World Book Encyclopedia*, and several other encyclopedia publishing houses. For sheer volume of printed pages, probably no other book publishing operation equals the bulk of encyclopedia printing. Also, several of the largest paperback houses use Chicago printers, adding further to the city's leadership in the graphic arts.

There are many outstanding publishing houses in the state and Chicago holds high rank in textbook and other educational publishing operations, as well as publication of educational and industrial tests.

For a time Chicago held the leadership in network radio broadcasting. The first "dramatic production" over television was sent out by the experimental television station W9XAP in 1931. Just as in radio, Chicago took an early lead in commercial television broadcasts, especially when network television first became practical. Many of the early television pioneers started in Chicago, but New York and Hollywood eventually took over the leadership in this field.

What Do You Make of That?

Until recently, Illinois was third among all the states in value of manufacturing, and most sources still claim that rank for Illinois. However, in the latest available figures for value of manufactures (1963), Illinois ranked behind New York, California and Ohio. The value of manufacturing in Illinois was $14,385,000,000 in 1963.

GROWTH OF MANUFACTURING

What a contrast to this gigantic flow of production was Illinois' first industry. The Indians had used the salt springs near Shawneetown to make salt, drying the salty water in large pottery containers, pieces of which may still be found in the area. Early Europeans in the region soon adapted this practice, leading to Illinois' first true industry—the making of salt. Great iron kettles were used, and the briny water was evaporated over wood fires, leaving salt crystals in the bottom of the kettles. To aid the endeavor, the state had reserved 180,000 acres of timber to assure adequate fuel. The slave labor considered essential to the saline industry was guaranteed to that industry by the 1818 constitution.

The saline industry attained its peak during the early 1800's with a daily production of about 500 bushels of salt. Then less expensive supplies of salt were found in great quantities elsewhere, and the salines vanished. However, Illinois' large reserves of brine are still important in the petroleum industry, where they are used in the flush-ing and reviving of old wells and in a wide variety of chemical industries.

The second great industrial boom in Illinois was the extraordinary growth of the Galena area due to the lead mining.

Other early manufacturing in Illinois depended mainly on the land. Mills for grinding grain and sawing timber supplied the needs of the people for food and lumber. When the enormous rafts of timber from the northern forests were floated down the Mississippi, many Illinois river towns became leaders in mill work, furniture and other wood products. Illinois, in fact, still ranks about third in the nation in furniture manufacturing.

The state's leadership in agriculture and transportation also spurred other manufacture. John Deere fulfilled the need for a plow that would knife through the tough prairie soil of Illinois and laid the foundation for the Quad Cities area to become the world capital of agricultural machine manufacturing. Cyrus McCormick's reaper heralded the beginning of the mechanization of agriculture.

Illinois' greatest single asset in manufacturing has been, once again, its key location. When the country's largest supplies of prime iron ore were developed in Minnesota, it was apparent that the ore could not be turned into iron and steel near where it was mined because of the lack of fuel supplies to fire the blast furnaces. High-grade fuel was accessible in Pennsylvania, not too far from the Chicago area, and the ore could also come to Chicago and northern Indiana cheaply in huge ore boats. This combination

Steelworks on the Calumet River.

of circumstances has made the Chicago area the "steel capital of the world."

MODERN GIANT

Chicago Heights was the first major steel manufacturing community in the Chicago area; the industry went from there to more convenient locations, and now the southern skyline of the city and suburbs is dominated by the cylindrical domes of mighty blast furnaces. Expansion and modernization have kept Illinois in the forefront of steel making. Such developments as the new $150,000,000 Jones and Laughlin steel mill at Hennepin are anticipated to retain leadership in the industry.

The Chicago area is also one of the largest fabricators of iron and steel products, a business which got its start in 1865 when the Chicago Rolling Mills made the first steel railroad rails ever produced in this country.

Altogether the Chicago complex can boast of a total of almost 20,000 manufacturing plants, which account for about three-fourths of the total manufacturing of the state—making it the second most important manufacturing region of the United States.

Many Illinois cities are preeminent in important and interesting fields of manufacture. The world's largest maker of glass is Owens-Illinois at Alton. This firm is also the largest producer of bottles. The fantastic bottle machinery spits out several bottles each second.

The first completely automatic hosiery producing machinery was made in Rockford and has helped that city maintain its lead as a large producer in that field. The Corn Products Company plant at Summit is the largest of its type anywhere. Peoria turns out a sea of whiskey in the world's largest bourbon plant; Caterpillar, also at Peoria, is the largest in its field; and Joliet continues to lead all other cities in covering the nation's walls with wallpaper.

SUBSURFACE WEALTH

Although Illinois is not usually thought of as a mining state, it holds eighth place among all the states in mineral production, according to the latest available figures (1965). The value of mineral production has exceeded $600,000,000 each year for the past ten years, and in 1965 it reached $618,500,000. The mineral fuels, coal and petroleum are the leading products, accounting for more than 65 percent of the total mineral value of the state.

From the nation's largest reserves of coal, Illinois produces more of that fuel than any except three other states. The largest single shaft underground coal mine in the world, Peabody mine number 10, is located at Pawnee in Sangamon County. From this mine alone come more than 5,550,000 tons a year.

Less than half of Illinois' coal now comes from underground mines. Strip mines—

where the topsoil layer is taken off, the coal exposed to the surface and then stripped away by great machines—accounts for 56 percent of all Illinois' coal production. These mines are in operation mostly around the edge of the Illinois basin, where the coal lies at shallow depths.

In 1965 there were 97 mines, both underground and strip, operating in 29 counties reporting production. Coal burning electric generating plants are the single largest consumers of Illinois coal.

Until 1964 oil had taken over as the leading mineral of Illinois, but in that year coal took back the lead it once had held, and production of more than 60,000,000 tons of coal brought revenues of $217,789,475 to the state in 1965.

Illinois' first commercial oil wells began producing in 1883, and there are about 400 producing oil fields, or pools, in the state. In 1965 Illinois produced 63,700,000 barrels of oil for a total value of $186,700,000. This gave Illinois eighth place among the nation's crude oil producing states. Oil production came from 41 counties.

For many years Illinois has led the nation in the production of fluorspar (used for hydrofluoric acid and in coloring), accounting for about two thirds of the entire national production of this mineral. The fluorspar district is centered in Hardin County with smaller deposits in Pope County. Illinois producers shipped a total of 159,140 tons of finished fluorspar in 1965. The state's output of this mineral is not reflected in the relatively low dollar value of the product each year—$7,861,165 in 1965.

Illinois is the second largest producer of crushed and broken limestone and dolomite in the country, ranking after Pennsylvania. In 1965 the state's commercial quarry operators produced a reported 43,300,000 tons, which was valued at $57,800,000. Although 60 counties reported production of stone, the top three—Cook, St. Clair, and Kankakee—accounted for 41 percent of the total.

Clay and clay products have fourth rank among the mineral products of Illinois. This is a widespread industry, with 48 plants located in 25 counties reported in operation in 1965. These plants produced pottery, stoneware, drain tile, sewer pipe, building tile, face and common brick, special heat-resistant bricks and processed clay for absorbent uses. Total value of clay products manufactured in Illinois in 1965 was $52,500,000.

In terms of dollar value, production of cement ranks as Illinois' fifth mineral industry. The four plants located in La Salle, Lee and Massac counties produced $30,600,000 worth of Portland cement and $1,900,000 worth of masonry cement.

Gravel production in Illinois totaled $16,508,000 in 1965, and sand was worth $11,356,000. The metropolitan Chicago area was the largest producing region, accounting for more than half of the state totals. Use of sand and gravel is tied closely to construction, which of course is the greatest in large population centers. Leading sand and gravel producing counties were McHenry and Will.

Illinois is one of the leading producers of high quality silica sand in the United States. Production is concentrated in La Salle County, with lesser production from Ogle County. About half of this sand is used in the manufacture of glass. In 1965 Illinois' silica sand production totaled $11,990,000.

Following in the tradition of historic Galena, lead and zinc are still produced in Illinois, with lead valued at about a million dollars a year and zinc at $5,347,688 in 1965. Metal mines in Joe Daviess County produce lead and zinc concentrates, and these come as coproducts from the fluorspar mines of southeastern Illinois.

Other minerals in the value of $17,251,042 in 1965 included tripoli (amorphous silica), lime, natural bonded molding sand and some natural gas.

A Good Crop of Dollars

Farmland still occupies about 85 percent of Illinois. Approximately 141,000 farms in the state bear a price tag of $11,000,000,000—their estimated value. They grow 40 crops on an acreage totaling 20,000,000, with another 10,000,000 acres of lush pasture, which helps to support the state's 4,000,000 cattle, half a million milk cows, 600,000 sheep and lambs and 8,000,000 hogs.

An especially interesting and valuable feature of Illinois agriculture is its unusual variety, due to the soil, climate and topography, making possible crops ranging from cotton in the delta at the junction of the Ohio and Mississippi rivers, to sugar beets, spring wheat, vegetables, apples, peaches, winter wheat, rye, hay and oats, and, naturally, corn and soybeans.

The history of farming in Illinois dates back to the prehistoric peoples. Later the early French settlers grew crops of such size that people elsewhere marveled. When settlement began in earnest in Illinois, settlers followed the pattern of the East and cleared the woodlands first, then went reluctantly to the prairies. Soldiers of the Revolutionary War were given land in the state, and other settlers were offered many inducements. Even as late as the 1850's good land could still be had in Illinois for $1.25 an acre.

The original McCormick reaper, invented in 1831.

The Chicago Union Stockyards in the 1860's.

At one time, it was necessary for almost everyone in Illinois to grow crops to provide food. Now only about one person in five works on a farm. During the last 40 years, 750,000 people have left farms in Illinois. The comparatively small number left can still provide more than enough manpower to grow food for the people and enough in addition to help make Illinois first among the states in agricultural exports. One man with machines can do the work of many laboring by hand. A hundred years ago one farm worker produced enough food and fiber for five persons. Today, at national rates he produces enough for 37 persons. New seeds and new kinds of crops such as hybrid corn, the use of fertilizers and the knowledge of scientific agriculture—all have made it possible for each acre of rich Illinois farmland to grow far more than it did before. Corn yields offer a good example of

this. At one time 20, 30, 40 bushels of corn per acre would have been satisfactory. Now yields of 125 bushels are not unusual. Illinois has doubled its corn yield per acre in only the last ten years.

Corn is still the most important crop of Illinois. Iowa and Illinois compete for the corn championship each year. Sometimes one state will come out ahead and then the other. Iowa has been ahead in more years than Illinois, but in the last year that figures were available (1965) Illinois moved to first place with 891,664,000 bushels. The importance of corn is based on the fact that it is the staple feed for livestock, and across the country almost three times as much of it is grown as the next largest crop. The vastly important livestock industry is vitally dependent on corn production.

One of the pioneers in greater corn production was Lester Pfister of El Paso, Illinois, who spent ten years developing his hybrid corn, mortgaging his farm to get the money for his experiments and bringing himself almost to starvation. At last in 1935 his efforts began to pay off when he introduced his Pfister Hybrid to the market. Another hybrid pioneer was James Holbert of Funk Brothers, Bloomington. Hybrid corn, of course, is responsible for greatly increased yields on the same acreage.

At one time wheat was more important in Illinois than it is today. Illinois led all the states in wheat production in 1860 when a vast flood of ripe grain poured into Chicago. Buying and selling this grain, as it still buys and sells much of the grain of the country, was the job of the Chicago Board of Trade, opened in 1848, the world's biggest grain exchange. Of all the world's grain futures, 90 percent of them are traded in Chicago.

Another leading crop is soybeans, and the state produces almost 20 percent of the entire United States total of this crop. Decatur claims the title of "Soybean Capital of America." Less important but interesting "firsts" for Illinois are those in Swiss cheese, horseradish and onion sets.

Illinois is also important in vegetable and orchard crops. Average annual production exceeds 2,500,000 bushels of apples, 260,000 bushels of peaches and 141,000 tons of to-

matoes. An unusual first for Illinois is its leadership in the growing of bleached asparagus, an industry centered at Belleville. The small town of Pana is a marketing center of another kind. Sixty acres of greenhouses near Pana grow nothing but roses. Twenty million cut roses each year go out from Pana to the flower lovers of the world.

Illinois is third in total production of livestock, ranking after Iowa and California. Illinois raises more hogs than any other state except Iowa. The state is a leader in the confinement method of hog raising. The animals are constantly on concrete and never touch the ground. Their diet is completely controlled, and they are protected by antibiotics and other medicines and growth is encouraged by vitamins.

Altogether, the income from agriculture in Illinois was $2,400,626,000 in 1965. This probably would have surprised the modest observer who in 1908 noted that at Prophetstown even "the tillers of the soil have automobiles. . . . It is said that in town and country around here are nearly twenty of these destructive machines." Today machinery and equipment average many thousands of dollars per farm, and some are so highly mechanized that almost nothing is done by hand. Production expenses for feed, seed, fertilizer, livestock, fuel, labor and other materials exceed a billion dollars a year.

They'd Rather Be "Wright"

The place of Illinois in world architecture is so distinctive that it is one accomplishment of the state that is recognized with little or no argument. Certainly no similar area has ever pioneered in design and construction over such a period of years.

The earliest architecture in Illinois was not distinguished from that of other areas— the caves of prehistoric peoples, the bark lodges of the Indians covered with woven mats or skins, and the log cabins of the early settlers. It is interesting to note that the French settlers built their cabins of vertical logs and the English and Americans used a horizontal type of construction. For many years logs were used for almost all construction in Illinois.

The first hint of things to come in new and daring methods of construction was unveiled at Chicago, naturally enough, in 1832, when George W. Snow invented a new method of building small houses and other buildings of wood. Until this time, wooden frames required bulky corner posts of large timbers and much bracing. Snow's simpler method placed smaller studs closely together, held by a sheath under the clapboards.

This "balloon frame" construction called for much less wood, was lighter and stronger, and became almost universally used. This was the skeleton construction still so familiar today in new housing projects and other places where small frame buildings are going up. Although little recognized, George Snow certainly deserves great credit for devising a technique which has been used and is still being used in millions of buildings throughout the world.

The first skyscraper, designed by William LeBaron Jenney, gained world fame for Chicago.

For a great many years Illinois architects were content to copy the reigning styles of architecture in Europe and the East—much of this being ugly, bulky and often overdone.

It was in 1885 that Chicago made a contribution to architecture that made the whole world gasp and completely transformed the faces of cities around the globe. Architect William LeBaron Jenney's Home Insurance Building made history by using upright steel framework to support steel floor beams. Before this time, the height of buildings had been limited because the higher the building the heavier and thicker the outside masonry walls had to be to carry the great weight. The 16-story Monadnock Building in Chicago, the last tall building of this type, required six-foot-thick walls at the ground.

In Jenney's building the outer walls were only a "skin" to provide a cover for the building and they supported no weight. The great steel skeletons of such buildings are so familiar today it is hard to realize how startling and revolutionary this type of construction was at first. It soon became apparent that with such steel skeletons there was almost no limit to the height of buildings. Crowds at the World's Columbian Exposition made special trips downtown to gaze in awe at the 22-story Masonic Temple Building, designed by the famous firm of Daniel H. Burnham and John Root in 1892.

There is little question that the invention of the skyscraper still remains Chicago's most significant contribution to modern city life. When the word skyscraper came into use to describe such a structure, the *Dictionary of American Slang* of 1891 defined the new term: "A very tall building such as are now being built in Chicago."

In addition to the firm of Burnham and Root, another famed Chicago architectural firm was that of Dankmar Adler and Louis Sullivan. Their great Auditorium Building, one of the most famous anywhere, showed the ornate decorations for which Sullivan was so famous. The building contained a hotel, office building and theater. Architects throughout the world cheered when it was announced in 1967 that the famed Auditorium Theater, long in disuse, had been restored at a cost of several millions and would be reopened. The artwork, brilliant designs in gold and muted colors, and all the splendid features of Sullivan's old concert hall have been carefully restored.

At one time a young architect, Frank Lloyd Wright, worked in the offices of Adler and Sullivan. He soon went out on his own and became, possibly, the best-known architect of his time. Few men have been more controversial than Wright. His works were strange, different, even bizarre. Many called him the greatest architect who ever lived, and others felt that his work was frightful. His early work was done in Chicago, and his famed houses and buildings in the city and suburbs are still pointed out as landmarks of architecture.

After World War II, Illinois was to take another step in providing new directions for architecture. Renowned architect-designer Ludwig Mies van der Rohe became director of Armour Institute (now Illinois Institute of Technology) at Chicago in 1938. He designed a new campus for the Institute. The first new skyscrapers put up in Chicago after the war were designed by Mies van der Rohe. His two apartment buildings on Lake Shore Drive seem to be nothing but steel framework and glass. They were acclaimed as a whole new concept in skyscraper construction, in which superficial siding and facing materials were eliminated and only

With its brilliant gold and red coloring and simple horizontal design, Louis Sullivan's Transportation Building contrasted sharply with the classic architecture of the many white buildings at the Columbian Exposition in 1893.

the essential elements of the building remained. When Mies van der Rohe designed the Seagram Building in New York along the same lines, the rush was on, and most of the tremendous new crop of skyscrapers all over the world owe much of their design to the pattern once more pioneered in Chicago.

The round "corncob" towers of Chicago's Marina City, now being imitated in many other cities, the pyramidal shapes of the First National Bank Building, John Hancock Center and the triangular form of Lake Point Tower, all reaching skyward in Chicago, have excited the imagination of another generation of architects, who contend that Chicago is still the leader in architecture.

Another widely acclaimed Illinois building rests on the flat land of the campus of the University of Illinois at Urbana, much like a tremendous flying saucer about to take off. This is the University's bowl-shaped Assembly Hall, which has been called an "architectural triumph" of its designer R. Buckminster Fuller.

"Cool, Clear Water"

"There can be no doubt that the arrival of man was one of the worst calamities that ever happened to all the creatures of this lovely earth," recently wrote Dr. W. J. Beecher, head of the Chicago Academy of Sciences. He had in mind, of course, man's destruction of the world's natural resources. However, since man also has to exist as one of the creatures of the world, he has recognized, at least to some extent, that he must take steps to avoid ruining his world completely by carelessness and ignorance.

Earliest destruction brought by man to the lush lands of Illinois was the ruthless cutting down and burning of trees. Large areas of forests were destroyed on land which was not really good for anything else, and the soil soon began to erode. In less than a century, 14,000,000 acres of forest were reduced to less than 4,000,000 acres.

Wildlife soon suffered, also. In time the large herds of deer almost completely disappeared from the state. Great flocks of wild birds were killed to be sold commercially. Other species, such as the wild turkey, and more recently the prairie chicken, disappeared or almost vanished. Recent count showed only 2,000 of the highly prized prairie chicken remaining in Illinois.

Unexpected natural disasters, brought about by man in other ways, sometimes occurred. An example of this was the lamprey eel, admitted into the Great Lakes with the opening of the St. Lawrence Seaway. The lamprey has almost completely destroyed the once numberless and highly valued lake trout and whitefish. As a consequence, both commercial fishing interests and sportsmen have suffered.

REVERSING THE DESTRUCTION

To see what could be done about reversing the destruction of natural resources the Illinois Department of Conservation was established. Its Division of Forestry helps to protect the existing forests and to encourage replanting on both public and private lands which should be forested, as well as overseeing the protection against forest fires.

A tract of 800,000 acres of Illinois woodland also is now protected in Shawnee National Forest by the Federal government.

The divisions of Game Management and Game Propagation are devoted to protecting and increasing Illinois wildlife. For wildlife to live, they must be given refuge. Land is bought for refuges; farmers are encouraged to leave cover in fence rows and other areas; trees and shrubs are planted in strategic places; swamps and other favorable wildlife areas are protected in their natural state. Hundreds of thousands of pheasant, quail and other birds are raised and released in game areas, as are animal species which may once again thrive in Illinois. The Division of Game Propagation has been trying to establish a wild turkey flock in the Shawnee National Forest and other areas, and the turkey population is once again growing.

A similar program has been carried out by the Division of Fisheries. Intensive study of the lamprey eel by Federal, state and private agencies raises the hope that this unwanted guest may soon be eliminated or controlled and good numbers of commercial and game fish once again may flourish in Lake Michigan.

The Department of Conservation has many other activities, such as the creation

Water recreation resources in Illinois.

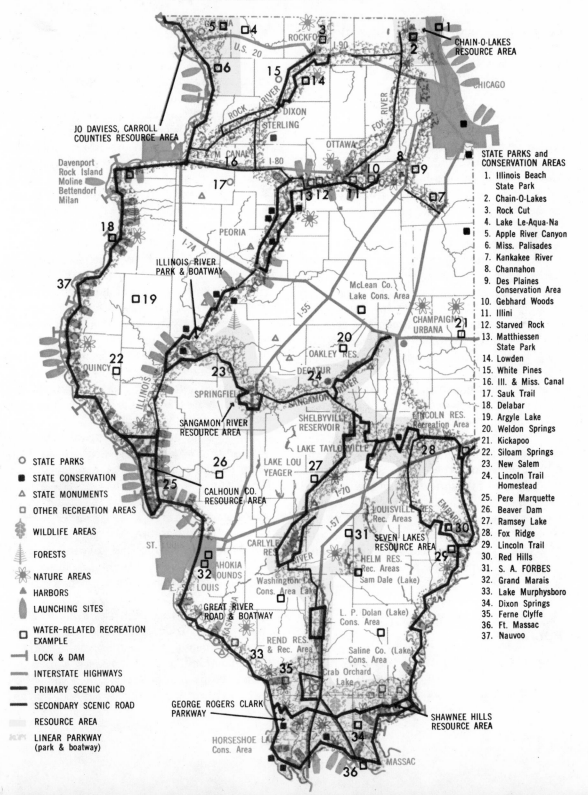

CHAIN-O-LAKES
RESOURCE AREA

JO DAVIESS, CARROLL
COUNTIES RESOURCE AREA

Davenport
Rock Island
Moline
Bettendorf
Milan

ILLINOIS RIVER
PARK & BOATWAY

McLean Co.
Lake Cons. Area

CHAMPAIGN
URBANA

OAKLEY RES.

DECATUR

SANGAMON RIVER

SPRINGFIELD

SHELBYVILLE
RESERVOIR

LINCOLN RES.
Recreation Area

SANGAMON RIVER
RESOURCE AREA

LAKE TAYLORVILLE

LAKE LOU
YEAGER

CALHOUN CO.
RESOURCE AREA

LOUISVILLE RES.
Rec. Areas

SEVEN LAKES
RESOURCE AREA

ST. LOUIS

CAHOKIA
MOUNDS

E. ST.
LOUIS

Washington Co.
Cons. Area Lake

HELM RES.
Rec. Areas

Sam Dale (Lake)

GREAT RIVER
ROAD & BOATWAY

CARLYLE
RES.

L. P. Dolan (Lake)
Cons. Area

REND RES.
& Rec. Area

Saline Co. (Lake)
Cons. Area

Crab Orchard
Lake

GEORGE ROGERS CLARK
PARKWAY

SHAWNEE HILLS
RESOURCE AREA

HORSESHOE LA.
Cons. Area

MASSAC

STATE PARKS and CONSERVATION AREAS

1. Illinois Beach State Park
2. Chain-O-Lakes
3. Rock Cut
4. Lake Le-Aqua-Na
5. Apple River Canyon
6. Miss. Palisades
7. Kankakee River
8. Channahon
9. Des Plaines Conservation Area
10. Gebhard Woods
11. Illini
12. Starved Rock
13. Matthiessen State Park
14. Lowden
15. White Pines
16. Ill. & Miss. Canal
17. Sauk Trail
18. Delabar
19. Argyle Lake
20. Weldon Springs
21. Kickapoo
22. Siloam Springs
23. New Salem
24. Lincoln Trail Homestead
25. Pere Marquette
26. Beaver Dam
27. Ramsey Lake
28. Fox Ridge
29. Lincoln Trail
30. Red Hills
31. S. A. FORBES
32. Grand Marais
33. Lake Murphysboro
34. Dixon Springs
35. Ferne Clyffe
36. Ft. Massac
37. Nauvoo

Legend

○ STATE PARKS
■ STATE CONSERVATION
△ STATE MONUMENTS
□ OTHER RECREATION AREAS

WILDLIFE AREAS
FORESTS
NATURE AREAS
HARBORS
LAUNCHING SITES

□ WATER-RELATED RECREATION EXAMPLE
LOCK & DAM
INTERSTATE HIGHWAYS
PRIMARY SCENIC ROAD
SECONDARY SCENIC ROAD
RESOURCE AREA
LINEAR PARKWAY (park & boatway)

of new lakes and other recreational areas, as well as the improvement of existing recreational areas and supervision of state parks.

EROSION PROBLEMS

In the field of agriculture, one of the greatest dangers is the washing or blowing away of the rich land by erosion, leaving poor soil unsuited for crops, or cutting great gullies or gashes, which increase as erosion continues.

Another danger is the wearing out of the soil by constant use when crops are not properly rotated or when nutrition is not added to the soil. Many agencies of Federal, state and local government are working on these problems, including the Division of Soil Conservation of the Illinois Department of Agriculture. The modern farmers of Illinois are aware of these dangers and study and practice the most up-to-date means of protecting and improving the soil.

Another problem concerns man-made "erosion" of the soil. The huge strip mines of Illinois cover large acreages. When the coal has been exhausted in an area, and the miners move on, they leave a vast wasteland. Many of these areas have been planted with trees, shrubs and grasses and lakes have been created in them for fishing and recreation. State law now requires that some kind of restoration be undertaken in every area where strip mining is now abandoned.

WATER, AIR AND GROUND POLLUTION

The older, more traditional problems in the saving of the land and its resources were difficult enough, but modern man has added a whole new collection of harmful practices.

One of these is the pollution of water. Pure fresh water is necessary to all life, including man. However, pure lakes and fresh running streams are almost as necessary for man's enjoyment of his surroundings as they are for life itself. When factories empty strong chemicals into a river, or sewage and other wastes are poured in constantly, the river dies, just as if it had been a living thing. Vegetation and trees die along its shore. Fish, frogs, turtles and wildlife disappear. The odor generally is foul. The river no longer can be used as a source of water; fishing is no longer possible; boating and swimming are unthinkable. What once was a thing of beauty and value is now not only useless but actually disagreeable.

River after river, creek after creek, stream after stream, lake after lake have followed one by one in this awful pattern of water death. At one time the Illinois River was one of the most important fishing rivers in the country. Now the Illinois in many stretches has few or no fish.

Polluted streams and lakes cannot be used for drinking water. In the early days of Chicago, sewage was poured into the Chicago River and Lake Michigan. Chicago's water was called by one observer a "filthy, slush, miscalled water . . . a nauseous chowder." To cure this and to preserve the Lake Michigan beaches, Chicago had to turn its river around in a costly process and create a sanitary canal to take the sewage downstream.

In some ways the poisoning of the air has become even worse than the killing of the living waters. Industrial smokestacks belching dense clouds of poisonous smoke, and the burning of millions of furnaces sometimes makes the air almost unbearable. Even worse, and the most dangerous threat to good air, is the internal combustion engine, pouring off exhaust fumes from millions of automobiles, buses, trucks and diesel engines.

Another grave problem is the increasing use of insecticides. Widespread and indiscriminate use of DDT and other long-lasting poisons to kill Dutch elm disease beetles and other pests has resulted in killing alarming numbers of birds and also in killing insects which are useful in controlling other insects. Some insecticides kill not only birds but also mammals, fish, reptiles, amphibians, insects and crustaceans. Rabbits are wiped out; foxes, armadillos, squirrels and mice killed. After one recent "treatment" the deaths of 697 chickens, 20 turkeys, 11 cats, 2 ducks and more than 50 dogs were reported.

SOLVING THE PROBLEM

The problem of dealing with the vast sources of water and air pollution is only now being faced in Illinois, and the cost of the solution has been estimated at a billion dollars. Governor Otto Kerner received in 1967 the report of a costly three-year survey undertaken by the state with funds from the United States Department of Housing and Urban Development. The 450-page report proposed a plan for action, calling for a statewide referendum in November, 1968, on a $1,000,-000,000 bond issue to finance specific projects and provide funds for administration: $160,000,000 for air pollution control; $250,000,000 for water pollution control; $200,000,000 for water-related recreation; $100,000,000 for flood control; and $290,-000,000 for water management.

Of the total, $300,000,000 would go for loans to private industry and local government which eventually would be recovered by the state. The program is also expected to generate $850,000,000 in Federal aid.

The money for air pollution control would be distributed in long-term, low-interest loans to industries and local governments for new pollution abatement equipment or modifications of existing equipment.

The allocation for water pollution abatement would be used for grants to communities to supplement Federal aid for construction of waste treatment plants. Most of the water recreation money would go for 25 new lakes to be created near urban centers, and for providing new access to areas for boating and swimming, as well as for developing fishing and fish-rearing units.

The plan calls for the creation of a State Water Resources Board, to coordinate water resources programs.

Lessons To be Learned

One of Illinois' most important resources—perhaps most important of all—is its great collection of more than 125 public and private colleges, universities and junior colleges.

The first institution of higher education in Illinois was Illinois College at Jacksonville, founded in 1829. Other colleges and universities followed, but higher education grew slowly in the state.

Knox College, chartered at Galesburg in 1837, is often listed as one of the ten leading liberal arts colleges in the United States. A college was one of the lures offered to settlers in the new community being created by the Rev. George Washington Gale. A scholarship was provided for each farm sold in the area, and the Knox boys worked hard on the college farm to earn their board. In the distinguished history of Knox College are such student names as Don Marquis and Eugene Field. The famous "Old Siwash" fiction by George Fitch, in the *Saturday Evening Post*, was supposed to be based on Knox College, and gave the world a new nickname for a small city college.

The University of Illinois began as Illinois Industrial College, which was chartered at Urbana-Champaign in 1867 and began operation in March, 1868. Through the Morrill Act, the United States government assisted the states to provide practical education in the fields of agriculture, engineering and other mechanical fields, and science. Illinois Industrial College received Illinois' share of the Morrill funds.

Many felt that a Morrill school could only teach the subjects covered in the act, while others contended that the institution should be broadened to become a general university. The state provided little help for the college until Governor John Altgeld's term. It then began its rapid expansion into a complete state university, and continued this advance even more rapidly in the early 1900's. Although the University of Illinois was the last of the great Midwestern state universities to begin complete operation, its growth and expansion have been astonishing.

Mushrooming enrollment has caused an almost unbelievable expansion of the main campus, with large modern buildings springing up so rapidly that even local residents find it difficult to keep up. In addition, the Chicago Circle Campus of the University of Illinois recently was built as a tremendous collection of modern buildings on Chicago's near southwest side, in what was once a slum area. Because it was built as a completely planned campus and educational operation, the Chicago Circle Campus has received many visitors from other states and abroad to study the planning and techniques which brought this unique educational center into being. Striking modern buildings continue to go up on the Circle Campus, but because of what the officials call an "education explosion" university leaders claim that the campus is "inadequate before it is completed."

Near the Chicago Circle Campus are the famous medical schools of the University of Illinois, associated with the vast medical concentration grouped around Presbyterian-St. Luke's and Cook County hospitals. The medical campus includes schools of pharmacy, dentistry and nursing as well as medicine. Called the medical center, this area

Knox College still uses this historic building which was the scene of the fifth Lincoln-Douglas debate.

also includes the Stritch School of Medicine of Loyola University and the Chicago Medical School. The American Medical Association and the American Dental Association have their headquarters in Chicago.

Only one other American university, the University of California, has a larger faculty than the 6,749 faculty members who serve at the University of Illinois at Urbana-Champaign and Chicago.

Altogether Illinois has six state universities. Others are Southern Illinois University at Carbondale and Edwardsville, Illinois State at Normal, Northern Illinois at De Kalb, Eastern Illinois at Charleston and Western Illinois at Macomb. Latest figures showed the total student population of the state universities of Illinois to be 93,751; by now it is probably well over 100,000.

Perhaps the most amazing growth of all has been that of Southern Illinois University, now enrolling almost 26,000 students. Only twenty years ago, enrollment in the drowsing institution was 3,000. The present student body consists of about 18,000 at the older Carbondale campus and about 8,000 at the new Edwardsville unit. The growth of Southern Illinois reflects, perhaps, the revitalization of the entire southern portion of the state from which it draws many of its students. The national spotlight was turned on Southern Illinois University in March, 1967, when its basketball team, the Salukis, carried off the National Invitational Tournament championship at New York.

In addition to the state universities the state recently has taken over the operation of the entire complex of Chicago State College and Northeastern Illinois State College and several junior colleges administered at one time by Chicago's school system, with several more scheduled to be built soon.

COSMOPOLITAN COMPLEX

The metropolitan Chicago area has been described as "the world's greatest concentration of higher education."

The oldest of the great universities in Chicago's metropolitan area is Northwestern University, founded in 1851 by a group led by John Evans, who had a unique personal history as an educational and civic leader in several states. Other Northwestern founders were Grant Goodrich and Orrington Lunt. Modern Northwestern is engaged in a multi-million dollar fund drive with plans designed to transform much of its land in Evanston. The university has been responsible for one of the largest landfills in Lake Michigan in recent years, bringing 2,000,000 cubic yards of sand to create the entirely new James Roscoe Miller campus adjoining the older campus and almost doubling the campus size.

The University of Chicago has been called "the most youthful of all the great universities in the world." It was founded in 1890 by the American Baptist Education Society, under the sponsorship of John D. Rockefeller. Under the direction of its first president, William Rainey Harper, a faculty of some of the leading names in higher education was assembled. According to a newspaper of the time, "President Harper's fondest wish was realized when the university started upon its practical life of instruction yesterday morning with the same confidence and absence of parade as if it had been running half a century." Happy students went about the campus singing, "John D. Rockefeller, wonderful man is he,/ Gives all his spare change to the U. of C.—" That spare change amounted to $35,000,000 then, and almost double that has since come from Rockefeller foundations and organizations.

One of the most publicized periods in the life of the University of Chicago came with the hiring of twenty-nine-year-old Dr. Robert Maynard Hutchins, then the youngest president ever to take over a great university. The new president was said to have "turned the world of education upside down, and there are some educators who wonder if it has ever righted itself." Under his direction the University of Chicago tried such new plans as letting students enter the college whether they had finished high school or not if they could pass the entrance tests—no matter what their age.

Surrounded by a decaying neighborhood, the University of Chicago seemed for a period to be losing stature, but it has recently transformed much of its surroundings and again embarked on a plan to build a faculty composed of the world's great scholars, as well as to build all the necessary new facilities. To accomplish this goal the university has made a good start on the largest fund drive ever conducted by a private educational institution—$360,000,000.

The almost endless list of Chicago area institutions includes Roosevelt University, Wheaton College, the National College of Education at Evanston, and three highly regarded Catholic institutions—De Paul University, Loyola University and Mundelein College. The area is also noted as one of the leading centers for theological education, including McCormick Theological Seminary, Chicago Theological Seminary, Moody Bible Institute and Hebrew Theological College, all in Chicago, and Garrett Theological Institute and Seabury Western Seminary in Evanston.

One of the country's leading scientific educational institutions is the Illinois Institute of Technology located on Chicago's South

Side. This school was formed in 1940 by the merger of Lewis Institute and Armour Institute of Technology.

THE SCHOOLS OF ILLINOIS

As early as 1785 a Federal land ordinance had reserved certain lands in Illinois for the "common" schools. The farseeing Northwest Ordinance in 1787 asserted: "Schools and the means of education shall forever be encouraged." At the time of Illinois statehood, Congress had provided an unusual opportunity for schools in Illinois by setting aside for education three percent of all the money from the sale of state land.

The first school law was not passed until 1825, when school districts were provided for, along with a compulsory tax to finance an education for white children between 6 and 21, but the taxation clause was removed in 1829, making the law almost meaningless. For a considerable period there were some public schools in Illinois, but very poorly supported. Chicago's first public school opened in 1841.

Until 1856 high school education was provided by a few private academies. In that year, Chicago High School became one of the first public high schools to be established west of the Alleghenies. It was later renamed Central High School and was eventually discontinued.

An expanded public school law was not passed until 1855, under the urging of Ninian W. Edwards, who had been appointed a special public instruction officer. Public schools in Illinois progressed after that time.

The Constitution of 1870 provided for an elected State Superintendent of Public Instruction, and each county has an elected superintendent of schools. The "business" of education has grown to such an extent that in modern Illinois the largest portion of the state's income is required for educational purposes. In addition, large sums are provided by the Federal government for a great variety of special educational programs.

In addition to public schools there are many well-known private schools and large numbers of parochial schools. Among private schools with a national reputation may be listed the North Shore Country Day School at Winnetka; Faulkner, Latin and Francis Parker schools in Chicago; and many such specialized schools as the School of the Art Institute of Chicago, said to be the largest of its kind anywhere, with classes for all ages as well as graduate work.

Among the several religious denominations which maintain schools, the Roman Catholic school system is by far the largest.

Land of Lincoln

"My friends, no one not in my situation can appreciate my feelings of sadness at this parting. To this place and the kindness of these people I owe everything. Here I have lived a quarter of a century, and have passed from a young to an old man. . . ." As he said these words, the tall, sad man stood on the observation platform of the train on the siding at the depot in Springfield preparing to leave Illinois to take on the fierce responsibilities of the presidency of a desperately troubled United States. Thus did Abraham Lincoln express publicly the debt he felt to the city of Springfield, to the state of Illinois, and to the people who meant so much to him.

In its turn, modern Illinois is proud to express in every conceivable way the influence this magnificent American has had on the state and the powerful, almost magical effect which his memory still exerts in what its residents now fondly think of and proclaim to the world as the Land of Lincoln.

The number and variety of places in Illinois dedicated, restored or preserved to the memory of Abraham Lincoln and his family or cherished for some association with him, no matter how fleeting, is truly remarkable. Probably nowhere else does the influence of one man so dominate a countryside. Certainly nowhere else is there such complete coverage and documentation of the multitude of associations of one man with such an area.

EARLY MEMORIES

The modern automobile can carry tourists in a few hours across almost the same route which required 15 days of toil and distress for the Lincoln family. Probably there are few who make the trip today without giving at least a moment's thought to this pioneer family coming to a new state for a new life. Most of the memories are still there, on the well-marked Lincoln Heritage Trail.

A striking bronze statue marks the beginning of this Memorial Highway in Illinois, near Lawrenceville. It shows Lincoln in bold relief from the rest of the monument, walking sturdily beside the family's covered wagon.

Fifteen days after they left Indiana, the Lincoln family settled on government land on the Sangamon River southwest of Decatur. The place is now maintained as Lincoln Trail Homestead Park. A large boulder marks the location of the family cabin.

After a year at the first Illinois home, Lincoln's father and stepmother settled near Charleston, in a location which is now Lincoln Log Cabin State Park. The Thomas Lincoln home has been reconstructed there on the original foundations. Not far from this cabin is the Moore Home State Memorial, where Lincoln ate his last meal with his stepmother, Sarah Bush Lincoln, in the home of Mrs. Matilda Moore, daughter of Mrs. Lincoln. Nearby is Shiloh Cemetery where Lincoln's father and stepmother are buried.

NEW SALEM

The most poignant Lincoln memories in Illinois are connected with the tiny town where he made his start. The restoration of New Salem brings back to life a ghost town and endows it with a feeling of the presence of the young man who went on to greatness.

Here Lincoln lived for six years and, strangely, those six years included most of the life of the town, which faded and died soon after Lincoln left, after being inhabited for only about ten years. New Salem had been founded with the hope that it would become prosperous because of river traffic up the Sangamon River. Lincoln himself had been asked to pilot the steamboat *Talisman* which came up the river loaded with goods and arrived at Portland Landing. On the return trip they had to tear down part of the dam at New Salem to let the boat pass. When it became clear that this part of the Sangamon was not deep enough for steamboats, the prospects of the town declined.

New Salem, never with more than 100 inhabitants, became a ghost town, and only one original building, the Onstot cooperage shop, was standing in 1906 when the land was purchased by newspaper magnate William Randolph Hearst, who gave it to the Old Salem Lincoln League. Later it was presented to the state. The old records of Sangamon County were studied; descendants of settlers were consulted and every effort was made to rebuild the town exactly as it was in Lincoln's time.

Thirteen cabins, six shops and the Rutledge Tavern compose the town, with the buildings furnished as much as possible as they once were. A post office is operated in the Lincoln-Berry store building where Lincoln once served as postmaster. Visitors enjoy riding about the park in a covered wagon pulled by oxen. A museum in New Salem State Park features items in use in the period when Lincoln called New Salem his home. A replica of the *Talisman* floats in the river, and the famed Robert Sherwood play *Abe Lincoln in Illinois* is given each summer in Kelso Hollow of New Salem State Park.

More than a million visitors come to the park each year to visit the scenes of Lincoln's bachelor years and pay tribute to him.

"I CHRISTEN THEE LINCOLN!"

Not far from New Salem and only 23 miles northeast of Springfield is the town of Lincoln, Illinois, the only town named for Lincoln while he was still living. The story of how this town received its name is one of the most revealing of all the Lincoln anecdotes. Lincoln was the lawyer for the founders of the town, who decided to give their new project the name of their lawyer. Lincoln protested, saying, "I never knew anything named Lincoln that amounted to anything." He finally agreed, however, and after the town site had been laid out, a crowd gathered to dedicate it, with Abraham Lincoln as master of ceremonies.

He took a large watermelon, which he neatly cut open with his pocketknife and split in two on the wagon where he was standing. Taking out the core, Lincoln squeezed the watermelon juice into a tin cup. "I now christen this town site. Its name is Lincoln!" he proclaimed and poured the watermelon juice on the ground in humorous dedication. Then he continued, "I have also prepared a feast for this occasion." He pulled a covering off a wagonload of watermelons, and the crowd did have a feast. The town now has an annual watermelon-day feast in honor of its dedication by Abraham Lincoln.

BELOVED SPRINGFIELD

Probably there are more Lincoln memories in his beloved Springfield than anywhere else in Illinois. There, at Eighth and Jackson, is the only house Lincoln ever owned. Lincoln purchased the home in 1844 for $1,500, with a $900 mortgage, and moved there that year. It originally was a story and a half, but Mrs. Lincoln had it remodeled into two stories while Lincoln was away from home. She is supposed to have used money received from her father. Lincoln's son, Robert Todd Lincoln, presented it to the state in 1887.

Made of native hardwoods, the house has framework and floors of oak, with laths of hand-split hickory. The original shingles were hand-split walnut. Wooden pegs and handmade nails were used in its construction. Today it is painted Quaker brown, as it was when the Lincolns lived there. Some of the original Lincoln furnishings can be seen in the house. Other furnishings have been collected, as nearly like the originals as possible.

The former state capitol, the one used just before the present statehouse, stood in the square in Springfield. In later years another and inappropriate floor had been added to it. Recently it was decided to tear it down and rebuild it exactly as it was when Lincoln made his famous speech there on his nomination for Senator, in 1858, when he said, "A house divided against itself cannot stand. I believe this government cannot endure permanently, half slave and half free."

Throughout Springfield, plaques, bronze tablets, and preserved architecture point to the Lincoln presence. The railroad station where he bade farewell is now the Lincoln Depot Museum. There is an Abraham Lincoln Museum and an Abraham Lincoln Memorial Garden.

Probably the most-visited spot at Springfield is the magnificent tomb where the 16th President and Mrs. Lincoln and three of their four sons are buried. Robert Todd Lincoln, whose grave is in Arlington National Cemetery, is the only one of the Lincoln sons not buried in the tomb in Oak Ridge Cemetery at Springfield. The citizens of Springfield organized the National Lincoln Monument Association and started a drive for funds to build a tomb and memorial. Construction of the tomb was started in 1869 and the memorial, costing $180,000, was dedicated in 1874.

Just two years later one of the most bizarre episodes in American history occurred. Counterfeit engraver Ben Boyd was in prison. His gang needed him to continue their illegal operations, so they planned to steal Lincoln's body, inform Boyd of where it was hidden, and he would then be able to use this information to blackmail his way out of prison. Officials learned of the plot and planned to catch the plotters as they stole the body. The thieves actually had the casket removed from its covering when they heard the officers and escaped. Two were later captured.

OTHER MEMORIES

In many other parts of Illinois the cherished memories of Abraham Lincoln are preserved. The Lincoln Heritage Trail winds throughout the scenic wonderland of central and southern Illinois. Courthouse memorials mark the route traveled by Lincoln, the circuit rider. The former courthouse in Beardstown recalls the famous Duff-Armstrong trial in which Lincoln served as defense attorney. The air still echoes with the ringing words of the seven Lincoln-Douglas debates in Ottawa, Freeport, Jonesboro, Charleston, Galesburg, Quincy and Alton, each place marked with a memorial.

Ratcliff Inn in Carmi marks another episode of Lincoln's travels in Illinois. Now a museum, it once served as his lodging twenty years before he became President.

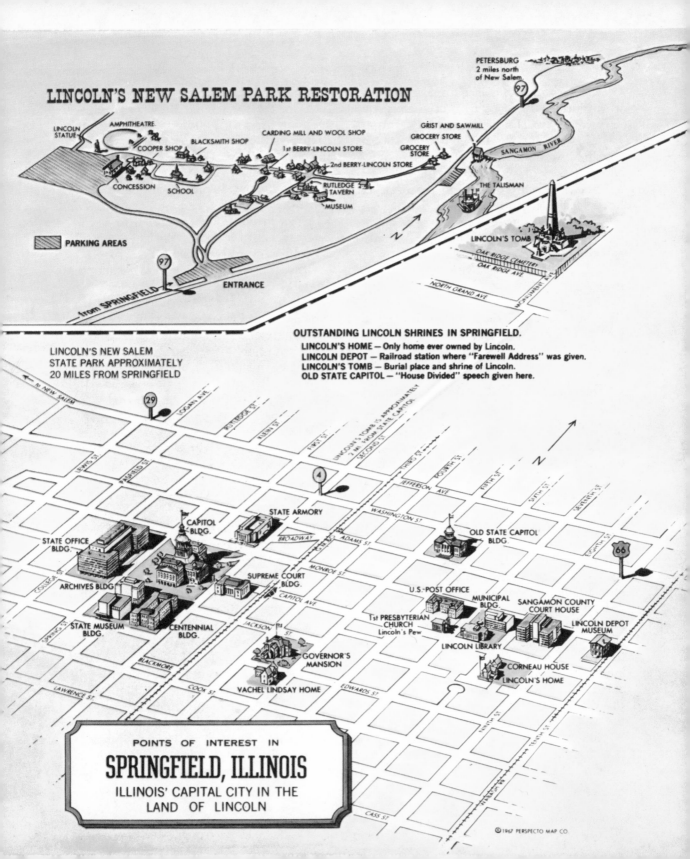

LINCOLN'S NEW SALEM PARK RESTORATION

PETERSBURG
2 miles north
of New Salem

97

SANGAMON RIVER

LINCOLN STATUE
AMPHITHEATRE
COOPER SHOP
BLACKSMITH SHOP
CARDING MILL AND WOOL SHOP
1st BERRY-LINCOLN STORE
2nd BERRY-LINCOLN STORE
CONCESSION
SCHOOL
RUTLEDGE TAVERN
MUSEUM
GRIST AND SAWMILL
GROCERY STORE
GROCERY STORE
THE TALISMAN

LINCOLN'S TOMB
OAK RIDGE CEMETERY
OAK RIDGE AVE.
NORTH GRAND AVE.
MONUMENT AVE.

PARKING AREAS

97

ENTRANCE

from SPRINGFIELD

N

LINCOLN'S NEW SALEM
STATE PARK APPROXIMATELY
20 MILES FROM SPRINGFIELD

OUTSTANDING LINCOLN SHRINES IN SPRINGFIELD.
LINCOLN'S HOME — Only home ever owned by Lincoln.
LINCOLN DEPOT — Railroad station where "Farewell Address" was given.
LINCOLN'S TOMB — Burial place and shrine of Lincoln.
OLD STATE CAPITOL — "House Divided" speech given here.

TO NEW SALEM

29

LOGAN'S AVE.
RUTLEDGE ST.
KLEIN ST.
FIRST ST.
SECOND ST.
THIRD ST.
FOURTH ST.
FIFTH ST.
SIXTH ST.
SEVENTH ST.

LINCOLN'S TOMB IS APPROXIMATELY
2 MI. FROM STATE CAPITOL

4

LEWIS ST.
PASFIELD ST.
SPRING ST.
COLLEGE ST.

JEFFERSON AVE.
WASHINGTON ST.

N

STATE ARMORY

CAPITOL BLDG.

BROADWAY

ADAMS ST.

OLD STATE CAPITOL BLDG.

66

STATE OFFICE BLDG.

MONROE ST.

ARCHIVES BLDG.

SUPREME COURT BLDG.

U.S. POST OFFICE

MUNICIPAL BLDG.

SANGAMON COUNTY COURT HOUSE

LINCOLN DEPOT MUSEUM

CAPITOL AVE.

1st PRESBYTERIAN CHURCH
Lincoln's Pew

STATE MUSEUM BLDG.

CENTENNIAL BLDG.

JACKSON ST.

LINCOLN LIBRARY

CORNEAU HOUSE

BLACKMORE

GOVERNOR'S MANSION

LINCOLN'S HOME

LAWRENCE ST.

COOK ST.

VACHEL LINDSAY HOME

EDWARDS ST.

EIGHTH ST.
NINTH ST.
TENTH ST.

CASS ST.

© 1962 PERSPECTO MAP CO.

POINTS OF INTEREST IN
SPRINGFIELD, ILLINOIS
ILLINOIS' CAPITAL CITY IN THE LAND OF LINCOLN

The memories of Lincoln's associations with Chicago can, and have, filled books.

Rushville recalls Lincoln being thrown twice in wrestling; Waukegan remembers the speech of April 2, 1860, which was interrupted by the cry of "fire!" It was thought his opponents had tried to break up the meeting, but at last Lincoln said, "Well, gentlemen, let us all go, as there really seems to be a fire, and help to put it out." This was the only speech Lincoln failed to finish.

Millions of people each year will read Secretary Stanton's words carved on Lincoln's tomb: "Now He Belongs To the Ages," but the Illinoisan will paraphrase this in a more personal way to say, "Now he belongs also to Illinois!"

CENTRAL ILLINOIS HIGHLIGHTS

Springfield, of course, has many points of interest not connected with Lincoln.

The first thing seen by visitors approaching Springfield from almost any direction is the 361-foot dome of the Illinois capitol. Statues of both Lincoln and Douglas stand on the nine-acre capitol grounds, along with those of Richard Yates, Pierre Menard and John M. Palmer.

The present statehouse was finished in 1887 at a cost of over $4,000,000. It is in the form of a Latin cross. The foundation for the great dome is 92½ feet across and is set 25½ feet below the ground level on solid rock. Walls supporting the dome are 17 feet thick to the first story. The walls are of various kinds of limestone, coming from several parts of the state. The statue of *Illinois Welcoming the World* was brought to the first floor of the capitol from the Illinois building of the World's Columbian Exposition. Other statues, murals and paintings throughout the building add to the story of Illinois.

Other important state buildings at Springfield are the Centennial Building, Archives Building, Armory Building, Supreme Court Building, Illinois State Office Building and the Governor's Mansion, erected in 1855.

The Illinois State Museum of Natural History and Art is one of the finest state-supported museums, and similar praise can be given to the Illinois State Historical Library, which has one of the finest Lincoln collections ever assembled.

Other Springfield museums include the Grand Army of the Republic Memorial Musuem; the Springfield Art Association's Historic Edwards Place, furnished in nineteenth century style; and the Vachel Lindsay home, residence of the poet, featuring exhibits of his original manuscripts and drawings.

In the Urbana-Champaign region, the University of Illinois offers many points of interest—the Natural History Building with its museum; the Vivarium; the spectacular, circular Assembly Hall; Memorial Stadium; Classical and European Culture Museum; and Krannert Art Museum. In Carle Park, Champaign, is Lorado Taft's statue of Lincoln as a lawyer.

The Robert Allerton Park, at Monticello, contributed to the university by Allerton, is noted for famous statuary in an outdoor park setting. Also at Monticello is the Pioneer Land Museum of Platt County, displaying pioneer items.

Decatur's well-known Art Center features traveling exhibits, mostly of paintings, changed monthly. The Lincoln Log Cabin Courthouse was once in the heart of the city but has been moved to Fairview Park.

It is claimed that the annual Easter time Passion Play held at Bloomington was the first Passion Play in the United States. In addition, Bloomington is the center for the training of trapeze performers. More than

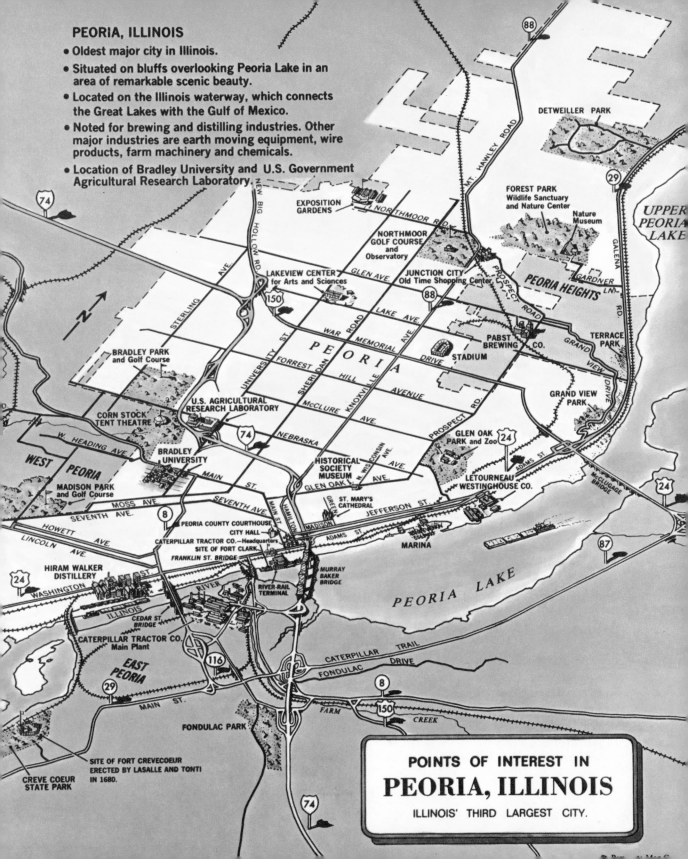

PEORIA, ILLINOIS

- Oldest major city in Illinois.
- Situated on bluffs overlooking Peoria Lake in an area of remarkable scenic beauty.
- Located on the Illinois waterway, which connects the Great Lakes with the Gulf of Mexico.
- Noted for brewing and distilling industries. Other major industries are earth moving equipment, wire products, farm machinery and chemicals.
- Location of Bradley University and U.S. Government Agricultural Research Laboratory.

POINTS OF INTEREST IN PEORIA, ILLINOIS

ILLINOIS' THIRD LARGEST CITY.

The city of Quincy, as illustrated in the book Das Illustrirte Mississippithal.

200 leading trapeze artists have trained at Bloomington since the Green brothers first practiced in a haymow and later became a featured act in Barnum's circus.

Peoria's Lakeview Center for the Arts and Sciences combines features of recreation, education, fine arts and science. There is a museum, art gallery, 300-seat auditorium for traveling exhibit area and museum shop, with a planetarium nearby. Metamora Court House State Memorial recalls Lincoln's circcuit days. The original building and chapel of one of Illinois' first colleges are preserved in the nearby Jubilee College State Memorial.

Near Lewiston is Dickson Mounds State Memorial, where more than 200 skeletons of mound builders have been uncovered and are to be seen in the positions in which they were put in their graves.

Other burial mound relics are displayed in Indian Mounds Park at Quincy, which includes Erroke Indian Burial Mounds. A 17-room home of former Governor John Woods is headquarters for the Historical Society of Quincy and Adams County.

A branch of the Mormon church, Nauvoo Restoration, Inc., is now restoring much of Nauvoo to the condition when it was the largest city in Illinois. When this is accomplished with 40 or 50 buildings restored over the next 10 years, Nauvoo will be one of the major restorations in the country. It is expected to be one of the principal tourist attractions of Illinois.

An information center shows visitors a historical movie of the city and its restoration. Among the points of interest now open is the Joseph Smith Homestead. This is Smith's original log cabin and the oldest building in Nauvoo. It is furnished with original items owned by the family. Near the house are the long-secret graves of Joseph Smith, Emma his wife, and his brother Hyrum. The Mansion House, also occupied by Smith, is open, with period furnishings. The Times and Seasons Building and the splendid brick home once owned by Elder Heber C. Kimball are other completed restorations at Nauvoo. In nearby Carthage the jail where the Smiths were murdered is maintained as a Mormon shrine.

"CITY OF THE BIG SHOULDERS"

"Chicago has the finest skyline in the world!" exclaimed the Duke of Windsor, as he stood on the steps of the Adler Planetarium. Most other knowledgeable visitors would probably agree with the former king of England. The tremendous vista of Chicago, with its skyscrapers towering for miles along the lake cannot be duplicated.

Without question, also, the tremendous department stores clustered on State Street form the greatest concentration for shopping to be found anywhere. On its outer edges Chicago also has more fine shopping centers.

The stretch of Michigan Avenue's "Magnificent Mile" can be compared favorably with any splendid boulevard in the world. The mile upon mile of lakeshore drive, enhanced by a border of parks as envisioned by the Chicago Plan, is another feature which sets Chicago apart from every other city. It is, in the words of Carl Sandburg, the "City of the Big Shoulders."

MUSEUMS WITHOUT PEER

Yet another premiere distinction of Chicago is the collection of great museums. Two or three of Chicago's museums are, individually, among the finest of their types in the world. Taken together, Chicago's museums, collections and zoos are recognized to form one of the finest groups of such institutions in the world.

Both laymen and experts alike recognize the supremacy of the magnificent Field Museum of Natural History, housed in one of the largest marble buildings ever built. Its collections are among the most complete ever assembled, and it has pioneered in the creation of display techniques which attract and hold the rapt attention of visitors. From the first Marshall Field, the museum received almost $10,000,000, and additional amounts were given by long-time president of the museum, Stanley Field. The Field Museum's Hall of the Races of Mankind, a complete collection of authentic sculpture by Malvina Hoffman, is the only exhibit of its kind. The museum began operations in the Fine Arts Building of the World's Columbian Exposition and then was moved to its present building.

The Fine Arts Building, originally only of temporary construction at the World's Columbian Exposition, was re-done in stone and now makes one of the finest modern examples of classical Greek architecture. Its present occupant is the Chicago Museum of Science and Industry, with exhibits covering 14 acres of floor space, recognized around the world as the largest and finest institution of this type anywhere. To provide its start, it received an initial gift from Julius Rosenwald. The museum's attendance is probably the world's largest. Skillful and delightful exhibits, such as a World War II submarine, a model farm, a coal mine or chickens hatching draw crowds of Chicagoans and tourists to the museum daily.

Another "first" for Chicago in the field of exhibit and display is the Adler Planetarium, the first of its kind to be operated in the United States. It also offers an unusual mu-

POINTS OF INTEREST IN

CHICAGO, ILLINOIS

DOWNTOWN AND NEAR NORTH AREA

▨ MUNICIPAL PARKING FACILITIES
╌ SUBWAY UNDER STREET

© PERSPECTO MAP CO.

seum of astronomical objects. Sharing the lakefront with the Planetarium is the John G. Shedd Aquarium, with the world's largest collection of marine animals.

The Art Institute of Chicago has in recent years added large new halls to increase its already impressive size. The Institute's collection of impressionistic works is one of the finest anywhere, as are its world-famous American and Oriental collections. Completely unique is the exquisite collection of miniature rooms donated to the museum by Mrs. James Ward Thorne. These 67 miniatures are considered the finest of their type— exact reproductions in perfect scale, with every detail in miniature, of some of the most beautiful rooms of well-known houses. In addition, the new Museum of Contemporary Art recently opened in Chicago.

One of the oldest and largest privately endowed historical societies in the United States is the Chicago Historical Society, founded in 1856. Its museum is noted for its Lincoln dioramas and other Lincoln material, its costumes, antique vehicles, other dioramas, period rooms, Civil War memorabilia, weapons, prints and pictures, as well as for its complete library.

Chicago Academy of Sciences, founded in 1857, is known as the "first museum of the west" and is one of the oldest scientific bodies of Illinois.

Another very fine museum is the world-famed Oriental Institute of the University of Chicago, with one of the finest collections of materials of ancient civilizations in the western hemisphere. Chicago has an almost endless collection of specialized museums. These include the Archives and Historical Library of the Evangelical Covenant Church

Wolf Point, on the Chicago River, as it appeared early in the nineteenth century.

(Above) The Kinzie house in Chicago in 1832.
(Below) A bird's-eye view of Chicago in 1868.

CHICAGO IN 1868.

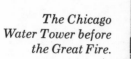

The Chicago Water Tower before the Great Fire.

of America; Medical Museum of the International College of Surgeons Hall of Fame, only one of its kind in the world; Ling Long Museum, Chinese exhibits in Chinatown; Mary R. Harvey Doll Museum and Orphans of the Attic Doll Museum and Antiques; Museum of Negro History and Art; Polish Museum of America, one of the world's largest collections of Polish historical and cultural objects; and the Ukrainian National Museum.

Two of the country's finest specialized libraries are the Newberry Library (history and literature) and John Crerar Library (science, medicine and engineering).

Not content with one great zoo, Chicago has two. The Chicago Zoological Society's zoo at Brookfield was one of the pioneers in the display of animals in their natural habitats, without bars. It has one of the largest collections of animals and some of the rarest in captivity. The zoo boasts one of the few inland oceanariums. It is pioneering, once more, this time in techniques of breeding rare animals in a special breeding farm, so that many species threatened with extinction may be saved. It also has a large expansion program. While not quite as large as Brook-

field, Lincoln Park Zoo is still one of the largest, and its collection is also outstanding.

"URBS IN HORTO"

Chicago's motto is "Urbs in Horto" ("City in a Garden"), and with a complete inner circle of parks and an outer circle of forest preserves it is just that. At the front door of Chicago is Grant Park, rimmed by the towers of Michigan Avenue and the city's leading museums. In Grant Park is renowned Buckingham Memorial Fountain, gift of Kate Buckingham in memory of her brother, Clarence. It is said to be the largest illuminated fountain in the world, with a central jet of over 100 feet, and "concerts" of changing colored lights are played on the dancing waters each summer night.

Burnham Park connects Grant Park with Jackson Park, making a lake front of park area extending south to 67th Street. Giant Lincoln Park, largest in the city, extends almost as far along the lake front to the north. One of the distinctions of Chicago is the fact that it has kept the largest portion of its waterfront open for beauty and for public use and enjoyment.

Chicago offers everything from a chrysanthemum show at Garfield Conservatory (top) to a home run at White Sox Park, formerly Comiskey Park, (bottom).

The Lincoln Park area as it appeared in 1858 when J. W. O'Brien did this painting.

Chicago parks offer one of the finest collections of sculpture. Among the most notable are the standing statue of Lincoln in Lincoln Park and the seated statue of the great Illinoisan in Grant Park, both by Augustus Saint-Gaudens; Lorado Taft's huge Fountain of Time at the end of the University of Chicago Midway; the memorial shaft topped by the Stephen A. Douglas statue, guarding the tomb of another great Illinoisan at 35th and South Lake Shore Drive, now a state memorial; and the memorial to the children's poet, Eugene Field, in the zoo at Lincoln Park.

Recreation in the parks covers everything from the Grant Park symphony concerts through concerts in other parks, professional and amateur theater, crafts and hobbies and almost every sport. Recreation in the city in general ranges from the concerts of the Chicago Symphony and the Lyric Opera, downtown professional theater and many theater-restaurants, the attractions of the Rush Street nightclub area to the excitement of the Cubs and Sox baseball teams, professional basketball, soccer and football. The Chicago Bears football team has such an enthusiastic and loyal following that season tickets rank among the most cherished possessions, often being handed down formally in wills from one generation to another.

OTHER POINTS OF INTEREST

One of the newest attractions of Chicago is Old Town, a revived section of Wells Street where a great effort has been made to develop a "Bohemian" atmosphere. Antique shops, a variety of restaurants, folk singers, jazz, opera, paintings, pottery, motorcycle rides, quaint gift courts and a rapidly growing variety of other attractions bring out colorful crowds to swarm the streets and courts.

Other Chicago points of interest include the Merchandise Mart, largest commercial building anywhere; the striking Elks National Memorial; the Glessner House, one of the country's best-known early architectural examples; First Methodist Temple, the tallest skyscraper church in the world; Conrad Hilton Hotel, world's largest; Insull's "throne," home of the Lyric Opera, built by Samuel Insull in the shape of an armchair, now the Kemper Insurance Building; historic Hull House, now restored, the only old building on the Chicago Circle Campus of the University of Illinois; the huge buildings of the national headquarters of both the Ameri-

*Modern Chicago, looking from the Prudential Building
to the Outer Drive East apartments and harbor (above)
contrasts sharply with the Chicago of 1850 (below)
as shown in an old aquatint of the second Fort Dearborn.*

can Medical and Dental associations; the historic old Water Tower; towering Marina City; and Navy Pier with its promenade deck, offering a glimpse of the port activities.

The year 1967 saw the dedication of an attraction which many feel may become the principal point of interest in the city. Famed artist Pablo Picasso contributed a design for a tremendous metal sculpture to be erected in the spacious plaza of the city's new Civic Center. It is so large that its parts had to be built by the American Bridge division of United States Steel Company, then assembled in the plaza. The steel used in the sculpture is the same oxidized steel used in the Civic Center. Because the artist did not explain his design, which appeared to be a tremendous head of some kind, there were angry shouts that Chicago had been hoaxed, but others contended that a five-story work by such a great artist entitled Chicago to front rank in the art world. Whatever its merits as art, it must rank as an attention-getter. The daring of Chicago in plunging ahead with such a controversial work demonstrates to many that the city still maintains its youth and imagination as well as its slogan, "I will!"

HIGHLIGHTS OF THE RINGS

The striking dome of the Baha'i Temple at Wilmette is one of the major tourist attractions of the near-Chicago region. The temple's nine sides represent the nine major world religions. The dome of the temple is decorated with a novel kind of concrete "lace," which was invented especially for it. The building is placed in one of the most beautiful garden settings in the Chicago area. It is the United States headquarters for the faith.

Wilmette takes its name from Antoine Ouilmette, a trapper who built his log cabin on the lake shore there. Poet Eugene Field's grave occupies a plot in the Church of the Holy Comforter in Kenilworth. Present residents of Highland Park might be surprised to know that their homes rest on the former site of two Potawatomi villages. Ravinia Park is the home of the famous summer music festival featuring the Chicago Symphony, ballet groups, theater and other musical attractions.

One of the notable small art museums of the state is the Laura Davidson Sears Academy of Fine Arts at Elgin. St. Charles is noted for Mooseheart, the orphanage sponsored by the Loyal Order of Moose. Near Wheaton is Cantigny War Memorial Museum of the First Division, established by Colonel Robert R. McCormick, former publisher of the *Chicago Tribune*. One of the unusual attractions of this museum is a full-scale World War I trench through which visitors may walk.

Another unique museum is the Hinsdale Health Museum, featuring human biology and physiology, with audio-visual animated exhibits on the brain and other organs. Graue Mill and Museum is another Hinsdale feature. Timke Circle-T Indian Museum at Downers Grove features exhibits representing 70 different Indian tribes. Freedom Hall at Oak Park is part of the Institute of Human Relations, and undertakes to show how freedom was obtained in many parts of the world. River Forest is known for its Trailside Museum, a combination zoo and museum.

Another unusual specialized museum is the Lizzadro Museum of Lapidary Art with displays and studies of gems, minerals and fossils, animals carved from precious stones and Oriental art objects. Aurora's Historical

POINTS OF INTEREST IN
ROCKFORD, ILLINOIS
ILLINOIS' SECOND LARGEST CITY

MERIDAN RD

S FORK

SAFFORD RD

AUBURN AVE

SPRINGFIELD AVE

KILBURN AVE

CENTRAL AVE

RIVERSIDE BLVD

ROCKTON AVE

BROWN CK

MACHESNEY AIRPORT

HARLEM RD

N MAIN ST

SECOND ST

SAND PK.

COTTONWOOD AIRPORT

SEARLES MEM. PK.

KENT CREEK

INGERSOLL MEMORIAL PARK

ANDREWS PK.

PAGE TALCOTT PK.

W STATE

SCHOOL ST

LAWNDALE

C M & ST P RR

AUBURN ST

OXFORD PLAYGROUND

BROWN PK.

BROWN AVE.

PRESTON ST

SUNSET PK.

JOHNSTON

FAIRGROUNDS PK.

ST

PRESTON ST

WINNEBAGO ST

HARLEM BLVD

C & NW RR

CUNNINGHAM RD

LAKE

S FORK

KENT CK

MORGAN ST

BEATTIE PK. (Indian Mounds)

COURT HOUSE

CHURCH ST

MAIN ST

ART MUSEUM

ROCK RIVER

SPRING CREEK RD

SPRING CK

HIGHCREST RD

LEVINGS PK.

MONTAGUE RD

TINKER'S COTTAGE

MONTAGUE ST

DAM Site of Original Ford

STATE ST

JEFFERSON

SINNISSIPPI PARK

REGAN ST

PARKVIEW AVE.

RURAL ST

OGILBY RD

WATER POWER DISTRICT Site of J. Manny Mower Co. and G. Kent Sawmill.

Site of Stagecoach Barn

ROCKFORD COLLEGE

SEMINARY

S MAIN ST

E. STATE ST (PART OF ORIGINAL STAGECOACH ROAD)

ROCKFORD ST

KEITHS CK

REUBEN ALDEEN PARK

LAKE

PRAIRIE RD

15th AVE.

2nd ST

CHURCHILL PK.

20th ST

VALLEY PK.

ROCKFORD COLLEGE

BLACKHAWK PARK

KISHWAUKEE ST

SOUTHEAST END PK.

BROADWAY ST

ALPINE PK.

ALPINE RD

S MAIN

C B & Q RR

HARRISON AVE.

MULFORD RD

C & NW RR

GREATER ROCKFORD AIRPORT

C RR

C & NW RR

N
W E
S

ROCKFORD, ILLINOIS:

- Founded in 1834 by New Englanders, it was named for the rock bottomed ford, which was a stagecoach stop on the route between Chicago and Galena.
- Located in the beautiful Rock River valley midway between Chicago and the Mississippi River, 17 miles from the Wisconsin line.
- Manufactured products include machine tools, furniture, hardware, farm implements, appliances, leather goods, and paint. Rockford is the second largest machine tool manufacturing center in the world.
- Home of Rockford College.

PERSPECTO MAP CO

Museum shows items of the area along with mastodon bones and geological exhibits. The dense woods in some areas of the Palos Park region have changed little from the time when the area was the grand council ground of the Potawatomi and Sauk tribes.

ROCKFORD HIGHLIGHTS

Illinois' second largest city, Rockford, recalls its predominately Scandinavian background with an annual Scandinavian Midsummer Festival at Sinnissippi Park in late June. Also popular is the Midwestern States Championship Powerboat Regatta on the Rock River over the Labor Day weekend.

The home built at Rockford by Robert Tinker in 1865 in the style of a Swiss chalet and furnished with art objects he collected throughout the world is now open as Tinker Swiss Cottage. There are also local historical items in the cottage.

Burpee Gallery of Art displays the art collection of the Rockford Art Association, especially contemporary American items. The Rockford Natural History Museum shows zoology, geology, mineralogy, archaeology, and has a fine collection of Indian objects and mounted birds. Erlander Home Museum recalls early Rockford history, with emphasis on the Swedish period and culture.

Sinnissippi Park and nearby Rock Cut State Park are fine outdoor recreation areas. The Rock River Valley in this region is noted for its scenery, especially during the fall when the river valley turns to flame.

NORTHERN HIGHLIGHTS

An outstanding collection of retired railroad equipment, steam engines, streetcars and interurban vehicles is shown in the Illinois Railway Museum at Union near Belvidere. One of the state's notable state parks is White Pines, preserving the southernmost stand of that noble tree in the United States. Looming on the bluff across the river from nearby Oregon is the famous heroic Indian statue by Lorado Taft, often said to be a statue of Black Hawk. Sterling-Rock Falls Historical Society Museum has a display of local history, especially Indian heritage.

Among the attractions of Freeport are three museums: Rawleigh Museum, displaying coins, sculpture, paintings, mosaics, primitive art from Africa and Oriental crafts; Stephenson County Historical Society Museum, displaying local industrial products, toys, a Jane Addams room, and an arboretum; and the Farm Museum, showing farm exhibits and a blacksmith shop.

Historic, compelling Galena is a must on any tourist's list of Illinois attractions. President Grant's home has been kept as a memorial and the building is open to the public. Many other old homes are open for tourists to explore. The Galena Historical Society operates a historical museum, the Grant Leather Store and the restored Firehouse Number One. The museum is notable for its historical paintings. Market House State Memorial is the oldest remaining market house in the Midwest. Galena's old buildings, the very hilly streets and remembrances of the past are all tourist attractions.

On both sides of Galena, Highway 20 becomes one of the most scenic routes in Illinois. For much of the way from Freeport, the road follows Terrapin Ridge, a crest of land almost level along the top. It extends for miles, sometimes through oak forests, then through clearings with deep and beautiful valleys dropping off on either side as far as the eye can see.

Galena, pictured at the height of its mining boom in the first part of the nineteenth century.

One of the principal attractions of Moline is the world's largest farm equipment plant, the International Harvester works, with 46 acres under one roof. Here, corn pickers, combines and other equipment are manufactured. The administrative center of Deere and Company at Moline has been designed by architect Eero Saarinen and has a picturesque location of 1,700 acres overlooking the Rock River Valley. A 400-seat auditorium and display building showing a history of Deere products is also open to the public.

No less an authority than Black Hawk declared Rock Island to be the "best island on the Mississippi." On the island is a large national cemetery and the burial ground of thousands of Confederate prisoners. Also on the island is the John M. Browning Memorial Museum, a military museum displaying small arms, artillery, field equipment, machine guns and automatic rifles developed by Browning.

Another museum near Rock Island is the Hauberg Indian Museum at Black Hawk State Park, displaying mementoes of Black Hawk and his tribe. An Indian powwow is held at the state park on Labor Day, with a parade through the streets of Rock Island.

Lake Depue preserves memories of the visit of poet William Cullen Bryant who stayed at his brother John Howard Bryant's home at Princeton. The lake near the town of Depue is said to have been the inspiration for one of William Cullen Bryant's most famous poems, *To a Waterfowl.* Peru, La Salle and Ottawa are other cities on the Illinois River above its big bend to the southwest. Near La Salle is Matthiessen State Park Nature Area. At the park a stockade and blockhouse have been reconstructed, and there is a deer reservation. Ottawa is located where the Fox and Illinois rivers meet—a manufacturing city with glass works, plastics plant and silica mining activities.

Historic Fort Armstrong on Rock Island in the Mississippi River.

SOUTHERN HIGHLIGHTS

The huge missionary area which centered in Cahokia during the French period once included even far-off Chicago; today Cahokia is a village on the outskirts of East St. Louis. Old Holy Family Church, which was finished in 1799, has been restored, with the original logs standing vertically, as the French built their log buildings. Cahokia Court House State Memorial preserves the oldest structure in the state, while the Jarrot Mansion is the oldest brick building in Illinois.

Near Cahokia is Cahokia Mounds State Park. Only a few of the more than 300 mounds in the area have been saved, with Monk's Mound, 1,000 feet long and 700 feet wide, the largest earth work on the continent. The museum at the park displays many exhibits of the Indians and explanations of the prehistoric sites nearby.

The industrial, railroad and meat-packing city of East St. Louis is headquarters for many of the Illinois sightseeing tours of the area. At the approach to Eads Bridge is one of the most historic parts of the city. This was known as Bloody Island. Here duels were fought, cock fights and other illegal activities were held. One of the worst duels was that fought by Congressmen Spencer Pettis and Thomas Biddle who stood only five feet apart. Writer Charles Dickens visited the island in 1842 and wrote "Bloody Island . . . so designated in honor of the last fatal combat fought there, which was with pistols, breast to breast. Both combatants fell dead upon the ground; and possibly some rational people may think . . . that they were no great loss to the community." Bloody Island once was an island, but improvements by army engineers in the main channel in order to save the port of St. Louis, Missouri, caused the Illinois channel to fill up. Thus Bloody Island became a part of East St. Louis. One of the engineers on this project was a young West Point graduate named Robert E. Lee.

Pere Marquette State Park, largest in the state, where the Illinois River meets the Mississippi north of East St. Louis, is named for the explorer-priest who camped on the site with Louis Jolliet and their party.

At Belleville, just south of East St. Louis, is "the world's largest outdoor Catholic shrine—the National Shrine of Our Lady of the Snows."

Old Fort de Chartres, once the strongest fortification on the continent, has been partially restored. Indian relics and other items from the French period are displayed in the museum in the guard house.

One of Illinois' most historic areas is what is now known as Kaskaskia Memorial State Park. Kaskaskia, the first capital of Illinois, had the strangest fate of any state capital. The Mississippi River cut through the narrow neck of land occupied by the town and washed away its historic buildings. Today the rivers covers most of the land where the capital of Illinois once stood. On the island left by the river when it cut its new channel is a fine memorial building recalling the stirring times of those early years in Illinois. The building houses the "Liberty Bell of the West." This was the bell which rang out proudly when George Rogers Clark captured the town of Kaskaskia for America during the Revolutionary War. The bell is older than the famous Liberty Bell in Philadelphia. Strangely enough, Kaskaskia Island is now the only part of Illinois to lie west of the Mississippi River. This is true because the boundary was fixed before the river changed its course, and the old boundary was kept, even though the river moved.

One of the attractions of Carbondale is the Museum of Southern Illinois University, which covers anthropology, zoology, and pioneer and Indian history. It also has extensive archaeological collections from the Midwest and Mexico, as well as collections of

An early watercolor of Starved Rock, the scenic bluff which takes its name from an Indian legend.

These two illustrations provide a good example of
the way in which historic ruins are restored.
(Above) The ruins of the powder magazine in Fort
de Chartres. (Below) The same building after restoration.

art of the South Pacific. Near Carbondale is Crab Orchard National Wildlife Refuge, wintering area for the Canadian goose. Also near Carbondale is Giant City State Park, noted for its strange rock formations, which looks like a lost prehistoric city.

From Bald Knob, high point of the Illinois Ozarks, a tourist can see three states—Illinois, Missouri and Kentucky. On the crest of Bald Knob is the prized giant cross, erected by people of the region, the site of Easter services. In Shawnee National Forest is an Illinois area known as the Garden of the Gods, a colorful wonderland during the fall.

Cairo is known for its annual Magnolia Festival, with a pilgrimage to fine homes of the area, and a Magnolia Ball, at which the Magnolia Queen is crowned. One of the showplaces of Cairo is Magnolia Manor, once the home of a leading merchant. It is noted for its Christmas decorations, and after Thanksgiving is called Holiday House.

Fort Massac, near Metropolis, knew many historic events. One of the most interesting was the stationing of Captain Zebulon Pike there, with his son Zebulon Montgomery Pike, who later became noted as an explorer of the north and west. A dramatic statue of George Rogers Clark stands in Fort Massac State Park in memory of his entrance into Illinois at this point on his way to Kaskaskia to capture Illinois for America.

Cave-in-Rock State Park is named for the large cave that goes back 108 feet into the river bank. This was once the lair of bloodthirsty river pirates who preyed upon the river traffic. Later the notorious Harpe Brothers used the cave as headquarters for their outlaw band, and a gang of counterfeiters operated here until 1831. Several years ago the TV series *Davy Crockett and the River Pirates* was filmed there.

Centralia's claim to national fame is its location as the population center of the United States. With its neighbors, Central City and Wamac, Centralia forms an almost completely built-up urban area, a labor and trading center for four counties.

The Olney *Times* of November 1, 1858, carried a headline reading "For President in 1860, Abraham Lincoln of Illinois." The newspaper proudly claims to have been the first in the nation to support Lincoln for President. Olney is a city of splendid old mansions and attracts wide-eyed tourists to see its multitude of white squirrels.

At Vandalia stands the Madonna of the Trail monument, which marks the end of the old National Road. This is one of a series of Madonna statues across the nation which pay tribute to America's pioneer women. The Little Brick House at Vandalia is typical of houses built during the period when Vandalia was the capital of Illinois, and the house now is open as a museum.

One of America's most historic structures is the old capitol at Vandalia, where Abraham Lincoln received his license to practice law and where both Lincoln and Douglas gained local fame as legislators. The old building is now open as a state museum, and few can visit the hallowed halls without a feeling of pride and awe for the great men and great state which were cradled there.

The Sweep of History in Illinois

1673—Marquette and Jolliet are first Europeans to reach Illinois country
1675—Marquette returns to teach Illini Indians
1680—La Salle comes to Illinois country
1690—De Tonti receives trading rights in the area
1696—Father Pierre Pinet's mission established at what is now Chicago
1699—Cahokia founded, first permanent settlement in Illinois country
1703—Jesuits establish Kaskaskia
1717—Illinois country becomes part of French Colony of Louisiana
1720—First Fort de Chartres finished
1730—Fox tribesmen massacred near present Plano
1756—Fort de Chartres, rebuilt, most formidable on continent
1763—Illinois country ceded to Britain by France
1765—French flag lowered over Fort de Chartres
1769—Chief Pontiac murdered by Illini
1778—George Rogers Clark secures Illinois country for Virginia
c1779—Jean Baptiste Point du Sable establishes a trading post at Chicago;
　　　　Illinois region becomes a county of Virginia
1783—Treaty of peace with Britain recognizes title of the United States
　　　　to the Illinois Country
1784—Virginia gives up claim to Illinois; beginning of cruel rule of
　　　　John Dodge at Kaskaskia
1787—Northwest Ordinance establishes government for Illinois as part of
　　　　Northwest Territory
1800—Illinois becomes part of the Indiana Territory
1803—Fort Dearborn established
1809—Illinois Territory organized by Congress
1811—First steamboat; great earthquake
1812—People of Fort Dearborn massacred, fort destroyed by
　　　　Potawatomi Indians
1813—Beginning of modern Peoria, Fort Clark built
1814—First Illinois newspaper published
1815—Beginnings of Alton
1816—Fort Armstrong begun, initiates Rock Island;
　　　　new Fort Dearborn built
1818—Illinois becomes 21st state, Dec 3; Albion founded
1820—Capital moved from Kaskaskia to Vandalia
1821—Springfield selected County Seat of Sangamon County
1822—Quincy and Urbana settled
1825—First school law in Illinois

1828—First steamboat reaches Peoria
1829—Illinois College founded at Jacksonville
1829—Decatur founded
1830—Abraham Lincoln comes to Illinois
1831—Joliet founded
1832—Black Hawk War; George W. Snow invents balloon type of construction
1833—Chicago chosen as terminal of Illinois and Michigan Canal, organized as town
1834—Aurora settled
1835—Waukegan's modern settlement begins; Elgin settled
1837—General Assembly passes bill making Springfield State Capital; Chicago incorporated as city; Cairo settled; Knox College chartered; John Deere designs effective steel plow
1838—First railroad operates in Illinois
1839—Nauvoo founded; Rockford incorporated
1840—Illinois Liberty Party organized
1843—Bloomington founded; Elmhurst settled; Catholic Diocese (now Archdiocese) of Chicago founded
1844—Joseph and Hyrum Smith murdered
1846—Lincoln elected to Congress
1847—First McCormick reaper plant built at Chicago
1848—New state constitution forbids slavery, bans free Negroes from state; Illinois and Michigan Canal opens; Chicago Board of Trade opened; Galena and Chicago Union Railroad begins
1850—Chicago "raises the grade"
1853—First State Fair
1854—Evanston founded
1855—First comprehensive school law in Illinois passed; Kankakee begun; Northwestern University founded
1856—Illinois Republican Party organized at Bloomington
1858—Lincoln-Douglas debates; Lincoln loses election
1860—Lincoln nominated, elected as President
1861—Civil War begins; East St. Louis incorporated
1864—President Lincoln reelected; Grant placed in command of Union armies
1865—War ends; Lincoln buried; Chicago Union Stock Yards established
1866—First GAR post established at Decatur; Cicero founded
1867—Beginnings of University of Illinois
1869—Grant becomes President
1870—Present Illinois constitution (third) adopted

1871—Great Chicago Fire
1874—Segregation forbidden in public schools
1875—Swift and Armour packing companies open in Chicago
1876—State Capitol begun
1885—Jenney creates first skycraper in Chicago
1886—Haymarket Riot
1888—State Capitol completed
1889—Jane Addams opens Hull House; Auditorium opens
1890—University of Chicago chartered
1892—Granite City established
1893—World's Columbian Exposition, Chicago; severe depression
1896—Bryan delivers Cross of Gold speech at Chicago
1897—Chicago Loop created by new "L" lines
1899—Dowie establishes Zion
1900—Chicago Sanitary and Ship Canal finished
1903—First effective child labor law passed by Illinois; Millikin
       University founded at Decatur; Iroquois Theater Fire, Chicago
1905—Hennepin Canal, also known as Illinois and Mississippi Canal,
       completed
1906—Hearst buys site of New Salem, restoration initiated
1910—Beginning of Civil Service in some state jobs
1911—Beginning of workmen's compensation acts
1913—Women's suffrage law passed by General Assembly
1915—Steamer *Eastland* disaster, Chicago
1917—U.S. enters World War I
1921—Cahokia Mounds scientifically studied for first time
1931—First dramatic television program broadcast from Chicago
1933—Illinois Waterway opened
1933-1934—Century of Progress, Chicago
1937—Oil discovered in Marion County, start of southern Illinois oil
       boom; Cairo escapes greatest Ohio River flood
1941—World War II begins; 900,000 from Illinois serve, 27,000 killed
1959—Chicago becomes deep-water port
1960—Dresden nuclear power plant begins operation
1961—Fair Employment Practices Commission created
1964—First at-large election of members of Illinois House of
       Representatives
1965—Sesquicentennial Commission created by General Assembly
1967—Weston chosen for nuclear accelerator; "Water for Illinois"
       program presented; Auditorium theater restored; Picasso statue
       dedicated at Chicago
1968—Illinois celebrates 150th anniversary of statehood

Information Roundup

Area—56,400 square miles (including 55,930 land, 470 inland water)
Extreme length (north to south)—380 miles
Extreme width (east to west)—205 miles
Highest Point—1,241 feet (Charles Mound near East Dubuque)
Lowest Point—279 feet (at the delta at Cairo)
Temperature Extremes—High: 117° (East St. Louis); low: minus 35° (Mt. Carroll)
Growing Season—North, 150 days; South, 210 days
Average Annual Number of Tornadoes—24
Statehood—21st State, December 3, 1818
Counties—102
U.S. Senators—2
U.S. Representatives—24
Capital—Springfield, settled 1819
State Symbols—Tree: Oak
              Flower: Wood violet
              Bird: Cardinal
State Song—*By Thy Rivers Gently Flowing, Illinois*, Words by Charles H. Chamberlin, new verses by Win Stracke, music by Archibald Johnson
State Slogan—*Land of Lincoln*
State Motto—State Sovereignty, National Union
Familiar Name—Prairie State
Population—10,722,000 (1966 estimate)
Population Density—180.3 persons per square mile
Major Cities—Chicago, 3,550,404 (1960 census)
              Rockford, 132,109
              Peoria, 103,162
              Springfield, 83,271
              East St. Louis, 81,712
              Evanston, 79,283
              Decatur, 78,004
              Cicero, 69,130
              Skokie, 67,865
              Joliet, 66,780
              Aurora, 63,715
              Oak Park, 61,093

Per Capita Income—$3,280 (1965)

Great Seal of Illinois—Authorized March 7, 1867; first used October 26, 1868

State Flag—Designed by Rockford Chapter of D.A.R., became official July 6, 1915

Principal Rivers—Illinois, 273 miles long

Mississippi, 581 miles (Illinois boundary)

Ohio, 113 miles (Illinois boundary)

Principal Manufacturing Industries—Machinery (nonelectric), electrical machinery, fabricated metal products, food and related products, primary metals, printing and publishing, chemicals, transportation equipment, apparel

Principal Minerals—Coal (bituminous), crude oil, limestone and dolomite, clay products, portland cement

Principal Agricultural Products—Corn, soybeans, apples, hogs, cattle

Index

Museum of Southern Illinois
University, 189
Museums, 28, 73, 76, 82, 169,
170, 172, 174, 175, 178, 180,
184, 186, 187, 188, 189, 191
Music, 89, 90, 129
Muskrat, 136

Names, derivation of, 34, 86, 105
Naperville, 84, 94
National cemetery, 187
National College of Education,
166
National Enameling and
Stamping Company, 105
National Forest, Shawnee, 160
National Guild of Community
Music Schools, 129
National historic landmark, 130
National Invitational
Tournament, 165
National League (baseball), 97
National Lincoln Monument
Assn., 170
National Road, 146, 191
National Shrine of Our Lady
of the Snows, 189
Natural History Building, Univ.
of Illinois, 172
Natural resources, 136-138
Nauvoo, 59, 60, 107, 174
Nauvoo Restoration, Inc., 174
Naval Training Station, Great
Lakes, 80, 84
Navy Pier, Chicago, 184
Negro Digest, 114
Negroes, 61, 62, 63, 86, 111-114,
180
Nelson, David, 63
Nevins, Allan, 85, 127
Newberry Library, Chicago, 180
New Design (town), 115
New Jersey, 66
Newman, Ralph G., 85
New Orleans, La., 45, 52, 117,
139
New Orleans, steamboat, 142
New Philadelphia, 112
New Salem, 117, 119, 168, 169,
171
New Salem State Park, 169, 171
Newspapers, Illinois, 62, 113,
125, 147, 191
New York City, 14, 66, 123
New York *Evening Post*, 64
New York State, 58
Niagara Falls, 84
Niagara limestone, 23
Niedringhaus, William F., 105
Nile River, Egypt, 15, 103
Niles, 94
Nobel Prizes, 83, 127, 130, 131
Normal (North Bloomington),
103, 165
North Bloomington (Normal),
103, 165

Northeastern Illinois State
College, 165
Northern Cross, steam engine,
144
Northern Illinois University, 165
North Shore Country Day
School, 167
Northwestern University, 94,
125, 130, 166
Northwest Ordinance of 1787,
51, 53, 61, 167
Northwest Territory, 49, 50,
51, 52, 61, 123
Norway, Ill., 110
Norwegian people, 110
Nuclear accelerator, Weston, 85,
94
Nuclear power plant, Dresden,
85

Oak Lawn, 94
Oak Park, 94, 127, 184, 195
Oak Ridge Cemetery,
Springfield, 100, 170
Oak Street, Chicago, 90
Oakwood Mound, 33
O'Brien, J. W., 182
Offut, Denton, 117
Ogden, William Butler, 88
Ogle County, 153
Oglesby, Richard J., 71, 75, 124
O'Hare, Edward (Butch), 145
O'Hare International Airport,
93, 145
Ohio, 48, 51, 53, 122
Ohio River, 14, 15, 48, 51, 52,
56, 61, 82, 107, 108, 139
Ohio River, flood, 1937, 82
Oil, 138, 152
Oil processing, 96
Oklahoma, 37
Old Holy Family Church,
Cahokia, 188
Old Main, Knox College, 66
Old St. Mary's Church,
Chicago, 73
Old Salem Lincoln League, 169
"Old Siwash," 164
Old Town, Chicago, 182
O'Leary, Patrick, 73
O'Leary cow, 73
Olney, 138, 191
Olney *Times*, 191
Onion sets, 156
Onstot cooperage shop, New
Salem, 169
Open-housing legislation, 114
Orchestra Hall, Chicago, 90
Ordinance of 1787, 51, 53, 61,
167
Oregon, Ill., 186
Oregon Territory, 120
Oriental Institute, University
of Chicago, 178
Oriental Theater, Chicago, 91

Orphans of the Attic Doll
Museum and Antiques,
Chicago, 180
Ottawa, Ill., 56, 64, 170, 187
Ottawa Indians, 36, 46
Ouilmette, Antoine, 184
Outer Drive East apartments,
Chicago, 183
Owens-Illinois Company, 152
Ozark range, 14, 24, 33, 191

Paducah, Ky., 82
Palmer, John M., 71, 124, 172
Palmer, Potter, 126, 127
Palmer, (Mrs.) Potter, 127
Palmer House, Chicago, 127
Palos Hills, 94
Palos Park, 26, 186
Pana, 156
Paris, Ill., 46, 70
Park, Francis, 131
Park Forest, 94, 106
Park House, Albion, 110
Park Ridge, 94
Parks (see also State parks),
168, 172, 174, 175, 180, 182,
184, 186
Parochial schools, 167
Parsons, James B., 114
Passion Play, Bloomington, 172
Paul, Maud, 129
Pawnee, 152
Peabody mine No. 10, Pawnee,
152
Peace pipe (calumet), 34, 128
Peaches, 156
Pease, Theodore C., 62
Peattie, Donald Culross, 127
Peerson, Cleng, 110
Pekitanoui River (Missouri), 38
Penitentiary, state, 96
Pennsylvania, 68
Peoria, 33, 40, 42, 51, 97, 98,
100, 115, 142, 152, 173, 174,
195
Peoria, lake, 37, 41-2
Peoria County, 98
Peoria Indians, 34, 41, 97
Peouarea (Peoria), 40
Peourea Indians, 97
Percy, Charles H., 125
Pere Marquette State Park, 189
Peru, Ill., 187
Petroglyphs, 33
Petroleum, 24, 138, 152
Pettis, Spencer, 188
Pfister, Lester, 156
Pheasants, 136
Philharmonic society, Chicago,
89
Physiographic regions, 14
Piankashaw Indians, 36
Piasa Bird, 29, 30, 33
Picasso, Pablo, statue, 184
Pictographs, 33

ILLUSTRATION ACKNOWLEDGMENTS

Grateful acknowledgment is made to the following organizations for permission to use the illustrations in this book:

American Heritage and the National Gallery of Art (p. 35); Chicago Academy of Science (pp. 22, 25, 27); Chicago Historical Society (pp. 10, 18, 30, 32, 36, 37, 39 inset, 41, 42, 44, 45, 47, 49, 50, 53, 54, 55, 57, 58, 59, 61, 62, 65, 66, 67, 69, 72, 74, 75, 76, 78, 79, 81, 82, 86, 87, 88, 89, 91, 98, 100, 102, 104, 105, 107, 108, 109, 110, 111, 113, 116, 118, 121, 122, 124, 125, 126, 131, 134, 142, 143, 144, 145, 146, 147, 148 top, 149, 154, 155, 157, 159, 165, 174, 178, 179, 180, 182, 183 bottom, 187, 188, 189, 190); Illinois Industrial Planning and Development (p. 137); Illinois Technical Advisory Committee on Water Resources (pp. 19, 20, 23, 161); Outdoor Recreation in Illinois (p. 21); Peoria Journal Star and First Federal Savings and Loan Association of Peoria (p. 128); Perspecto Map Company (pp. 16, 17, 140, 171, 173, 176, 177, 185); Talman Federal Savings and Loan Association (pp. 93, 95, 148 bottom, 151, 181, 183 top); William Blair & Company (p. 39).